LITERATURE AND LIFE

FREDERICK DENISON MAURICE.

LITERATURE AND LIFE

BY

EDWIN P. WHIPPLE

Essay Index Reprint Series

BOOKS FOR LIBRARIES PRESS
FREEPORT, NEW YORK

First Published 1899
Reprinted 1972

Library of Congress Cataloging in Publication Data

Whipple, Edwin Percy, 1819-1886.
   Literature and life.

   (Essay index reprint series)
   First published under title: Lectures on subjects
connected with literature and life.
   Reprint of the 1899 ed.
   1. Literature--Addresses, essays, lectures.
I. Title.
PN511.W55 1972   814'.3   72-8540
ISBN 0-8369-7340-2

PRINTED IN THE UNITED STATES OF AMERICA

CONTENTS.

———◆———

AUTHORS IN THEIR RELATIONS TO LIFE.*

THERE has existed in all ages a class of men, called at different periods by different names, but generally comprehended under the name of authors. They hold the same relation to the mind of man that the agriculturist and manufacturer bear to his body; and by virtue of their sway over the realms of thought and emotion, they have exercised a vast influence upon human affairs, which has too often been overlooked or denied by earth's industrial and political sovereigns. Operating as they do on unseen substances, and working silent and mysterious changes in the inward man, without altering his external aspect, they have strangely puzzled the whole horde of bigots and tyrants, and have written their Mene, Mene, Tekel, Upharsin on the walls of earth's proudest palaces. On the occasion of a literary anniversary like yours, I am aware of no more appropriate

* Delivered before the Literary Societies of Brown University Sept 1, 1846.

subject, — none which is more likely to bear, remotely
or immediately, on your own future pursuits and professions, — than this of Authors; and in tracing out some
of tneir relations to life, I think I can inflict less tediousness upon you than if I had selected some topic with a
more resounding name, and admitting of more ambitious
disquisition. My object will be to set forth their moral
and intellectual influence, the physical necessities which
have modified the direction of their powers, and the dis-
crepancies observable between their internal and external
existence. This will involve a consideration of their
relations to their age, to booksellers, and to domestic and
social life. You must pardon the remediless superficiality of my view, as each division might well exhaust a
volume.

And first, let us refer to the influence of authors, and
the position they have occupied in the world.

Without taking into view the lives and thoughts of
authors, history becomes an enigma, or a many-volumed
lie. We read of wars, crusades, persecutions, ameliora-
tions, of mighty and convulsive changes in opinions and
manners, without obtaining any clue to the real causes
of events, any insight into the laws of God's providence.
Without inweaving literary into civil history, we gain no
knowledge of the annals of human nature. We have
the body of history without the soul, — events without

ideas, — effects without causes, - the very atheism of narrative. The abridgments we study at schools are commonly made up of incidents jumbled together like beads, and unconnected by any thread of reason and reality. It is hardly possible for a boy, studying these works, to grasp any other idea of man than the idea of a being with legs, arms, and appetites.

Now it is a fact that Thought, true or false, beneficial or pernicious, has borne the sceptre of influence in this world's affairs. Impulse, whim and chance, have not been the blind guides of the generations of men. Above all the fret and tumult of active existence, above the decrees of earth's nominal sovereigns, above all the violence and evil which render what is called history so black a record of folly and crime — above all these, there have ever been certain luminous ideas, pillars of fire in the night of time, which have guided and guarded the great army of humanity, in its slow and hesitating, but still onward, progress in knowledge and freedom. It is not the ruler that makes the most noise in the world, that most shapes the world's fortunes. Ten rockets, sent violently into the air, by their blaze and impotent fury, attract all eyes, and seem much finer and grander than the eternal stars; but after their short and rushing life has burnt out, and they have noised themselves into nothingness, the stars still shine serenely on, and seem almost to look down with contempt on the crowd who have been fooled into fear or admiration. Thus is it in history. The being to whose commands is given a brief omnipotence, — whose single word moves myriads of men, — on whom power and glory are lavished without measure, — is often but the mere instrument of some idea or principle, mightier than he; and to find his master and king, we must travel back years, and perhaps ages, and seek him in the lonely cell of some poor and despised student, whose busy brain is shaping in silence those immaterial substances, destined to shake the world; to fall like fire upon the hearts of men, and kindle in them new life and energy; to overthrow and to rebuild thrones; to be the roots of new moral and intellectual dynasties; and, keeping their way through generation after generation, to come out in the end gloriously or infamously, according as they are founded in justice and truth, or falsehood and wrong. Thus the thinker ever precedes the actor. Thoughts ever have to battle themselves into institutions. The passage of a paradox into a truism is attended with numberless commotions. With these commotions, rather than with the ideas and feelings whence they spring, history has chiefly chosen to deal; and it rarely notices the ten thousand agencies operating on a nation's mind, until revolutions have passed from thoughts into facts, and made themselves

known on fields of stricken battle. Every great originating mind produces in some way a change in society;
every great originating mind whose exercise is controlled
by duty, effects a beneficial change. This effect may be
immediate, may be remote. A nation may be in a tumult
to-day, for a thought which the timid Erasmus placidly
penned in his study more than two centuries ago.
Thought may be first written in an unintelligible jargon,
in Benthamese or Kantese, for instance; but every Ben-
tham finds his Dumont, and every Kant his Cousin. An
author may affect his race through conductors. He may
be mysterious; others will translate him to the people.
He may be a coward; others will do the fighting. He
may be a wretch, studious of infamy; Humanity takes
the thought, and spurns the man. Many poets who have
led lives of luxury and effeminacy, and sat honored
guests at the tables of tyrants, have still exalted our conceptions of intellectual excellence, refined our manners,
extended the range of our sympathies. They have modified the institutions of society by modifying the mental
character of society, of which institutions are the outward expression. A change in thought or prejudice
works out, in the end, a change in governments and
laws. "Beware," says a brilliant essayist, "when the
great God lets loose a thinker on this planet. Then all
things are at risk."

Authors are thus entitled to a prominent rank among the producing classes, and their lives deserve a more intelligent scrutiny from the practical men who stigmatize them as dreamers. Their importance has rarely been correctly estimated, either in summing up a nation's wealth or a nation's dangers. Society has played with them its most capricious game of coquetry. The same generation which neglects or tortures a man of letters, will often supply a whole army of admiring commentators to distort his works.

> " Ten ancient towns contend for Homer dead,
>   Through which the living Homer begged his bread."

No language can fitly express the meanness, the baseness, the brutality, with which the world has ever treated its victims of one age and boasts of the next. Dante is worshipped at that grave to which he was hurried by persecution. Milton, in his own day, was " Mr. Milton, the blind adder, that spit his venom on the king's person ;" and soon after, " the mighty orb of song." These absurd transitions from hatred to apotheosis, this recognition just at the moment when it becomes a mockery, sadden all intellectual history. Is it not strange that the biography of authors should be so steeped in misery, -- that while exercising the most despotic dominion that man can wield over the fortunes of his race, their own lives should so often present a melancholy spectacle of unrest, unhappiness, frailty, beggary, and despair ?

What has been the fate of those who have striven hard to bring the actual world nearer to ideal perfection ? Has not fidelity to ideas, the exercise of moral courage in the cause of truth, when it could not be pensioned into apostacy, been too often rewarded with persecution into heaven ?   The cold, lifeless axiom, so inoffensively ineffective, and so securely announced from the dull soul of the pedant—how has it been, when it came hissing hot from the gushing heart of genius, tearing and ripping up the surface concealments of tolerated sins ?   Wherever a great soul has raised the banner of revolt against accredited fraud or honored duncery, thither has flown Ignorance with her bats and owls, thither has sped Power with his racks and gibbets.   Do you wonder that so much of the world's intellect has been chained, like a galley-slave, to the world's corruptions, when you find its free and honest exercise so often thus rewarded with poverty or death ?

Time, to be sure, that consecrates all things, consecrates even the lives of authors.   When the great man is laid in his grave, lies of malice are apt to give way to lies of adulation.   Men feel his genius more, and his faults less.   The cry then is, to bury the evil he has done with his bones, — to forbear dragging his frailties from their dread abode. Then steps forth a debonair biographer, to varnish his errors or crimes, in order that he may appear respectably before that dear public whose stupidity or caprice may have urged him to their commission. It is well, after calumny has feasted and fattened on his name, that he should undergo the solemn foolery of a verbal beatitude ! Indeed, it seems strange, that the old maxim declaring no human being to have arrived at perfection on earth should still be heard from the pulpit, when even every newspaper obituary gives it the lie !

There is, indeed, a natural disposition with us to judge an author's personal character by the character of his works. We find it difficult to understand the common antithesis of a good writer and a bad man. We dislike to believe that any of those gifted beings who have been the choicest companions of our best and happiest hours, who have kindled or exalted our love of the beautiful and good, who have given us knowledge and power, and whose words rebuke us for our own moral as well as mental inferiority, should have ugly spots of meanness or baseness blotting their bright escutcheons. We instinctively lend a greedy ear to the weakest apologies offered in behalf of our favorites, and side with them against any who may have been their adversaries or victims. The greater the writer, the more pertinaciously we sophisticate away the faults of the man. We side with Pope in his quarrel with Cibber, with Addison in his quarrel with Steele. We give little credence to the fact that Bacon took bribes, or that Byron took gin. No notoriety given to Campbell's vices can make us believe the creator of Gertrude, envious, malignant and sottish. Let mediocrity commit similar faults to those we pardon in genius, and we should hurl at it our loudest thunders of rebuke. Forgetting that writers are men, exposed to more than common trials and temptations, we fondly believe their external life always in harmony with their internal ideals. A little reflection teaches us that the truisms of thought are the paradoxes of action. If this be true, then the ideals of thought may be almost classed among the prodigies of conduct; and in literature we must often be indebted for priceless benefits to men personally unworthy of our esteem; to have our courage kindled by the oratory of cowards; our confidence in virtue strengthened by the poetry of debauchees; and our loftiest sentiments of liberty and disinterestedness ennobled by imaginations shaped by the servile and the mean.

To reconcile this monstrous anomaly with nature, we must recollect two things: first, that the possession of great energies of mind does not suppose the absence of bad passions; and second, that authors are compelled like other men, to labor for a subsistence. In some cases, it is true, the man of genius is blasted from within; his genius becoming the slave of unbitted passions and satanic pride. Thus Campbell compared the unwearied fire that burned in the breast of Byron to the "robe and golden crown which Medea, in Euripides, sends Glaucè, the wife of Jason; their beauty and magic loveliness did not prevent them from consuming to ashes the victim whom they so gorgeously adorned." In some cases, too, the lust of the intellect has been stronger than the lust of the flesh, and put iron wills into evil hearts,

> "Whose steep aim
> Was, Titan-like, on daring doubts to pile
> Thoughts which should draw down thunder, and the flame
> Of heaven."

But poverty, perhaps, has been the most fertile source of literary crimes. Men of letters have ever displayed the same strange indisposition to starve common to other descendants of Adam. The law of supply and demand operates in literature as in trade. For instance, if a poor poet, rich only in the riches of thought, be placed in an age which demands intellectual monstrosities, he is tempted to pervert his powers to please the general taste. This he must do or die, and this he should rather die than do; but still, if he hopes to live by his products, he must produce what people will buy, — and it is already supposed that nothing will be bought except what is brainless or debasing. The opposite of this is likewise true. If a man of mental power and moral weakness be placed in an age which demands purity in its literature, his writings may exhibit a seraphical aspect, while his life is stained with folly and wickedness. Thus it is that many writers who have lived decently good lives have written indecently bad works; and many who have lived indecently bad lives have written decently good works; and the solution of the mystery lies not in the brain, but in the physical necessities, of the man. Poets are by no means wingless angels, fed with ambrosia plucked from Olympus, or manna rained down from heaven.

This brings us to one great division in every author's life, — his relation to the public. This can be best illustrated by a pertinent example from a corrupt age. John Dryden had a clear perception of moral truth, and no natural desire to injure his species. He was an eminent professional author during the reign of Charles II. The time in which he lived was one of great depravity of taste, and greater depravity of manners. Authors seemed banded in an insane crusade to exalt blasphemy and profligacy to the vacant throne of piety and virtue. Books were valuable according to the wickedness blended with their talent. Mental power was lucrative only in

2

its perversion. The public was ravenous for the witty
iniquities of the brain; and, to use the energetic invective of South, laid hold of brilliant morsels of sin, with
" fire and brimstone flaming round them, and thus, as
it were, *digested death itself, and made a meal upon per-
dition.*" Now, it is evident, in such a period as this, a
needy author was compelled to choose between virtue
attended by neglect, and vice lackeyed by popularity.
One of Sir Charles Sedley's profligate comedies, one of
Lord Rochester's ribald lampoons, possessed more mercantile value than the Paradise Lost. In such a period
as this, the poet should have descended upon his time,
like Schiller's ideal artist, "not to delight it with his presence, but terrible, like the son of Agamemnon, to purify
it." Dryden was placed in this age, and, for a long period
of his life, was its pander and parasite. The author
of Alexander's Feast condescended to write comedies
whose ferocious licentiousness astounds and bewilders
the modern reader. Yet, had he lived in the reign of
George III., he would not have been more immoral than
Churchill; had he lived in our day, his muse would
have been as pure as that of Campbell. He could not,
or would not, learn that it is better to starve on honesty
than thrive on baseness. "It is hard." says an old
English divine, "to maintain truth, but still harder to
be maintained by it."

Now this mercantile or economical element, this disposition to let out talent as a jaded hack in the service of
Satan, when Satan pays the price, looks out upon us constantly from literary history. In this connection it would
be unjust not to pay a passing tribute to that long-eared
wisdom which obtains in our country, of starving authors
down into despair in order that they may be lifted thence
by sin — that sagacious philosophy which sees no danger
in neglecting a poor novelist or poet, and then contrives
to be astonished at the ability displayed in an atheistic
pamphlet or an agrarian harangue. The merchant, who
sneers at literary pursuits, shuts his purse when a new
volume appears, and clamors for the protection of all
manufactures but those of the mind, might, perhaps,
if he were logically inclined, trace some connection between his foolish illiberality and a financial storm which
stripped him of half his fortune, or a quack medicine
which poisoned his wife, or a bad book which ruined the
morals of his son. It is this senseless and disgraceful
contempt for the power of authors which causes much
of the perversion of talent so common in our day. Let
us suppose the case of a man who, led by some inscrutable inward impulse, adopts the profession of American
authorship. Of course, this act would furnish indubitable proof of insanity in any candid court of justice; but
waiving that consideration, let us hear the advice given

to him after his first book has gone the way of the trunk-
maker's, after a sale of ten copies. He is told that he
made a mistake in the selection of his subject; that
the people want something in the " flash line." It is
well for him if he can reconcile the flash line with the
line of duty. However, he proceeds in his course, until
all notion of the dignity of authorship vanishes from his
mind. Literature, to him, is the manufacture of ephem-
eral inanities and monstrous depravities, to serve as food
for fools and vagabonds. He is ready to write on any
subject which will afford him bread, — moral or immoral,
religious or atheistic, solid or flash. He lets out his pen
to the highest bidder, as Captain Dalgetty let out his
sword. You may hire him to write transcendentalism;
you may hire him to write brain-sick stories for namby-
pamby magazines; you may hire him to write quack
advertisements. And this is a successor of John Milton,
— as Pope Joan was a successor of Saint Peter! But
where lies the blame? The "respectable" portion of
society aver that the blame lies in the author; reason
seems to assert that the blame lies in the "respectable"
portion of society.

Indeed, it seems impossible for men to realize the importance and influence of authors, as purifiers or poisoners of the public taste and morals. For evil or good
they exercise a vast and momentous dominion. But

they are not generally men distinguished from other men by superior strength of principle. If neglected and despised, they teach the lesson, that if virtue and truth decline paying wages to talent, falsehood and profligacy are not so parsimonious.

Burke, no superficial reader of men and books, says, in one of his immortal pamphlets, that " he can form a tolerably correct estimate of what is likely to happen in a character chiefly dependent for fame and fortune on knowledge and talent, both in its morbid and perverted state, and in that which is sound and natural. Naturally, such men are the first gifts of Providence to the world. But when they have once cast off the fear of God, which in all ages has been too often the case, and the fear of man, which is now the case ; and when, in that state, they come to understand one another, and to act in corps, a more fearful calamity cannot arise out of hell to scourge mankind." Now, whether American authors are to be scourges or blessings rests with those who are to be injured or benefited. But one thing is certain, that social order, good government, correct morals, cannot long be preserved after well-fed and well-principled mediocrity has divorced itself from ill-fed and loose-principled talent. And it is perfectly right that it should be so. It is according to the heaven-ordained constitution of things. A nation which

places implicit reliance on steam-engines and mill-privi-
leges will find that in all that affects the weal or woe of
communities mind-power is greater than steam-power
— a truth which should be held up in the faces of our
shrewd and prudent worldlings, till, like the poet's mirror
of diamond, " it dazzle and pierce their misty eye-balls."
It is doubtless very pleasant, and very agreeable, to shoot
out the tongue at the mere mention of a national literature, to belittle and degrade the occupation of letters; but
let those complacent gentlemen who practise the jest look
to it that the sparks they would trample under foot fly
not up in their own faces.   " Literature," said Mr. Pitt to
Robert Southey, " will take care of itself."—" Yes," was
the reply, " and take care of you too, if you do not see
to it."

But there is a class of authors different from those
who cringe to prevalent tastes, and pander to degrading
passions; men whom neither power can intimidate, nor
flattery deceive, nor wealth corrupt; the heroes of intellectual history, who combine the martyr's courage with
the poet's genius, and who, in the strength of their fixed
wills and free hearts, might have scoffed as divinely a
the threats of earth-born power as the Virgin Martyr of
Massinger at the torturers of Diocletian and Maximi
aus : —

" The visage of the hangman frights not me ;
    The sight of whips, racks, gibbets, axes, **fires**,
    Are scaffoldings on which my soul climbs up
    To an eternal habitation."

This class, it must be confessed, is small.   **It does not
include** many men of unquestioned genius.   **It does not
include** many whose works will be read and loved **forever.**
But such an one was Dante, to whose raised **spirit,**
even in this life, the world had passed away.   Such was
Schiller, toiling for twenty years up the topless pinnacle
of thought, unconquered by constant physical pain, his
upward eye ever fixed on his receding ideal.   Such was
Shelley, who made his stricken life, with all its stern
agonies and cruel disappointments,

" A doom
As glorious as a fiery martyrdom."

Such was Wordsworth, unmoved by ridicule and neglect
calmly writing poems for another generation **to read.**
And such, above all, was Milton.   No eulogy, **though**
carved in marble, can rightly celebrate his **character and**
genius : —

" Nothing can cover his high fame, but **Heaven ;**
    No monument set off his memories,
    But the eternal substance of his greatness."

The austere grandeur of his life may well **excite the**
wonder of the traders, panders and parasites of **literature.**
His patience and conscience were tried by all the calami-

ties which break down the spirits of common men, — by
sickness, by blindness, by poverty, by the ingratitude of
his children, by the hatred of the powerful, by the malice
of the base.   But the might of his moral nature overcame
them all.   No one can fitly reverence Milton who has not
studied the character of the age of Charles II., in which
his later fortunes were cast.   He was Dryden's contemporary in time, but not his master or disciple in slavishness.   He was under the anathema of power: a republican, in days of abject servility; a Christian, among men
whom it would be charity to call infidels; a man of pure
life and high principle, among sensualists and renegades.   On nothing external could he lean for support.
In his own domain of imagination perhaps the greatest
poet that ever lived, he was still doomed to see such
pitiful and stupid poetasters as Shadwell and Settle
bear away the shining rewards of letters.   Well might
he declare that he had fallen on evil times!   He was
among his opposites, — a despised and high-souled Puri-
tan-poet, surrounded by a horde of desperate and dissolute scribblers, who can be compared, as an accomplished
critic has eloquently said, "to nothing so fitly as the
rabble in Comus, grotesque monsters, half bestial,
half human, dropping with wine, bloated with gluttony, reeling in obscene dances.   Amidst these his
muse was placed, like the chaste lady of the masque

ofty, spotless and serene, — to be chattered at, and pointed at, and grinned at, by the whole rabble of satyrs and goblins." Yet, from among such base environments, did Milton "soar in the high reason of his fancies, with his garland and singing robes about him;" and while suffering the bitterest penalties of honesty and genius, in that age of shallow wit and profound villany, his soul never ceased to glow with the grandeur of that earlier day, when he had stood forth foremost among the champions of truth, and like his own invincible warrior, ZEAL, "a spirit of the largest size and divinest mettle," had driven his fiery chariot over the heads of "scarlet prelates," "bruising their stiff necks under his flaming wheels." The genius of Milton is indeed worthy all the admiration we award marvellous intellectual endowment; but how much more do we venerate the whole man, when we find it riveted to that high and hardy moral courage which makes his name thunder rebuke to all power that betrays freedom, to all genius that is false to virtue! Dante, Schiller, Shelley, Milton, — poets, heroes, martyrs, — must the mournful truth be forced from our reluctant ips, —

> "Their mighty spirits
> Lie raked up with their ashes in their urns,
> And not a spark of their eternal fire
> Glows in a present bosom."

The relation of an author to his age is the most important of his life. We have seen what terrible temptations
beset him in this relation, — how apt are his principles to
break like bubbles into air, when tried by want and oblo-
quy. But, perhaps, with him it is more properly a relation to his publisher; and certainly few chapters of literary history are more curious than those relating to the
connection of writers and booksellers. In this division
of his life, the man of letters appears as a man of business. No two classes connected by ties of interest have
hated each other more cordially than these; and none
have had more reason. It is difficult to say which has
suffered most. The result of all inquiries may be
summed up in this, — that booksellers have realized fortunes out of works they purchased for a pittance, and
that on a majority of published books there has been a
loss. "Learning," pithily says old Dr. Fuller, "has
made most by those books on which the printers have
lost." On one side, we are told that booksellers are
grasping and knavish; capitalists who loan money on
mortgages of brain and conscience; bon-vivants, who
drink their wine out of authors' skulls. That fine old
poet, Michael Drayton, calls them "a base company of
knaves, whom he scorns and kicks at." Epithets as
contemptuous swarm in all printed books. Indeed, the
author heretofore has shown little sagacity in his deal

ngs with "the trade." He has sold his commodities when spurred by pressing necessities; and it is an universal rule, that when the author wants money the publisher never wants books. No writer who does not desire to end his life in beggary and despair, should ever treat with a bookseller when he is dunned by a washerwoman or dogged by a sheriff. In the present century, Scott, Byron, Moore, Mackintosh, and Dickens, have shown in this far more tact and shrewdness than their brethren of former times. Scott was nominally paid nearly a million of dollars for his works. Byron received ten dollars a line for the fourth canto of Childe Harold. Moore obtained two thousand pounds for his Life of Sheridan, three thousand pounds for Lalla Rookh, four thousand pounds for his Life of Byron. The list might be indefinitely extended. But, in fact, until the latter part of the last century, the science of book-making and book-publishing was imperfectly understood. The "reading public" is a creation of the last eighty years. Previously, writers depended for subsistence chiefly on the theatre, the patronage of the noble, the favor of sects and factions. The age of general intelligence, which makes the great body of the nation the dispensers of fame and fortune, had not commenced. The work best remunerated during the seventeenth and eighteenth centuries was Pope's translation of the Iliad.

for which he received about five thousand three hundred pounds. Most of Pope's contemporaries were but
poorly paid for their literary tasks, and he himself received but fifteen pounds for the Essay on Criticism, and
twenty-two pounds for the Rape of the Lock. Byron
calls the hacks of an eminent bookseller of that period
"Jacob Tonson's ragamuffins." Pope, in satirizing
them, dwelt with malicious emphasis on their rags
and their hunger. The age which succeeded that
of Queen Anne was still worse. The patronage of
nobles and politicians, which had been freely extended
to the best poets of the preceding generation, was
withdrawn. A large portion of the life of so eminent
a man as Dr. Johnson was spent in a desperate and
nearly fruitless attempt to keep up the connection between his body and soul, constantly threatened by
pressing want. The character of a considerable portion
of professional authors was little higher than that of
street beggars. Occasionally they would obtain a little
money. Riot and gaming soon relieved them of it.
With the proceeds of a successful pamphlet or servile
dedication to use the words of another, "they soon diced
themselves into spunging-houses, or drank themselves
into fevers." The art of dodging a bailiff and bilking a
landlord was more important to the poet than the art
of pointing an epigram or polishing a period. Some

of these men were fortunate enough to have residences m cellars or garrets; but most of them, with the blue tent of the sky pitched above their heads, must have waited all nigh', witn shivering frames, for the sweet influences fabled to fall from Orion and the Pleiades. The gulf that yawned between the mouth of a poet and the shop of a baker was almost as deep and wide as that which spread between Lazarus and Dives. Only by the fiercest exertion could the chasm be abridged, and a frail communication opened between the two. Of course, such persons, with five ravenous senses unsupplied, were ready to write anything which would afford them a few guineas. The booksellers, under whose " inquisitorious and tyran nical duncery no free and splendid wit could flourish," keeping them accurately poised between want and utter starvation, employed them to celebrate any remarkable event, any piece of domestic scandal, any assault upon decorum and decency, which would be likely to sell. This era, the darkest and most dreary in English letters, presents the most melancholy satire on authorship extant. There will you see the last infirmity and profanation of intellect, — sin shorn of its dazzling robes, and strutting no longer on its Satanic stilts, but creeping, shrivelled and shivering, to its slavish tasks, chained to the ever restless wheel of its objectless drudgery, to be tumbled down at last into the dust with poverty and shame.

We now come to a delicate part of the subject, which every prudent man would wish to avoid, — the relation of authors to domestic life, their glory or shame as lovers and husbands. One great fact here stares us in the face, — that the majority of those men who, from Homer downwards, have done most to exalt woman into a divinity, have either been bachelors or unfortunate husbands. Prudence forbid that I should presume to give the philosophy of this singular, and, doubtless, accidental occurrence, or find any preëstablished harmony between heaven-scaling imaginations and vixenish wives. Still, it must be said, that not only with regard to poets, but authors generally, a great many have been unhappily married; and a great many more, perhaps you would say, unhappily unmarried. The best treatise on divorce was written by the laureate of Eve and the creator of the lady in Comus. The biography of scholars and philosophers sometimes hints at voices neither soft nor low piercing the ears of men meditating on Greek roots. or framing theories of the moral sentiments. You all know the aidful sympathy that Socrates received from Xantippe, in his great task of confuting the lying ingenuities of the Greek sophists, and bringing down philosophy from heaven to earth   The face of one of Eng and's earliest and best linguists is reported to have often exhibited crimson marks, traced by no loving fingers; and Greek, Hebrew, Latin, and English, must often have met and run together in his brain, as it reeled beneath the confusing ring of a fair hand knocking at his ears. The helpmates of Whitelocke and Bishop Cooper were tempestuous viragos, endowed with a genius for scolding, who burnt their husbands' manuscripts, and broke in upon their studies and meditations with reproaches and threats. Hooker, the saint and sage of English divinity, was married to an acute vixen, with a temper compounded of vinegar and saltpetre, and a tongue as explosive as gun-cotton. Addison espoused a countess; and spent the rest of his life in taverns, clubs, and repentance.

Some men of genius, Molière and Rousseau, for example, have had unsympathizing wives. Sir Walter Scott, walking once with his wife in the fields, called her attention to some lambs, remarking that they were beautiful. " Yes," echoed she, " lambs are beautiful, — boiled!" That incomparable essayist and chirping philosopher, Montaigne, married but once. When his good wife left him, he shed the tears usual on such occasions, and said he would not marry again, though it were to Wisdom herself. A young painter of great promise once told Sir Joshua Reynolds that he had taken a wife.

Married!" ejaculated the horrified Sir Joshua; "then
you are ruined as an artist." Michael Angelo, when
asked why he never married, replied, — "I have espoused
my art, and that occasions me sufficient domestic cares,
for my works shall be my children." The wives of
Dante, Milton, Dryden, Addison, Steele, shed no glory
on the sex, and brought no peace to their firesides. The
bitterest satires and noblest eulogies on married life have
come from poets. Love, indeed, has ever been the
inspiration of poetry. From Theocritus all the way
down to the young gentleman that drizzled in yesterday's
newspaper, it has provoked millions on millions of good
and bad verses, most of which have been kindly gathered
by Oblivion under her dusky wing. Among these
mountains of amatory poetry, there are doubtless some of
the finest imaginations and truest and noblest sentiments
ever breathed from the lips of genius; but the greater
portion only prove, that if love softens the heart, it does
not always decline performing a similar service to the
head. I know a very sensible man who preserves in an
iron box some of these metrical indiscretions of his youth,
in order, if he is ever accused of a capital crime, that he
may produce them as furnishing indubitable proofs of
insanity. The most notable instance of inconstancy
related in the "loves of the poets" is that of **Lucy
Sacheverell**, to whom Col. Lovelace, the Philip Sidney

of Charles I.'s court, was warmly attached. He celebrated her accomplishments in some exquisite poetry; but, on his being taken prisoner in one of the wars of the time, and reported to be dead, she hastily married another. He soon returned to his native land, imprecated divers anathemas on the sex, and declined into a vagabond, — dying perhaps of a malady, common enough in dark ages, but now happily banished from genteel society, a broken heart.

Perhaps the sweetest pictures in the poetry of human ife are those which represent the domestic felicity of those authors who married happily. The wives of Wieland, Buffon, Gesner, Herder, Priestley, Wordsworth, not to mention others, are especially honored among women. Who has not sometimes seen, in the wife of scholar or artist, that elusive and unutterable charm, which has made his heart echo the praise of Fletcher's ideal Panthea?—

> " She is not fair
> Nor beautiful ; these words express her not:
> They say her looks have something excellent,
> That wants a name yet."

Wordsworth, with that pensive spiritualism which characterizes all his poetry relating to the affections, has in three lines fitly immortalized r is own noble wife, as

> " She who dwells with me, whom I have loved
> With such commu .ion, that no place on earth
> Can ever be a solitude to me."

Wherever, in fact, a noble spirit has been fortunate in his domestic relations, he has left testimonials in his writings that those human affections, which are the monopoly of none, are more productive of solid happiness than wealth, or power, or fame ; than learning that comprehends all knowledge ; than understanding which sweeps over the whole domain of thought ; than imaginations which rise and run over regions to which the " heaven of heavens is but a veil."

Of the relations of authors to social life, of their habits manners, dispositions in society, as contrasted with those displayed in their writings, a great deal that is interesting might be said. A man of letters is often a man with two natures, — one a book nature, the other a human nature. These often clash sadly. Seneca wrote in praise of poverty, on a table formed of solid gold, with two millions of pounds let out at usury. Sterne was a very selfish man ; according to Warburton, an irreclaimable rascal ; yet a writer unexcelled for pathos and charity. Sir Richard Steele wrote excellently well on temperance, — when he was sober. Dr. Johnson's essays on politeness are admirable ; yet his " You lie, sir !" and " You don't understand the question, sir !" were too ʟommon characteristics of his colloquies. He and Dr. Shebbeare were both pensioned at the same time. The report immediately flew, that the king had pensioned two bears, — a he-bear and a she-bear. Young, whose gloomy fancy cast such sombre tinges on life, was in society a brisk, lively man, continually pelting his hearers with puerile puns. Mrs. Carter, fresh from the stern, dark grandeur of the Night Thoughts, expressed ʻer amazement at his flippancy. " Madam," said he, ' there is much difference between writing and talking." The same poet's favorite theme was the nothingness of worldly things ; his favorite pursuit was rank and riches. Had Mrs. Carter noticed this incongruity, he might have added, — " Madam, there is much difference between writing didactic poems and living didactic poems." Bacon, the most comprehensive and forward-looking of modern intellects, and in feeling one of the most benevolent, was meanly and wickedly ambitious of place. Of the antithesis between the thoughts of this great benefactor of mankind and the actions of this inquisitor and supple politician, Macaulay remarks, in his short, sharp way, — " To be the leader of his race, in the career of improvement, was in his reach. All this, however, vas of no avail while some quibbling special pleader was promoted before him to the bench ; while some heavy country gentleman took precedence of him by virtue of a purchased coronet; while some pandei happy in a fair wife, could obtain a more cordial salute from Buckingham; while some buffoon, versed in the latest scandal of the court, could draw a louder laugh from James."

But enough for the external life of authors. Their inward life is what most concerns posterity, and constitutes their immortal existence. We might, for instance, speculate on the outward life of Shakspeare, and obtain tolerably clear notions of his acts and conversation as they appeared to his contemporaries; but of those awful periods when the conceptions of Lear and Hamlet, of Macbeth and Timon, dawned upon his mind; of those moments when his shaping and fusing imagination traversed earth and heaven, "invisible but gazing;" of those hours of meditation when the whole chart of existence lay before his inward eye, and he sounded all its depths and shallows; — these we must seek in the immortal pages wherein they are chronicled. And here lies our indebtedness to authors, the undying benefactors of all ages. How shall we fitly estimate this vast inheritance of the world's intellectual treasures, to which all are born heirs? What words can declare the immeasurable worth of books, — what rhetoric set forth the importance of that great invention which diffused them over the whole earth to glad its myriads of minds? The

invention of printing added a new element of power to
the race. From that hour, in a most especial sense, the
brain and not the arm, the thinker and not the soldier,
books and not kings, were to rule the world; and weapons, forged in the mind, keen-edged and brighter than
the sunbeam, were to supplant the sword and the battle-
axe. The conflicts of the world were not to take place
altogether on the tented field; but Ideas, leaping from a
world's awakened intellect, and burning all over with
indestructible life, were to be marshalled against princi-
palities and powers. The great and the good, whose
influence before had been chiefly over individual minds,
were now to be possessed of a magic, which, giving
wings to their thoughts, would waft them, like so many
carrier doves, on messages of hope and deliverance to
the nations. Words, springing fresh and bright from
the soul of a master-spirit, and dropping into congenial
hearts like so many sparks of fire, were no longer to lose
this being with the vibrations of the air they disturbed,
or moulder with the papyrus on which they were written, but were to be graven in everlasting characters,
and rouse, strengthen, and illumine the minds of all
ages. There was to be a stern death-grapple between
Might and Right, — between the heavy arm and the
ethereal thought, — between that which *was* and that
which ought *to be;* for there was a great spirit abroad in

the world, whom dungeons could not confine, nor oceans check, nor persecutions subdue,—whose path lay through the great region of ideas, and whose dominion was over the mind.

If such were the tendency of that great invention which leaped or bridged the barriers separating mind from mind and heart from heart, who shall calculate its effect in promoting private happiness ? Books, — light-houses erected in the great sea of time, — books, the precious depositories of the thoughts and creations of genius, — books, by whose sorcery times past become time present, and the whole pageantry of the world's history moves in solemn procession before our eyes; — these were to visit the firesides of the humble, and lavish the treasures of the intellect upon the poor. Could we have Plato, and Shakspeare, and Milton, in our dwellings, in the full vigor of their imaginations, in the full freshness of their hearts, few scholars would be affluent enough to afford them physical support; but the living images of their minds are within the eyes of all. From their pages their mighty souls look out upon us in all their grandeur and beauty, undimmed by the faults and follies of earthly existence, consecrated by time. Precious and priceless are the blessings which books scatter around our daily paths. We walk, in imagination, with the noblest spirits, through the most sublime and enchanting regions, — regions which, to all **that is lovely in the** forms and colors of earth,

> " Add the **gleam,**
> The light that never was on sea **or land,**
> The consecration and the poet's dream."

A motion of the hand brings all Arcadia to sight. The **war** of Troy can, at our bidding, rage in the narrowest chamber. Without stirring from our firesides, we may roam to the most remote regions of the earth, **or soar** into realms where Spenser's shapes of unearthly beauty flock to meet us, where Milton's angels peal in **our ears** the choral hymns of Paradise. Science, art, literature, philosophy, — all that man has thought, all that man **has** done, — the experience that has been bought with the sufferings of a hundred generations, — all are garnered **up** for us in the world of books. There, among realities, in **a** " substantial world," we move with the crowned kings of thought. There our minds have a free range, **our hearts** a free utterance. Reason is confined within none of the partitions which trammel it in life. The hard granite **of** conventionalism melts away as a thin mist. We call things by their right names. Our lips give not the lie our hearts. We bend the knee only to the great **and** good. We despise only the despicable ; we honor **only** the honorable. In that world, no divinity hedges a **king,**

no accident of rank or fashion ennobles a dunce, or
shields a knave. There, and almost only there, do our
affections have free play. We can select our compan
ions from among the most richly gifted of the sons of
God, and they are companions who will not desert us in
poverty, or sickness, or disgrace. When everything
else fails — when fortune frowns, and friends cool, and
health forsakes us, — when this great world of forms
and shows appears a " two-edged lie, which *seems* but
is not," — when all our earth-clinging hopes and ambitions melt away into nothingness,

> " Like snow-falls on a river,
> One moment white, then gone forever," —

we are still not without friends to animate and console
us, — friends, in whose immortal countenances, as they
look out upon us from books, we can discern no change ·
who will dignify low fortunes and humble life with
their kingly presence ; who will people solitude with
shapes more glorious than ever glittered in palaces ;
who will consecrate sorrow and take the sting from
care · and who, in the long hours of despondency and
weakness, will send healing to the sick heart, and
energy to the wasted brain. Well might Milton exclaim.
in that impassioned speech for the Liberty of Unlicensed
Printing, where every word leaps with intellectual life
— " Who kills a man kills a reasonable creature, God's

image; but who destroys a good book kills reason itself, kills the image of God, as it were, in the eye. Many a man lives a burden upon the earth; but a good book is the precious life-blood of a master spirit, embalmed and treasured up on purpose for a life beyond life!"

NOVELS AND NOVELISTS.*
CHARLES DICKENS.

———◆———

MUCH has been said and written on the uses and
abuses of fiction. Novel-writing and novel-reading have
commonly been held in low estimation by grave and
sensible people, or rather by people whose gravity has
been received as the appropriate garment of sense.
Many are both amused, and ashamed of being amused
by this class of compositions; and, accordingly, in the
libraries of well-regulated families, untouched volumes
of history and philosophy glitter on prominent book-
shelves in all the magnificence of burnished bindings,
while the poor, precious novel, dog's-eared and wasted
as it may be by constant handling, is banished to some
secret but accessible nook, in order that its modest
merit may not evoke polite horror. It thus becomes
a kind of humble companion, whose prattle is pleas-

* Delivered before the Boston Mercantile Library Association
December, 1844.

ant enough when alone, but who must be cut in genteel company. And thus, many a person whose heart is beating hard in admiration of Mr. Richard Turpin's ride to York, or whose imagination is filled with the image of Mr. James's solitary horseman slowly wending up the hill, still in public vehemently chatters on subjects with which he has no sympathy, and on books which he has never read.

Against good novels, that is, against vivid representations or idealizations of life, character, and manners, in this or in any past age, there would seem to be no valid objection; but this department of literature has unfortunately been a domain in which the whole hosts of folly, stupidity, and immorality, have encamped. A good portion of the feeble things purporting to be novels are bad, and some of them execrably bad. Ink-wasters, who could write nothing else, whom nature never intended to write anything, have still considered themselves abundantly qualified to write fiction; consequently, all the nonsense and fat-wittedness in poor perverted human nature have been fully represented in the congress of romance. Of all printed books that ever vexed the wise and charmed the foolish, a bad novel is probably that which best displays how far the mind can descend in the sliding scale of sense and nature. In the art of embodying imbecility of thought and pettiness of sentiment in a style correspondingly mean and gauzy, all other men and women have been fairly distanced by certain novelists, not altogether unblessed now with popularity and influence.

This fact brings us to the distinctions existing between the widely different works classed under the common name of novels; namely, novels written by men of genius; novels written by commonplace men; and novels written by dunces. Commonplace and stupid novels, and commonplace and stupid admirers of them, every community can boast of possessing; but prose fictions of the higher class are rare. When, however, a man of genius embodies his mind in this form, it is ridiculous to allow any prejudice against the name to prevent us from acquiring the knowledge and enjoying the delight he is able to convey. If he be a great novelist, we may be sure that he has succeeded in a department of letters requiring a richly-gifted mind and heart, and that his success entitles him to some of the proudest honors of the intellect.

The novel, indeed, is one of the most effective, if not most perfect forms of composition, through which a com prehensive mind can communicate itself to the world exhibiting, as it may, through sentiment, incident, and character, a complete philosophy of life, and admitting a dramatic and narrative expression of the abstract princ ples of ethics, metaphysics, and theology. Its range is theoretically as wide and deep as man and nature. Life is its subject, life in all its changes and modifications, by climate, by national and local manners, by conventional usages, by individual peculiarities, by distance in time and space, by every influence, in short. operating on the complex nature of man. It is the most difficult of all modes of composition, for, in its perfection, it requires a mind capable of perceiving and representing all varieties of life and character, of being tolerant to all, and of realizing them to the eye and heart with vivid and vital truth. The great novelist should be a poet, philosopher, and man of the world, fused into one. Understanding man as well as men, the elements of human nature as well as the laws of their combinations, he should possess the most extensive practical knowledge of society, the most universal sympathies with his kind, and a nature at once shrewd and impassioned, observant and creative, with large faculties harmoniously balanced. His enthusiasm should never hurry him into bigotry of any kind, not even into bigoted hatred of bigotry ; for, never appearing personally in his work as the champion of any of his characters, representing all faithfully, and studious to give even Satan his due, he must simply exhibit things a their right relations, and trust that morality of effect will result from truth of representation.

It is evident that this exacting ideal of a novelist **has** never been realized. In most of the novels written by men of powerful talents, we have but eloquent expres- sions of one-sided views of life. In some, the author represents himself, ideals of himself, and negations of himself, instead of mankind. Others are rhetorical ad- dresses, in favor of vice or virtue, religion or irreligion, clumsily cast into a narrative and colloquial form, in which we have a view of the abstract feebly struggling after the concrete, but unable to achieve its laudable pur- pose. In some novels of a higher grade, we notice a predominance of the poetical, or philanthropic, or moral element, and though in these we may have pictures, the author constantly appears as showman. Perhaps Scott of all novelists, approaches nearest to the ideal, as far as his perceptions in the material and spiritual world ex- tended. Whatever lay on the broad mirror of his imag- ination he fairly painted; but there were many things which that mirror, glorious as it was, did not reflect. Fielding, within the range of his mind, approaches near absolute perfection; and if he had possessed as keen a sense of the supernatural as the natural, he might have taken the highest rank among great constructive and creative minds; but he had no elevation of soul, and little power of depicting it in imagination. As it is however, the life-like reality of the characters and scenes he has painted, indicates that his genius was bounded by nothing but his sentiments. Perhaps the greatest single novel, judged by this standard of comprehensiveness, is Goethe's Wilhelm Meister. It was the rich result of ten years' labor; and there is hardly a faculty of the mind, a feeling of the heart, or an aspiration of the soul, which has not contributed something to its interest, its value, or its beauty. Imagination, fancy, passion, humor, sentiment, understanding, observation, -- the shrewdest practical wisdom, the loftiest idealism, the acutest and most genial criticism on art and literature, the keenest satire on social foibles, — all have their place within the limits of one novel, without producing confusion or discord; for they are all but ministers working the will of one self-conscious and far-darting intelligence, that perceives with the clearest insight each shape and shade of many-colored life, without being swayed by any; delineating everything, yet seemingly advocating nothing; and allowing virtue and vice, knowledge and ignorance, enthusiasm and mockery, to meet and jostle, with a provoking indifference, apparently, to the triumph of either. But perhaps the range of the characterization including, as it does, so many varying types of humanity, from the vulgar sensualist to the mystic pietist, is more to be admired than the felicity with which each is individualized, and the English reader especially, while he cannot but wonder at the author's abundance of ideas, and be thrilled by the transcendent dramatic excellence displayed in the delineation of a few of the characters, will still miss that solid, substantial, indisputable personality he ever finds not only in the creations of Shakspeare, but in those of Addison and Goldsmith, of Fielding and Scott. In Wilhelm Meister, we generally think more of the knowledge of man and nature we acquire through the characters, than of the characters themselves, — a sign that the philosophic and the ideal have not been realized throughout with sufficient intensity to produce perfect forms of individual life.

Although English literature is now, in respect to novels of character and manners, the richest in the world, we still find that the novel had not acquired much eminence as a department of imaginative literature until about the middle of the last century. Prose fiction was generally abandoned to writers who lacked the ability to embody their folly or indecency in verse. Richardson was the first man of genius who put forth his whole strength in this department of composition, and Fielding began his admirable series of fictions rather with the design of ridiculing Richardson than of forming a new school of novelists. Smollett, without possessing Fielding's depth and geniality of nature, or Richardson's

intense sentiment and hold upon the passions, still exhibited so large a knowledge of the world, such immense
fertility of invention, such skill in the delineation of
humorists, and such power in awakening both laughter
and terror, that his works, though vitiated by the caustic
bitterness of his temper, and by a misanthropic vulgarity
calculated to inspire disgust rather than pleasure, have
won for him a position side by side with Richardson and
Fielding, as the founder of an influential school of novelists. Following these great men in rapid succession,
came Sterne, Goldsmith, Charles Johnstone, Fanny
Burney, Walpole, Clara Reeve, Robert Bage, Macken-
zie, and Mrs. Radcliffe, each of them possessing a vein
of originality, and occupying some new department of
fiction; and two of them, Sterne and Goldsmith, estab-
lishing a renown which promises to survive all mutations
of taste. As the tone of morality and delicacy in works
of fiction varies with the moral variations of society, and
as the Anglo-Saxon mind seems penetrated by an ine-
radicable love of coarseness, the writings of many mentioned on our list are not particularly characterized by
decorum. Indeed, until Miss Burney began to write, in
1778, decency was not considered a necessary ingredient
of romance. Richardson has a minute and ludicrously
formal method of dwelling upon licentious situations, and
Fielding and Smollett include a considerable amount of

4

profanity and ribaldry, which the least prudish reade.
must pronounce superfluous.   The dunces, as a matter
of course, adopted, with some additions, the vulgarity of
their betters, and superadded large quantities of stupidity
from their own minds.   Novels, therefore, soon came
under the ban of the religious and prudent; anathemas
were freely launched at them from the fireside and the
pulpit; and parents might be excused for some bitterness of invective transcending the cool judgments of
criticism, especially if a son was engaged in running the
career of Peregrine Pickle, or a daughter was emulating
the little eccentricities of Lady Betty Careless.

But about the beginning of the present century, a new
order of fictions came into fashion.   As novelties commonly succeed with the public, some enterprising authors
tried the speculation of discarding indecency.   Sentimentality, the opposite evil, was substituted, and the
dynasty of rakes was succeeded by the dynasty of flats.
Lady Jane Brazenface, the former heroine, abdicated in
favor of Lady Arabella Dieaway.   The bold, free, reckless libertine of the previous romances, now gave way to
a lavendered young gentleman, the very pink and
essence of propriety, faultless in features and in morals,
and the undisputed proprietor of crushed affections and
two thousand sterling a year.   The inspiration of this
tribe of novelists was love and weak tea ; the soul-shat

tering period of courtship was their field of action. Considered as a mirror of actual life, this school was inferior
to the worst specimens of that which it supplanted; for
the human race deserves this equivocal compliment to its
intelligence, that it has more rogues than sentimentalists.
However, the thing, bad as it was, had its day. Santo
Sebastiano, Thaddeus of Warsaw, The Children of the
Abbey, and other dispensations of a similar kind, exercised the despotism of sentimental cant over the circulating libraries, and their painfully perfect Matildas,
Annas, Theresas, and Lauras, became the ideal of the
sex. It is evident that these novels, as we see them now
enveloped in their moist atmosphere of sickly sensibility
required the smallest capital of intelligence that ever suf-
ficed for the business of literature. A hero, whose duty
it is to suffer impossible things and say foolish ones;
a heroine, oscillating between elegant miseries and genteel ecstacies; a testy old father, from whom the gout
occasionally forces a scrap of reason; a talkative maiden
aunt, who imagines the hero to be in love with herself;
a pert chambermaid, who fibs and cheats for her mistress, and, at the same time, looks after some John or
Peter on whom her own undying affections have settled;
and a deep villain, who is the only sensible person in
the book;—these shadows of character,—which the
uthor has the impertinence to call men and women,—

oined to an unlimited power to create and demolish fortunes, constitute about all the matter we have been able
to find in some scores of these novels. The style is
bountifully sprinkled with a kind of interjectional pathos,
consisting mainly of a frequent repetition of *ah!* and *oh!*
The whole wretched mixture, despicable in every respect, still passed for many years, with far the largest
portion of the reading public, for the genuine expression
of the human heart and imagination.

It is principally from this vapid class of novels that
the contemporary parental objection to works of fiction
has arisen.   Even at the period of their popularity, they
were mostly esteemed by persons at a certain age of life
and a certain stage of intellectual development; and
there are doubtless many still living who can recollect
the peevish disdain with which the master, and the voluble indignation with which the mistress, of a family,
beheld their entrance into the house.

But these fictions all fled, like mists before the sun
when Scott appeared with Waverley.   Since then, the
novel has risen to a new importance in literature, and
exerted a great influence upon departments of intellectual labor with which it seems to have little in common.
Thierry, one of the greatest of modern historians, con-
fesses that the reading of Ivanhoe revealed to him the
proper method of historical composition.   From being

the weak companion of the laziest hours of the laziest
people, the novel, under the impulse it received from
Scott, became the illustrator of history, the mirror and
satirist of manners, the vehicle of controverted opinions
in philosophy, politics, and religion.   In its delineations
of character and its romantic and heroical incidents, it
took the place of the drama and the epic.   But in becoming the most popular mode of communication with the
public, it induced an indiscriminate rush of mediocrity
and charlatanism into romance, so great as almost to
overwhelm the talent and genius travelling in the same
path.   In addition to this multitude of rogues and dunces,
there was another multitude of preachers and controver-
sialists, eager to inculcate some system, good or bad, relating to other departments of literature, and who should
have written treatises and sermons instead of novels.   Mr.
Plumer Ward desires to answer some arguments against
Christianity, and forthwith publishes a novel.   Professor
Sewall has a dislike to the law of supply and demand,
hates Lord John Russell and Sir Robert Peel, and considers Romanists and Dissenters as criminals; and the
result of these opinions and antipathies is a novel.   Dr.
Croly desires to give a narrative of some political and
military events, and to analyze the characters of some
prominent statesmen, during the present century; and
accordingly declaims, rhapsodizes, and pastes the purple

patches of his rhetóric on a long colloquial dissertation, and calls the agglomeration a novel. There is, of course, no objection to the matter of their works, provided it were treated dramatically; but this substitution of opinions for characters and incidents, is altogether from the purpose of novel-writing.

Of these various classes of fiction, that which, next to Scott's, attained for a few years the most popularity and influence, was the school of Bulwer, or the novel of fashionable life. The publication of Pelham heralded a new intellectual dynasty of fops and puppies. Bulwer's original idea of a hero was the greatest satire ever written by a man of talent on his own lack of mental elevation. He attempted to realize in a fictitious character his notion of what a man should be, and accordingly produced an agglomeration of qualities, called Pelham, in which the dandy, the scholar, the sentimentalist, the statesman, the *roué*, and the blackguard, were all to be included in one "many-sided" man, whose merits would win equal applause from the hearty and the heartless, the lover and the libertine. Among these, however, the dandy stood preëminent; and scholarship, sentiment, politics, licentiousness, and ruffianism, were all bedizened in the frippery of Almacks. To this character Bulwer added another, who may be described in general terms as a man burning with hatred and revenge, misanthropica

and moody, whose life had been blasted by some terrible
wrong, and whose miserable hours were devoted to plots,
curses, lamentations, and "convulsing" his face. These
two types of character, the one unskilfully copied from
Don Juan, the other from Lara, both of them Byronic as
far as Bulwer could understand Byron, reäppeared, like
ghosts of ghosts, in most of his succeeding novels. However much his mind may have grown, and his experience of life increased, since his first plunge into romance,
he has never yet fully emancipated himself from these
original shackles. Indeed, Bulwer is rather an eloquent
and accomplished rhetorician than a delineator of life
and character. His intellect and feelings are both narrowed by his personal character, and things which clash
with his individual tastes he criticizes rather than delineates. Everything that he touches is Bulwerized. A
man of large acquirements, and ever ready to copy or
pilfer from other authors, he discolors all that he borrows
The two sisters in Eugene Aram are copied directly from
Scott's Minna and Brenda Troil, and their relative position is preserved ; but throughout there is manifested an
nability to preserve the features of the originals in their
ourity, and accordingly their natural bloom soon changes
to fashionable *rouge*. That a man thus without humor
and dramatic imagination should be able to attain a
wile reputation as a novelist, is a triumph of pretension

which must give delight to all engaged in experimenting on the discrimination of the public. If we compare him with any novelist possessing a vivid perception of the real, in actual or imaginary life, we see instantly the galf which separates his splendid narrative essays from true novels ; and his unreal mockeries of men and women, quickly passing from individualities into generalizations, stand out as embodied opinions on life and character, not representations of life and character.

In regard to the question which has been raised as to the morality of Bulwer's fictions, it is hardly possible for any person who, in reading a book. is accustomed to observe the biases of the author's mind, to come but to one conclusion. Their general tendency is not only immoral, but it is evident that the writer plumes himself on being superior to that vulgar code of practical ethics which keeps society from falling to pieces ; and, in its place, favors us with a far more elegant system, of which the prominent principle is a morbid voluptuousness, compounded of sensuality and noble sentiments, and admit ting many resounding epithets of virtue and religion when they will serve either to dignify a meanness c point a period. To those who have no objection t devils provided they are painted, this peculiar form t morality may have its attractions. Considered in rei tion to Bulwer's mind, it is one illustration of his defec as a novelist, especially as indicating his lack of intellectual conscientiousness, of that fine sagacity which detects the false through all disguises, and seizes on the true and real with the felicity and speed of instinct. Without this genius for the truth, no novelist can succeed in a consistent exhibition of character; and its absence in Bulwer is the cause of the unnatural mixture of vices and virtues in the personages of his novels. In the present day, at least, when immorality is not of itself a passport to popularity, moral obliquity ever indicates an intellectual defect.

The success of Bulwer stirred the emulation of a crowd of imitators, and for a considerable period the domain of fiction was deluged by a flood of fashionable novels. Bulwer possessed shining talents, if not a kind of morbid genius; but most of those who followed in his wake produced a class of vapid fictions, full of puppyism and conceit, illumined by hardly a ray of common sense r moral sense, and as unparalleled in their dulness as o their debility. How such dreary trash contrived to find readers, is one of those unexplained mental phenomena not solvable by any received theory of the mind. Fashionable life is, at the best, but a perversion of life, and represents human nature in one of its most unnatural attitudes; but still it is life and affords a fair though limited field for light satire and sketchy characterization. The authorlings who essayed to delineate it, from their parlors or their garrets, brought to the task a large stock of impudence and French phrases, perfect freedom from moral obligations, a weakness of feeling which it would be a compliment to call feminine, and an extensive acquaintance with the modes and mysteries of wearing apparel. The drawing-room and the boudoir, the coxcomb's drawl and the fine lady's simper, white waistcoats and top-boots, — these were their inspiring themes. The leading merit of these authors consisted in their complete knowledge of clothes; their leading defect, in forgetting to put men and women into them. Lady Montague, in reference to a titled family of her day named Hervey, said that God had created men, women, and Herveys. The fashionable novelists delineated the Herveys.

About the time that this way of writing nonsense had lost its attractiveness, and every respectable critic welcomed each new specimen of it with an ominous exclamation of disgust, Charles Dickens appeared with the Pickwick Papers. The immediate and almost unprecedented popularity he attained was owing not more to his own genius than to the general contempt for the school he supplanted. After ten years of conventiona. frippery and foppery, it was a relief to have once more a view of the earth and firmament, — to feel once more

ne of those touches of nature " which make the whole
world kin." Here was a man, at last, with none of the
daintiness of genteel society in his manner, belonging to
no clique or sect, with sympathies embracing widely
varying conditions of humanity, and whose warm heart
and observant eye had been collecting from boyhood
those impressions of man and nature which afterwards
gushed out in exquisite descriptions of natural scenery,
or took shape in his Pickwicks, Wellers, Vardens, Peck-
sniffs, and their innumerable brotherhood.

Dickens, as a novelist and prose poet, is to be classed
in the front rank of the noble company to which he belongs. He has revived the novel of genuine practical
life, as it existed in the works of Fielding, Smollett, and
Goldsmith, but at the same time has given to his materials an individual coloring and expression peculiarly his
own. His characters, like those of his great exemplars,
constitute a world of their own, whose truth to nature
every reader instinctively recognizes in connection with
their truth to Dickens. Fielding delineates with more
exquisite art, standing more as the spectator of his personages, and commenting on their actions with an ironical humor, and a seeming innocence of insight, which
pierces not only into but through their very nature, laying bare their inmost unconscious springs of action, and
in every instance indicating that he understands them

better than they understand themselves. It is this perfection of knowledge and insight which gives to his
novels their naturalness, their freedom of movement, and
their value as lessons in human nature as well as con-
summate representations of actual life. Dickens's eye
for the forms of things is as accurate as Fielding's, and
his range of vision more extended; but he does not
probe so profoundly into the heart of what he sees, and
he is more led away from the simplicity of truth by a
tricksy spirit of fantastic exaggeration. Mentally he is
indisputably below Fielding; but in tenderness, in pathos,
in sweetness and purity of feeling, in that comprehensiveness of sympathy which springs from a sense of
brotherhood with mankind, he is as indisputably above
him.

The tendency of Dickens's genius, both in delineating
the actual and the imaginary, is to personify, to individu-
alize. This makes his page all alive with character. Not
only does he never treat of man in the abstract, but he
gives personality to the rudest shows of nature, everything he touches becoming symbolic of human sympathies or antipathies. There is no writer more deficient in
generalization His comprehensiveness is altogether of
the heart, but that heart, like the intelligence of Bacon's
cosmopolite, is not "an island cut off from other men's
ands, but a continent which joins to them." His obser

ration of life thus beginning and ending with individuals, it seems strange that those highly sensitive and patriotic Americans who paid him the compliment of flying into a passion with his peevish remarks on our institutions, should have overlooked the fact that his mind was altogether destitute of the generalizing qualities of a statesman, and that an angry humorist might have made equally ludicrous pictures of any existing society. When his work on America was quoted in the French Chamber of Deputies, M. de Tocqueville ridiculed the notion that any opinions of Mr. Dickens should be referred to in that place as authoritative. There is a great difference between the criticism of a statesman and the laughter of a tourist, especially when the tourist laughs not from his heart, but his bile. The statesman passes over individual peculiarities to seize on general principles, while the whole force of the other lies in the description of individual peculiarities. Dickens, detecting with the nicest tact the foibles of men, and capable of setting forth our Bevans, Colonel Tompkinses, and Jefferson Bricks, in all the comic splendor of humorous exaggeration, is still unqualified to abstract a general idea of national character from his observation of persons. A man immeasurably inferior to him in creative genius might easily excel him in that operation of the mind. Indeed, were Dickens's understanding as comprehensive as his heart,

and as vigorous as his fancy, he would come near realizing the ideal of a novelist; but, as it is, it is as ridiculous to be angry with any generalizations of his on
American institutions and politics, as it would be to
inveigh against him for any heresies he might blunder
into about innate ideas, the freedom of the will, or original sin. Besides, as Americans, we have a decided
advantage over our transatlantic friends, even in the
matter of being caricatured by the novelist whom both
are rivals in admiring; for certainly, if there be any
character in which Dickens has seized on a national
trait, that character is Pecksniff, and that national trait
is English.

The whole originality and power of Dickens lies in
this instinctive insight into individual character, to which
we have already referred. He has gleaned all his facts
from observation and sympathy, in a diligent scrutiny
of actual life, and no contemporary author is less indebted to books. His style is all his own, its quaint
texture of fancy and humor being spun altogether from
his own mind, with hardly a verbal felicity which bears
the mark of being stolen. In painting character he is
troubled by no uneasy sense of himself. When he is
busy with Sam Weller or Mrs. Nickleby, he forgets
Charles Dickens. Not taking his own character as the
test of character, but entering with genial warmth into

the peculiarities of others, and making their joys and
sorrows his own, his perceptions are not bounded by his
personality, but continually apprehend and interpret new
forms of individual being; and thus his mind, by the
readiness with which it genially assimilates other minds,
and the constancy with which it is fixed on objects external to itself, grows with every exercise of its powers.
By this felicity of nature, the man who began his literary life with a condemned farce, a mediocre opera, and
some slight sketches of character, written in a style
which but feebly indicated the germs of genius, produced
before the expiration of eight years, The Pickwick Papers, Oliver Twist, Nicholas Nickleby, The Old Curiosity Shop, and Martin Chuzzlewit, in a continually
ascending scale of intellectual excellence, and achieved a
fame not only gladly recognized wherever the English
tongue was spoken, but which extended into France,
Germany, Italy, and Holland, and caused the translation
of his works into languages of which he hardly understood a word. Had he been an egotist, devoured by a
ravenous vanity for personal display, and eager to print
the image of himself on the popular imagination, his
talents would hardly have made him known beyond
the street in which he lived, and his mind by self-admiration would soon have been self-consumed. His fellow-
feeling with his race is his genius.

The humanity, the wide-ranging and healthy sympa
thies, and, especially, the recognition of the virtues
which obtain among the poor and humble, so observable
in the works of Dickens, are in a great degree characteristic of the age, and without them popularity can
hardly be won in imaginative literature. The sentiment
of humanity, indeed, or a hypocritical affectation of it,
has become infused into almost all literature and speech,
from the sermons of Dr. Channing to the *feuilletons* of
Eugene Sue. It is exceedingly difficult for a man to be
as narrow as he could have been had he lived a century
ago. No matter how bigoted may be the tendencies of
his nature, no matter how strong may be his desire to
dwell in a sulky isolation from his race, he cannot
breathe the atmosphere of his time without feeling occasionally a generous sentiment springing to his lips, without perceiving occasionally a liberal opinion stealing into
his understanding. He cannot creep into any nook or
corner of seclusion, but that some grand sentiment or
noble thought will hunt him out, and surprise his soul
with a disinterested emotion. In view of this fact, a
bigot, who desires to be a man of the tenth century, who
strives conscientiously to narrow his intellect and shut
his heart, who mumbles the exploded nonsense of past
tyranny and exclusiveness, but who is still forced into
some accommodation to the spirit of the age in which he

lives, is worthy rather of the tender commiseration than the shrewish invective of the philanthropists whom he hates but imitates.

Now Dickens has an open sense for all the liberal influences of his time, and commonly surveys human nature from the position of charity and love. For the foibles of character he has a sort of laughing toleration ; and goodness of heart, no matter how overlaid with ludicrous weaknesses, has received from him its strongest and subtlest manifestations. He not only makes us love our kind in its exhibitions of moral beauty, but also when frailties mingle with its excellence. Distinguishing, with the instinctive tact of genius, the moral differences of persons and actions, and having a nicely adjusted scale of the degrees of folly and wickedness, not one of his characters is just as wise or as foolish, as good or as bad, as another ; and he also contrives to effect that reconciliation of charity and morality, by which our sympathies with weakness and toleration of error never run into a morbid sentimentality. He deals in no sophistries to make evil appear good, and the worse the better reason. He does not, as Bulwer is apt to do, dress up a crowd of sharpers and adulterers in the purple and fine linen of rhetoric, and then demand us to wish them well in their business, — an example of abstinence from a common peccadillo of romancers worthy of especial

5

praise in an age which appreciates George Sand and
Dumas.   If he refrains from thus superadding noble sentiments to animal appetites, he evolves, with a sagacity
in which he is only excelled by Wordsworth, beautiful
and heroic qualities from humble souls, disguised though
they may be in unsightly forms, and surrounded by grotesque accompaniments.   He makes the fact that happiness and virtue are not confined to any one class a reality to the mind ; and, by shedding over his pictures the
consecrations of a heart full of the kindliest sympathies,

> " Rustic life and poverty
> Grow beautiful beneath his touch."

Kit Nubbles, in the Old Curiosity Shop, is a pertinent
example, among numerous others, of this searching humanity of Dickens.   Here is a boy, rough, uneducated,
ill-favored, the son of a washer-woman, the very opposite
of a common novelist's idea of the interesting, with a
name which at once suggests the ludicrous ; yet, as
enveloped in the loving humor of Dickens, he becomes
a person of more engrossing interest and affection than a
thousand of the stereotyped heroes of fiction.   We not
only like him, but the whole family, Mrs. Nubbles, Jacob
the baby and all ; and yet nothing is overcharged in the
description, and every circumstance calculated to make
Kit an object for laughter is freely used.   The materials

for numberless characters equally as interesting are within the reach of all novelists ; but most of them are ridden by some nightmare of dignity or gentility, which compels them to pass by the hero in the alley for some piece of etiquette and broadcloth in the drawing-room It is not the least of Dickens's merits that he excelled all his contemporaries, not by attempting to rival them on their own selected vantage-ground, but by availing himself of matter which they deemed only worthy of pitying contempt. He introduced the people of England to its aristocracy ; and though there were not wanting dainty and vulgar spirits to call his novels "low," he soon not only gained the popular voice, but he overthrew the fashionable novelists in their own circles, and his Wellers and Swivellers, edging their way into boudoirs and parlors, supplanted Pelhams and Cecils in the estimation of countesses.

In thus representing life and character, there are two characteristics of his genius which startle every reader by their obviousness and power, — humor and pathos ; but, in respect to the operation of these qualities in his delineations, critics have sometimes objected that his humor is apt to run into fantastic exaggeration, and his pathos into sentimental excess. Indeed, in regard to his humorous characters, it may be said that the vivid intensity with which he conceives them, and the overflowing

abundance of joy and merriment which springs instinctively up from the very fountains of his being at the
slightest hint of the ludicrous, sometimes lead him to the
very verge of caricature.   He seems himself to be taken
by surprise, as his glad and genial fancies throng into
his brain, and to laugh and exult with the beings he has
called into existence, in the spirit of a man observing,
not creating.   Squeers and Pecksniff, Sim Tappertit
and Mark Tapley, Tony Weller and old John Willett,
although painted with such distinctness that we seem to
see them with the bodily eye, we still feel to be somewhat overcharged in the description.   They are caricatured more in appearance than reality, and if grotesque
in form, are true and natural at heart.   Such caricature
as this is to character what epigram is to fact, — a mode
of conveying truth more distinctly by suggesting it
through a brilliant exaggeration.   When we say of a
man, that he goes for the greatest good of the greatest
number, but that the greatest number to him is number
one, we express the fact of his selfishness as much as
though we said it in a literal way.   The mind of the
reader unconsciously limits the extravagance into which
Dickens sometimes runs, and, indeed, discerns the actual
features and lineaments of the character shining the
more clearly through it.   Such extravagance is com
mon.y a powerful stimulant to accurate perception. espec

tally to readers who lack fineness and readiness of intel-
ect. It is not that caricature which has no foundation
but in

> " The extravagancy
> And crazy ribaldry of fancy ;"

but caricature based on the most piercing insight into
actual life ; so keen, indeed, that the mind finds relief or
pleasure in playing with its own conceptions. Shakspeare often condescends to caricature in this way, and
so do Cervantes, Hogarth, Smollett, and Scott. Though
it hardly approaches our ideal of fine characterization, it
has its justification in the almost universal practice of
men whose genius for humorous delineation cannot be
questioned.

That Dickens is not led into this vein of exaggeration
by those qualities of wit and fancy which make the caricaturist, is proved by the solidity with which his works
rest on the deeper powers of imagination and humor. A
caricaturist rarely presents anything but a man's peculiarity, but Dickens ever presents the man. He so preserves the keeping of character that everything said or
done by his personages is either on a level with the
original conception or develops it. They never go beyond the pitch of thought or feeling by which their personality is limited. Thus, Tony Weller, whose round
fat body seems to roll about in a sea of humor, makes us

augh at his sayings as much because he says them as for any merriment they contain in themselves. His .oddities of remark are sufficiently queer to excite laughter, but they receive their peculiar unction from his conception of his own importance and his belief in the unreachable depths of his own wisdom. Mr. Pickwick compliments the intelligence of his son Sam. "Werry glad to hear of it, sir," he replies; "I took a great deal o' pains in his eddication, sir; let him run the streets when he wos very young, and shift for hisself. It's the only way to make a boy sharp, sir." His infallibility in matters relating to matrimony and widows is a good instance of the method in which a novelist may produce ludicrous effect by emphasizing an oddity of opinion, and at the same time connect it with the substance of character. When Sam sends the Valentine to Mary, the old man's forecasting mind sees the consequences, and he bursts out in that affecting rebuke, — "To see you married, Sammy, to see you a deluded wictim, and thinkin' in your innocence it's all werry capital. It's a dreadful trial to a father's feelin's, that 'ere, Sammy." He is troubled by an obstinate suspicion that he himself is especially marked out as an object for the machina tions of widows. In a contemptuous account of a jour ney he made on a railroad, he says, "I wos locked up in a close carriage with a living widdur; and I believe

it wos only because we wos alone, and there wos no
clergyman in the conweyance, that that 'ere widdur
did n't marry me before we reached the half-way station." He is a coachman of forty years, standing, and
accordingly has a wise scorn of all railroads. "As for
the ingein," he says, "as is always a pourin' out red hot
coals at night, and black smoke in the day, the sensiblest
thing it does, in my opinion, is ven there's something in
the vay, and it sets up that frightful scream vich seems
to say, now here's two hundred and forty passengers in
the werry greatest extremity of danger, and here's their
two hundred and forty screams in vun." He is, indeed,
the very Lord Burleigh of low life; and from those par-
oxysms of inward chuckles, — which generally termi-
nated in "as near an approach to a choke as an elderly
gentleman can with safety sustain," — through all the
variety of his sayings and doings, to his earnest exhor-
tation that Sam should spell Weller with a V, he never
loses his substantial personality, never becomes anything
but Tony Weller.

Much of Dickens's most exquisite and most exube-
rant humor is displayed in representing characters compounded of vanity, conceit, and assurance. His Artful
Dodgers and Mr. Baileys are cases in point. They re-
mind you of the child who ran away from his parents
when he was only a year old, because he understood

they intended to call him Caleb.   The little, thievish ragged Dodger, when brought before the police court points to the judge, and politely requests to be informeα " who is that old file up there ;" and warns the court not to keep him long, as he has an engagement to dine with the " wice-president of the House of Commons."   This conceit, varied according to age and character, mingles with the other peculiarities of the two Wellers, John Willett, Mr. Mantalini, and a score of others.   There is Sim Tappertit, the sublime apprentice, conceit and bathos embodied, who is troubled by his soul's getting into his head, and disturbed by " inward workings after a higher calling" than making locks.   Mr. Kenwigs, in Nicholas Nickleby, is an elderly Tappertit, whose discourse is pitched on a more uniform key of fustian.   But Mr. Richard Swiveller is probably the most splendid specimen of the class, and is a fine example of the felicity with which Dickens can tread the dizziest edges of characterization without sinking into mere caricature.   Dick is a sort of shabby Sir Harry Wildair, a reckless, feather-brained, good-natured vagabond, with no depth of guile, and whose irregularities are the result of idleness, vanity, egotism, and a great flow of spirits.   With a vast opinion of his own abilities, he is still overreached by every knave he encounters, and his life is accordingly a descent from one " crusher" to another.   He is so vair that he almost believes his own self-exalting lies; and he cannot possibly see things as they are. When the old grandfather is disturbed by the demands of his graceless grandson for money, Dick is very much surprised that the "jolly old grandfather should decline to fork out with that cheerful readiness which is always so pleasant and agreeable at his time of life." His head is full of scraps of songs and plays, which he has a singular felicitous infelicity in quoting to sustain the sentiment of the moment; and his slang, ever accompanying his sentiment, is as characteristic as the soil on his linen, or the marks of Time's "effacing fingers" on his flash coat. When jilted by Miss Wackles, he says, in parting, "I go away with feelings that may be conceived, but cannot be described, feeling within myself the desolating truth that my best affections have received this night a stifler;" but he then adds, from the promptings of his vanity, and with reference to his proposed suit to little Nell, "that a young girl of wealth and beauty is growing up at the present moment for me, and has requested her next of kin to propose for my hand, which, having a kindness for some members of her family, I have consented to promise. It's a gratifying circumstance, that you'll be glad to hear, that a young and lovely girl is growing into a woman expressly on my account, and is now saving up for me." Dick's imaginative vanity

absolutely deceives his own senses.   He calls a fight, in
which his own face is damaged, a festive scene ; he asks
his companion in punch to pass the rosy wine ; he pays
for his liquor by solemnly advising the boy at the bar
never to touch spirits ; and tells a stranger, whom he
designs to dupe, that the wing of friendship must not
moult a feather.   Sir Epicure Mammon himself hardly
realizes with more fulness his gorgeous visions of gluttony and avarice, than the images of all that is unreal in
dissipation succeed each other as facts in poor Dick's
helter-skelter brain.

Among the various characters of Dickens, there is one
class, which, disagreeing in many things, agree in being
the tormentors of social life.   They are persons whom
the law does not touch, but, compared with some of
them, highwaymen may be considered public benefactors.   As ladies always have the precedence, we will
pass over the currish attorney, Brass, and the coarse
scoundrel, Squeers; the snapping, hissing hatred of
Quilp, and the creamy villany of Pecksniff; in order to
lo fit honor to that miracle of mingled weakness, pru-
dery, and malice, the incomparable Miss Miggs.   She
is an elderly maiden, who, by some strange neglect on
the part of mankind, has been allowed to remain unmar
ried.   This neglect might in some small degree be ac
counted for by the fact that her person and disposition

came within the range of Mr. Tappertit's epithet of " scraggy." She had various ways of wreaking her hatred upon the other sex, the most cruel of which was in often honoring them with her company and discourse. Her feeling for the wrongs of woman was deep and strong, and she had been known to wish that the whole race would die off, that men might be brought to appreciate the real value of the blessings by which they set so little store ; and averred, " if she could obtain a fair round number of virgins, say ten thousand, to follow her example, she would, to spite mankind, hang, drown, stab, or poison herself, with a joy past expression." When she watches at the window for the return of Sim Tappertit, with the intention of betraying him, she is described as " having an expression of face in which a great number of opposite ingredients, such as mischief, cunning, malice, triumph, and patient expectation, were all mixed up together in a kind of physiognomical punch ;" and as composing herself to wait and listen, " like some fair ogress, who has set a trap, and was waiting for a nibble from a plump young traveller." Dickens, in this character, well represents how such seemingly insignificant malignants as Miss Miggs can become the pest of families ; and that, though full of weakness and malignity, they can be proud of their vir-

tue and religion, and make slander the prominent ele
ment of their pious conversation.

Few novelists excel in the finer shades of character
in the exhibition of those minor traits which the eye of
genius alone can detect.   Much of the most refined
humor of Dickens comes from his insight into the subtle-
ties of the ludicrous.   This penetration of vision is often
shown when the humor seems broad even to farcical
excess, and especially when he makes a transparent
hypocrite speak as if he were playing a deep game.
Squeers, for instance, is a thoroughly vulgar rascal, but
he has a dim sense that some men are swayed by moral
and sympathetic considerations, and he accordingly
adopts what he deems the language of virtue and religion when he intends some peculiarly infamous trick.
His mode of translating morality and affection into his
own vocabulary of villany is richly ludicrous.   When
his hopeful son, Master Wackford Squeers, catches poor
Smike, the exulting parent exclaims, — "You always
keep on the same path, and do things that you see
your father do, and when you die you will go right slap
to heaven, and be asked no questions."   Snawley and
Squeers know each other to be scoundrels, yet they ever
preserve in their colloquies a clumsy affectation of senti
ment and conscience.   Snawley, who is hired to entrap
poor Smike, effects his purpose by claiming the boy as

his son. When he meets Squeers he indulges in a commendable strain of snivelling eloquence on the beauty of natural affection. "It only shows what natur is, sir," said Mr. Squeers. "She's a rum 'un, is natur."—"She is a holy thing," murmured Snawley.—"I believe you,' added Mr. Squeers, with a moral sigh; "I should like to know how we could get along without her Natur," he said, growing solemn, "is more easily conceived than described. O! what a blessed thing, sir, to be in a state of natur."

Brass, in the Old Curiosity Shop, a knave compounded of hawk and puppy, who fawns, cheats, and sentimentalizes through the whole book, has become so accustomed to this grotesque affectation of excellence, that it always flows from his lips when he speaks without reflection. He lays a trap to make poor Kit Nubbles appear a thief, and really appears measurelessly horror-stricken when the money is found in the boy's possession. "And this," he cries, clasping his hands, "this is the world, that turns upon its own axis, and has lunar influences, and revolutions round heavenly bodies, and various games of that sort! This is human natur, is it?" Pecksniff, again, is so thoroughly impregnated with the spirit of falsehood, that he is moral even in drunkenness, and canting even in shame and discovery.

Much of the humor of Dickens is identical with his

style. In this the affluence of his fancy in **suggestive**
phrases and epithets is finely displayed ; and he **often**
flashes the impression of a character or a scene upon the
mind by a few graphic verbal combinations.   When
Ralph Nickleby says "God bless you," to his nephew,
"the words stick in his thoat, as if unused to the passage."   When Tigg clasped Mr. Pecksniff in the dark,
that worthy gentleman " found himself collared by something which smelt like several damp umbrellas, a barrel
of beer, a cask of warm brandy and water, and a small
parlor full of tobacco-smoke, mixed."   Mrs. Todgers,
when she desires to make Ruth Pinch know her station
surveys her with a look of "genteel grimness."   A
widow of a deceased brother of Martin Chuzzlewit is
described as one, who, "being almost supernaturally dis-
agreeable, and having a dreary face, a bony figure, and a
masculine voice, was, in right of these qualities, called a
strong-minded woman."   Mr. Richard Swiveller no
sooner enters a room than the nostrils of the company
are saluted by a strong smell of gin and lemon-peel.
Mr. George Chuzzlewit, a person who over-fed himself,
is sketched as a gentleman with such an obvious disposition to pimples, that "the bright spots on his cravat
the rich pattern of his waistcoat, and even his glittering
trinkets, seemed to have broken out upon him, and not
to have come into existence comfortably." Felicities like

these, Dickens squanders with a prodigality which reduces their relative value, and makes the generality of style-mongers poor indeed.

It is difficult to say whether Dickens is more successful in humor or pathos. Many prefer his serious to his comic scenes. It is certain that his genius can as readily draw tears as provoke laughter, Sorrow, want, poverty, pain, and death; the affections which cling to earth and those which rise above it; he represents always with power, and often with marvellous skill. His style, in the serious moods of his mind, has a harmony of flow which often glides unconsciously into metrical arrangement; and is full of those words

> " Which fall as soft as snow on the sea,
> And melt in the heart as instantly."

One source of his pathos is the intense and purified conception he has of moral beauty, of that beauty which comes from a thoughtful brooding over the most solemn and affecting realities of life. The character of little Nell is an illustration. The simplicity of this creation, framed as it is from the finest elements of human nature, and the unambitious mode of its development through the motley scenes of the Old Curiosity Shop, are calculated to make us overlook its rare merit as a work of high poetic genius. Amid the wolfish malignity of Quilp, the sugared meanness of Brass, the roaring conviviality of Swiveller, amid scenes of selfishness and shame, of passion and crime, this delicate creation moves along, unsullied, purified, pursuing the good in the simple earnestness of a pure heart, gliding to the tomb as to a sweet sleep, and leaving in every place that her presence beautifies the marks of celestial footprints. Sorrows such as hers, over which so fine a sentiment sheds its consecrations, have been well said to be ill-bartered for the garishness of joy ; " for they win us softly from life, and fit us to die smiling."

In addition to this refined perception of moral beauty, he has great tragic power. It would be useless, in our limits, to attempt to give illustrations of his closeness to nature in delineating the deeper passions ; his profound observation of the workings of the soul when stained with crime and looking forward to death ; his skill in gifting remorse, fear, avarice, hatred and revenge, with their appropriate language ; and his subtle appreciation of the influence exercised by different moods of the mind in modifying the appearances of external objects. In these the poet always appears through the novelist, and we hardly know whether imagination or observation contributes most to the effect.

In closing these desultory remarks on Dickens, and the department of literature of which he is the greatest living representative, it may not be irrelevant to express

▲ regret that we have not a class of novels illustrative of American life and character, which does some justice to both. Novelists we have in perilous abundance, as Egypt had locusts ; some of them unexcelled in the art of preparing a dish of fiction by a liberal admixture of the horrible and sentimental ; and some few who display talents and accomplishments of a higher order; but a series of national novels, illustrative of the national life, the production of men penetrated with an American spirit without being Americanisms, we can hardly plume ourselves upon possessing. The American has heretofore appeared in romance chiefly to be libeled or caricatured. He has been represented as an acute knave, expressing the sentiments of a worldling in the slang of an ale-house, and principally occupied in peddling Connecticut nutmegs, wooden clocks, and tin ware. That Sam Slick, Nimrod Wildfire, and the Ethiopian Minstrels, do not comprehend the whole wealth and raciness of life as it is in the North, the South, and the West, might easily be demonstrated if a man of power would undertake the task. But one would almost suppose, from hearing the usual despairing criticism of the day, that in the United States the national novel was an impossible creation. Are there, then, no materials here for the romantic and heroic — nothing over which poetry can lovingly hover, — nothing of sorrow for pathos to

6

convert into beauty, — no fresh indi-idualities of disposi
tion over which humor, born of pathos, can pour its
floods of genial mirth, — no sweet household ties, no
domestic affections, no high thoughts, no great passions
no sorrow, sin, and death ?   Has our past no story to
tell ?   Is there nothing of glory in the present, nothing
of hope in the future ?   In no country, indeed, is there a
broader field opened to the delineator of character and
manners than in our own land.   Look at our society,
the only society where the whole people are alive, —
alive with intelligence and passion, — every man's individual life mingling with the life of the nation, — avarice, cruelty, pride, folly, ignorance, in a ceaseless contest with great virtues, and noble aims, and thoughts
that reach upward to the ideal.   In the noise and tumult
of that tremendous struggle, a man of genius not blinded
by its dust or deafened by its din, at once an actor in
life and a spectator of it, might discover the materials of
the deepest tragedy and the finest and broadest humor ·
might hear, amid the roar and confusion, the "still, sad
music of humanity;" might see, through all the rancor
and madness of partisan warfare, the slow evolution of
right principles ; might send his soul along that tide of
impetuous passion in which novelties are struggling with
prejudices, without being overwhelmed in its foaming
flood; and in the comprehensive grasp of his intellect

might include all classes, all sects, all professions, making them stand out on his luminous page in the clear light of reality, doing justice to all by allowing each its own costume and language, compelling Falsehood to give itself the lie, and Pride to stand abased before its own image, and guided in all his pictures of life and character by a spirit at once tolerant, just, **generous** **humane, and** national.

WIT AND HUMOR.*

It has been justly objected to New England society
that it is too serious and prosaic. It cannot take a joke.
It demands the reason of all things, or their value in the
current coin of the land. It is nervous, fidgety, unre-
posing, full of trouble. Striving hard to make even religion a torment, it clothes in purple and fine linen its
apostles of despair. Business is followed with such a
devouring intensity of purpose, that it results as often in
dyspepsia as in wealth. We are so overcome with the
serious side of things, that our souls rarely come out in
irrepressible streams of merriment. The venerable King
Cole would find few subjects here to acknowledge his
monarchy of mirth. In the foppery of our utilitarianism,
we would frown down all recreations which have not a
logical connection with mental improvement or purse
improvement. For those necessary accompaniments of

* Delivered before the Boston Mercantile Library Association
December, 1845.

all life out of the Insane Asylum, — qualities which the most serious and sublime of Christian poets has described with the utmost witchery of his fancy, —

> " Quips, and cranks, and wanton wiles,
> Nods, and becks, and wreathéd smiles,
> Sport, that wrinkled Care derides,
> And Laughter holding both his sides," —

for these we have the suspicious glance, the icy speech, the self-involved and mysterious look. We are gulled by all those pretences which require a vivid sense of the ludicrous to be detected ; and with all our boasted intelligence, there is hardly a form of quackery and fanaticism which does not thrive better by the side of our schools and colleges than anywhere else. And the reason is, we lack generally the faculty or feeling of ridicule, — the counterfeit-detector all over the world. We have, perhaps, sufficient respect for the great, the majestic, and the benevolent ; but we are deficient in the humorous insight to detect roguery and pretence under their external garbs. As we cannot laugh at our own follies, so we cannot endure being laughed at. A Grub-street scribbler, tossing at us from a London garret a few lightning-bugs of jocularity, can set our whole population in a flame. Public indignation is the cheapest article of domestic manufacture. There is no need of a tariff to protect tnat. We thus give altogether too much

importance to unimportant things, — breaking butterflies
on the wheel, and cannonading grasshoppers; and our
dignity continually exhales in our spasmodic efforts to
preserve it.

Now it is an undoubted fact that the principle of
Mirth is as innate in the mind as any other original
faculty. The absence of it, in individuals or communities, is a defect; for there are various forms of error and
imposture which wit, and wit alone, can expose and
punish. Without a well-trained capacity to perceive the
ludicrous, the health suffers, both of the body and the
mind; seriousness dwindles into asceticism, sobriety
degenerates into bigotry, and the natural order of things
gives way to the vagaries of distempered imaginations.
" He who laughs," said the mother of Goethe, " can commit no deadly sin." The Emperor Titus thought he had
lost a day if he had passed it without laughing. Sterne
contends that every laugh lengthens the term of our lives.
Wisdom, which represents the marriage of Truth and
Virtue, is by no means synonymous with gravity. She
is L'Allegro as well as Il Penseroso, and jests as well
as preaches. The wise men of old have sent most of
their morality down the stream of time in the light skiff
of apothegm or epigram; and the proverbs of nations
which embody the common-sense of nations, have the
brisk concussion of the most sparkling wit. Almost

every sensible remark on a folly is a witty remark. **Wit** is thus often but the natural language of wisdom, viewing life with a piercing and passionless eye. Indeed, nature and society are so replete with startling contrasts, that wit often consists in the mere statement and comparison of facts; as when Hume says, that the ancient Muscovites wedded their wives with a whip instead of a ring; as when Voltaire remarks, that Penn's treaty with the Indians was the only one ever made between civilized men and savages not sanctioned by an oath, and the only one that ever was kept. In the same vein of wise sarcasm is the observation that France under the Ancient Regime was an absolute monarchy moderated by songs, and that Russia is a despotism tempered by assassination; or the old English proverb, that he who preaches war is the devil's chaplain.

In view of this ludicrous side of things, perceived by Wit and Humor, I propose in this lecture to discourse of Mirth, — its philosophy, its literature, its influence. The breadth of the theme forbids a complete treatment of it, for to Wit and Humor belong much that is impor tant in history and most agreeable in letters. The mere mention of a few of the great wits and humorists of the world will show the extent of the subject, viewed simply in its literary aspect; for to Mirth belong the exhaust-less fancy and sky-piercing buffooneries of Aristophanes

the matchless irony of Lucian; the stern and terrible
satire of Juvenal; the fun-drunken extravagances of
Rabelais; the self-pleased chuckle of Montaigne; the
farcical caricature of Scarron; the glowing and sparkling verse of Dryden; the genial fun of Addison; the
scoffing subtilties of Butler; the aerial merriment of
Sterne; the hard brilliancy and stinging emphasis of
Pope; the patient glitter of Congreve; the teasing
mockery of Voltaire; the polished sharpness of Sheridan;
the wise drolleries of Sydney Smith; the sly, shy, elusive, ethereal humor of Lamb; the short, sharp, flashing
scorn of Macaulay; the careless gayety of Béranger;
the humorous sadness of Hood; and the comic creations,
various almost as human nature, which have peopled the
imaginations of Europe with everlasting forms of the
ludicrous, from the time of Shakspeare and Cervantes
to that of Scott and Dickens. Now all these writers
either represented or influenced their age. Their works
are as valuable to the historian as to the lover of the
comic; for they show us what people in different ages
laughed at, and thus indicate the periods at which forms
of faith and government, and social follies and vices,
passed from objects of reverence or respect into subjects
of ridicule and contempt. And only in Dr. Barrow's
celebrated description of facetiousness, " the greatest
proof of mastery over language," says Mackintosh, "ever

given by an English writer," can be represented the manifold forms and almost infinite range of their mirth. "Sometimes it lieth in pat allusion to a known story, or in seasonable application of a trivial saying, or in forging an apposite tale; sometimes it playeth in words and phrases, taking advantage from the ambiguity of their sense or the affinity of their sound; sometimes it is wrapped up in a dress of humorous expression; sometimes it lurketh under an odd similitude; sometimes it 's lodged in a sly question, in a smart answer, in a quirkish reason, in a shrewd intimation, in cunningly diverting or cleverly retorting an objection; sometimes it is couched in a bold scheme of speech, in a tart irony, in a lusty hyperbole, in a startling metaphor, in a plausible reconciling of contradictions, or in acute nonsense; sometimes a scenical representation of persons or things, a counterfeit speech, a mimical look or gesture, passeth for it; sometimes an affected simplicity, sometimes a presumptuous bluntness, giveth it being; sometimes it riseth only from a lucky hitting upon what is strange; sometimes from a crafty wresting obvious matter to the purpose. Often it consisteth in one hardly knows what, and springeth up one can hardly tell how, being answerable to the numberless rovings of fancy and windings of language."

To this description, at once so subtle and so comprehensive, little can be added. It remains, however, to indicate some characteristics which separate wit from humor. Neither seems a distinct faculty of the mind, but rather a sportive exercise of intellect and fancy, directed by the *sentiment* of Mirth, and changing its character with the variations of individual passions and peculiarities. The essence of the ludicrous consists in *surprise*, — in unexpected turns of feeling and explosions of thought, — often by bringing dissimilar things together with a shock; — as when some wit called Boyle, the celebrated philosopher, the father of Chemistry and brother of the Earl of Cork; or as when the witty editor of a penny paper took for the motto of his journal, — " The price of liberty is eternal vigilance, the price of the Star is only one cent." When Northcote, the sculptor, was asked what he thought of George the Fourth, he answered that he did not know him. " But," persisted his querist, " his majesty says he knows you." " Know me," said Northcote, " pooh! pooh! that's all his brag!" Again, Phillips, while travelling in this country, said that he once met a republican so furious against monarchs that he would not even wear a crown to his hat. The expression of uncontrolled self-will is often witty as well as wicked, from this element of unexpectedness. Peter the Great, observing the number of lawyers in Westminster Hall, remarked that he had but two lawyers ın his whole dominions, and that he intended to **hang** ▸ne of them as soon as he got home.

Wit was originally a general name for all the intel‑ ectual powers, meaning the faculty which kens, per‑ ceives, knows, understands; it was gradually narrowed in its signification to express merely the resemblance between ideas; and lastly, to note that resemblance when it occasioned ludicrous surprise. It marries ideas, lying wide apart, by a sudden jerk of the understanding. Humor originally meant moisture, a signification it met‑ aphorically retains, for it is the very juice of the mind, oozing from the brain, and enriching and fertilizing wherever it falls. Wit exists by antipathy; Humor by sympathy. Wit laughs *at* things; Humor laughs *with* them. Wit lashes external appearances, or cunningly exaggerates single foibles into character; Humor glides into the heart of its object, looks lovingly on the infirmi‑ ties it detects, and represents the whole man. Wit is abrupt, darting, scornful, and tosses its analogies in your face; Humor is slow and shy, insinuating its fun into your heart. Wit is negative, analytical, destructive; Humor is creative. The couplets of Pope are witty, but Sancho Panza is a humorous creation. Wit, when earnest, has the earnestness of passion, seeking to de‑ stroy; Humor has the earnestness of affection, and would .ift up what is seemingly low into our charity and love

Wit, bright, rapid and blasting as the lightn.ng, flashes strikes and vanishes, in an instant; Humor, warm and all-embracing as the sunshine, bathes its objects in a genial and abiding light. Wit implies hatred or con-tempt of folly and crime, produces its effects by brisk shocks of surprise, uses the whip of scorpions and the branding-iron, stabs, stings, pinches, tortures, goads, teases, corrodes, undermines; Humor implies a sure conception of the beautiful, the majestic and the true, by whose light it surveys and shapes their opposites. It is an humane influence, softening with mirth the ragged inequalities of existence, promoting tolerant views of life, bridging over the spaces which separate the lofty from the lowly, the great from the humble. Old Dr. Fuller's remark, that a negro is " the image of God cut in ebony,' is humorous; Horace Smith's inversion of it, that the taskmaster is " the image of the devil cut in ivory," is witty. Wit can coëxist with fierce and malignant pas-sions; but Humor demands good feeling and fellow-feel-ing, feeling not merely for what is above us, but for what is around and beneath us. When Wit and Humor are commingled, the result is a genial sharpness, dealing with its object somewhat as old Izaak Walton dealt with the frog he used for bait, — running the hook neatly through his mouth and out at his gills, and in so doing *using him as though he loved him!" Sydney Smith and Shakspeare's Touchstone are examples.

Wit, then, being strictly an assailing and destructive faculty, remorselessly shooting at things from an antagonist point of view, it not infrequently blends with great passions; and you ever find it gleaming in the van of all radical and revolutionary mo. ....ents against established opinions and institutions. In this practical, executive form, it is commonly called Satire; and in this form it has exercised vast influence on human affairs. Its character has varied with the character of individual satirists; in some taking the beak and talons of the eagle or the hawk, in others putting on the wasp and the dragon-fly. Too often it has but given a brighter and sharper edge to hatred and malignity. In a classification of satirical compositions, they may be included in two great divisions, namely, satire on human nature, and satire on the perversions and corruptions of human nature. The first and most terrible of these, satire on human nature, dipping its pen in " Scorn's fiery poison," represents man as a bundle of vices and weaknesses, considers his aspirations merely as provocatives of malignant scoffing, and debases whatever is most beautiful and majestic in life, by associating it with whatever is vilest and most detestable. This is not satire on men, but on Man. The laughter which it creates is impish

and devilish, the very mirth of fiends, and its **wit the**
gleam and glare of infernal light. Two great dramatists
Shakspeare and Goethe, have represented this phase of
satire artistically, in the characters of Iago and Mephistopheles ; and Dean Swift and Lord Byron have done it
personally, in Gulliver and Don Juan; — Swift, from following the instinct ᷽ a diseased heart, and the analogies of an impure fancy ; Byron, from recklessness and
capricious misanthropy.   Only, however, in Iago and
Mephistopheles do we find the perfection of this kind of
wit, — keen, nimble, quick-sighted, feelingless, under-
mining all virtue and all beauty with foul suspicions and
fiendish mockeries.   The subtle mind of Iago glides to
its object with the soft celerity of a panther's tread ; that
of Mephistopheles darts with the velocity of a tiger's
spring.   Both are malignant intelligences, infinitely
ingenious in evil, infinitely merciless in purpose ; and
wherever their scorching sarcasm falls, it blights and
blackens all the humanities of life

Now for this indiscriminate jibing and scoffing at hu
man nature there can be no excuse.   There is no surer
sign of a bad heart than for a writer to find delight in
degrading his species.   But still there are legitimate
objects for the most terrible and destructive weapons of
satire ; and these are the corruptions and crimes of the
world, whether embodied in persons or institutions

Here wit has achieved great victories, victories for humanity and truth. Brazen impudence and guilt have been discrowned and blasted by its bolts. It has overthrown establishments where selfishness, profligacy and meanness, had hived for ages. It has felt its way in flame along every nerve and artery of social oppressors, whose tough hearts had proved invulnerable to wail and malediction. It has torn aside the masks which have given temporary ascendency to every persecutor calling himself Priest, and every robber calling himself King. It has scourged the bigot and the hypocrite, and held up to "grinning infamy" the knaveries and villanies of corrupt governments. It has made many a pretension of despotism, once unquestioned, a hissing and a by-word all over the earth. Tyrannies, whose iron pressure had nearly crushed out the life of a people, — tyrannies, which have feared neither man nor God, and withstood prayers and curses which might almost have brought down Heaven's answering lightnings, — these, in the very bravery of their guilt, in the full halloo of their whole pack of unbridled passions, have been smitten by the shaft of the satirist, and passed from objects of hatred and terror into targets of ridicule and scorn. As men neither fear nor respect what has been made contemptible, all honor to him who makes oppression laughable as well as detestable. Armies cannot protect it then; and

walls which have remained impenetrable to cannon have
fallen before a roar of laughter or a hiss of contempt.

Satirists generally appear in the dotage of opinions
and institutions, when the state has become an embodied
falsehood, and the church a name ; when society has
dwindled into a smooth lie, and routine has become
religion ; when appearance has taken the place of reality,
and wickedness has settled down into weakness.   If we
take the great comic writers who represent their age, we
shall find that satire, with them, is the expression of
their contempt for the dead forms of a once living faith.
Faith in Paganism at the time of Homer as contrasted
with the time of Aristophanes, — faith in Catholicism in
Dante's age as contrasted with the age of Voltaire, —
faith in the creations of the imagination at the time of
Spenser as contrasted with the age of Pope, — in some
degree measure the difference between these writers, and
explain why the ridicule of the one should be pitched at
what awakened the reverence of the other.   Great satirists, appearing in the decay of an old order of civilization, descend on their time as ministers of vengeance,
intellectual Alarics, " planetary plagues,"

> " When Jove
> Shall o'er some high-viced city hang his poison
> In the sick air."

They prepare the way for better things by denouncing

what has become worn, and wasted, and corrupt, — that from the terrible wreck of old falsehoods may spring "truths that wake to perish never." With invincible courage they do their work, and wherever they see accredited hypocrisy or shameless guilt, they *will* speak to it,

> "Though Hell itself should gape,
> And bid them hold their peace."

Thus we shall find that many satirists have been radical legislators, and that many jests have become history. The annals of the eighteenth century would be very imperfect that did not give a large space to Voltaire, who was as much a monarch as Charles the Twelfth or Louis the Fourteenth. Satirical compositions, floating about among a people, have more than once produced revolutions. They are sown as dragon's teeth; they spring up armed men. The author of the ballad of Lilliburlero boasted that he had rhymed King James the Second out of his dominions. England, under Charles II., was governed pretty equally by roués and wit-snappers. A joke hazarded by royal lips on a regal object has sometimes plunged kingdoms into war; for dull monarchs generally make their repartees through the cannon's mouth. The biting jests of Frederick the Great on the Empress Elizabeth and Madame de Pompadour were instrumental in bringing down upon his dominions the

armies of Russia and France. The downfall of th
French monarchy was occasioned primarily by its becoming contemptible through its vices. No government,
whether evil or good, can long exist after it has ceased
to excite respect and begun to excite hilarity. Ministers
of state have been repeatedly laughed out of office.
Where Scorn points its scoffing finger, Servility itself
may well be ashamed to fawn. In this connection, I
trust no one will consider me capable of making a political allusion, or to be wanting in respect for the dead, if
I refer in illustration to a late administration of our own
government, — I mean that which retired on the fourth
of March, 1845. Now, during that administration meas-
ures of the utmost importance were commenced or con-
summated; the country was more generally prosperous
than it had been for years; there were no spectacles of
gentlemen taking passage for France or Texas, with
bags of the public gold in their valises.; the executive
power was felt in every part of the land; and yet the
whole thing was hailed with a shout of laughter, ringing
to the remotest villages of the east and the west. Every
body laughed, and the only difference between its nominal supporters and its adversaries was that whereas one
party laughed outright, the other laughed in their
sleeves. Nothing could have saved such an administra
tion from downfall, for whatever may have been its

intrinsic merits, it was still considered not so much a government as a gigantic joke.

And now, in further illustration of the political importance of satirists, and their appearance in periods of national degradation, allow me to present a few leaves from literary history. The great satirical age of English literature, as you are all aware, dates from the restoration of Charles II., in 1660, and runs to the reign of George II., a period of about seventy years. During this period flourished Dryden, Pope, Swift, Young, Gay, and Arbuthnot, and during this period the national morality was at its lowest ebb. It was an age peculiarly calculated to develop an assailing spirit in men of talent, for there were numberless vices which deserved to be assailed. Authors moved in, or very near, the circle of high life and political life, in the full view of the follies and crimes of both. They were accustomed to see Man in his artificial state, — busy in intrigue, pursuing selfish ends by unscrupulous means, counting virtue and honor as ornamental non-existences, looking on religion as a very good thing for the poor, conceiving of poetry as lying far back in tradition or out somewhere in the country, hiding his hate in a smile, pocketing his infamy with a bow. They saw that the star of the earl, the ermine of the judge, and the surplice of the prelate, instead of representing nobility, justice and piety, were often but the mere badge of apostasy, the mere livery o liberticide. They saw that every person seemed to have his price, and that if a man ascertained that he himself was not worth buying, he was perfectly willing to sell his sister or his wife, and strutted about, after the sale, bedizened with infamy, as happy and as pleasant a gentleman as one would wish to meet on a summer's day. It was from the depth of such infamy as this last that the Duke of Marlborough emerged, the first general of his time. In such a mass of dissimulation, effrontery, peculation, fraud, — in such a dearth of high thoughts and great passions, — in such a spectacle of moral nonchalance, dignified imbecility, and elegant shamelessness, — the satirical poet could find numberless targets for the scorn-winged arrows of his ridicule ; could sometimes feel that he, too, had his part in the government of the country ; and with honest delight could often exclaim, with Pope, —

> " I own I 'm proud — I must be proud, to see
> Men not afraid of God afraid of me."

Among these satirists, Pope, of the age of Queen Anne, was by far the most independent, unflinching and merciless. Inferior to Dryden, perhaps, in genius, he was still placed in a position which rendered him more independent of courts and parties, and his invective unlike that of Dryden, was shot directly at crime and

folly, **without** respect to persons. Although he **was**
terribly bitter when galled and goaded by personal opponents, and, in his satire, too often spent his strength
against mere imbecility and wretchedness ; yet, take him
as he is, the great representative writer of his time ; the
uncompromising smiter of powerful guilt, the sturdy
defender of humble virtue ; the satirist of dukes, but the
eulogist of the Man of Ross ; his works the most perfect
specimens of brilliant good sense, his life free from the
servility which hitherto had disgraced authorship ; and
though charity may find much in him that needs to be
forgiven, though justice may even sometimes class him
with those moral assassins who wear, like Cloten, their
daggers in their mouths, yet still great merit cannot be
denied to the poet and the man who scourged hypocrisy
and baseness, at a time when baseness paved the way
to power, and hypocrisy distributed the spoils of fraud.
The courage exercised by such a satirist was by no
means insignificant. The enmities which Pope provoked
were almost as numerous as knaves and fools. After
the publication of the Dunciad, he was generally accom-
panied in the street by a huge Irishman, armed with a
club, so that if any lean-witted rhymer or fat-fisted member of Parliament, whom he had gibbeted with his sarcasm. desired to be revenged on his person, the brawny
Hibernian had full commission to conduct that contro-

versy, according to the most approved logic of the shil-
laleh.

The other great satirist of the age of Queen Anne
was Dean Swift, a "darker and a fiercer spirit" than
Pope, and one who has been stigmatized as "the apos-
tate politician, the perjured lover, and the ribald priest,
— a heart burning with hatred against the whole human
race, a mind richly laden with images from the gutter
and the lazar-house." Swift has been justly called
the greatest of libellers, — a libeller of persons, a libeller
of human nature, and, we may add, a libeller of himself.
He delighted to drag all the graces and sanctities of life
through the pools and puddles of his own mind, and
after such a baptism of mud, to hold them up as specimens of what dreamers called the inborn beauty of the
human soul. He was a bad man, depraved in the very
centre of his nature ; but he was still one of the greatest
wits, and, after a fashion, one of the greatest humorists,
that ever existed. His most effective weapon was irony,
a kind of saturnine, sardonic wit, having the self-posses-
sion, complexity and continuity of humor, without its
geniality ; and, in the case of Swift, steeped rather in
the vitriol of human bitterness than the milk of human
kindness. Irony is an insult conveyed in the form of a
compliment ; insinuating the most galling satire under
the phraseology of panegyric ; placing its victim naked

ᴍn a bed of briars and thistles, thinly covered with rose-
leaves ; adorning his brow with a crown of gold, which
burns into his brain ; teasing, and fretting, and riddling
him through and through, with incessant discharges of
hot shot from a masked battery ; laying bare the most
sensitive and shrinking nerves of his mind, and then
blandly touching them with ice, or smilingly pricking
them with needles. Wit, in this form, cannot be withstood, even by the hardest of heart and the emptiest of
nead. It eats and rusts into its victim. Swift used it
with incomparable skill, sometimes against better men
ᵗhan himself, sometimes against the public plunderer and
the titled knave, the frauds of quackery and the abuses
of government. His morose, mocking and cynical spirit,
combined with his sharp insight into practical life, enabled him to preserve an inimitable coolness of manner
while he stated the most nonsensical or atrocious paradoxes as if they were self-evident truisms. He generally
destroyed his antagonists by ironically twisting their
ᴼpinions into a form of hideous caricature, and then set-
ᵗing forth grave mockeries of argument in their defence ;
imputing, by inference, the most diabolical doctrines to
his opponents, and then soberly attempting to show that
ᵗhey were the purest offspring of justice and benevolence.
Nothing can be more perfect of its kind, nothing more
vividly suggests the shallowness of moral and religious

principle which characterized his age, nothing **subjects**
practical infidelity to an ordeal of more tormenting **and**
wasting ridicule, than his ironical tract, giving a state
ment of reasons why, on the whole, it would be impolitic
to abolish the Christian religion in England.   This is
considered by Mackintosh the finest piece of irony in the
English language.

Swift's most laughable specimen of "acute nonsense"
was his prophecy that a certain quack almanac-maker,
by the name of Partridge, would die on a certain day.
Partridge, who was but little disposed to die in order to
give validity to the prediction of a rival astrologer, came
out exultingly denying the truth of the prophecy, after
the period fixed for his decease, and not he, had expired.
Swift, nothing daunted, retorted in another tract, in
which he set forth a large array of quirkish reasons to
prove that Partridge was dead, and ingeniously argued
that the quack's own testimony to the contrary could not
be received, as he was too notorious a liar to be entitled to belief on so important a point.

But perhaps the most exquisite piece of irony in modern literature, and, at the same time, the most terrible
satire on the misgovernment of Ireland, is Swift's pamphlet entitled, " A Modest Proposal to the Public, for
Preventing the Children of Poor People in Ireland from
being a Burden to their Country, and for making them

Beneficial to the Public ;" — which modest proposal consisted in advising that the said children be used for *food*.
He commences with stating that the immense number
of children in the arms, or on the backs, or at the heels,
of their starving mothers, has become a public grievance,
and that he would be a public benefactor who should
contrive some method of making them useful to the com-
monwealth. After showing that it is impossible to ex
pect that they should be able to pick up a livelihood by
stealing much before they are six years old, and saying
that he had been assured by merchants that a child
under twelve years was no saleable commodity, — that
it would not bring on 'change more than three pounds,
while its rags and nutriments would cost four times that
amount, — he proceeds to advise their use as food for their
more fortunate fellow-creatures ; and as this food, from
its delicacy, would be somewhat dear, he considers it all
the more proper for landlords, who, as they have already
devoured the parents, seem to have the best right to the
children. He answers all objections to his proposal by
nock arguments, and closes with solemnly protesting his
own disinterestedness in making it ; and proves that he
has no personal interest in the matter, as he has not
nimself a child by whom he can expect to get a penny,
the youngest being nine years old ! So admirably was
he irony sustained, that the pamphlet was quoted by a

French writer of the time, as evidencing the hopeless barbarity of the English nation.

It would be easy to trace the influence of satirical compositions further down the course of English history; but enough has already been said to indicate the check which social and political criminals have received, from the presence of men capable of holding them up to the world's laughter and contempt. This satire, in all free commonwealths, has a share in the legislation and policy of the government; and bad institutions and pernicious opinions rarely fall, until they have been pierced by its keen-edged mockeries, or smitten by its scathing invectives.

The lighter follies and infirmities of human nature, as seen in every-day life, have afforded numberless objects for light-hearted or vinegar-hearted raillery, gibe, satire, banter and caricature. Among the foibles of men, Wit plays and glances, a tricksy Ariel of the intellect, full of mirth and mischief, laughing at all, and inspiring all to laugh at each other. Egotism and vanity are prominent provocations of this dunce-demolishing fun; for a man, it has been truly said, is ridiculous "not so much for what he is, as for pretending to be what he is not." It is very rare to see a frank knave, or a blockhead who knows himself. The life of most men is passed in an attempt to misrepresent themselves, everybody being bitten by an ambition *to appear* instead of *to be.* Thus few can visit sublime scenery without preparing before-hand the emotions of wonder and awe they ought to feel, and contriving the raptures into which they intend to fall. We mourn, make love, console, sentimentalize, in cant phrases. We guard with religious scrupulousness against the temptation of being betrayed into a natural expression of ourselves. A perception of the ludicrous would make us ashamed of this self-exaggerating foible, and save us from the cuffs and pats by which Wit occa-sionally reminds us of it. " Dr. Parr," said a young student once to the old linguist, — " let 's you and I write a book." — " Very well," replied the doctor, " put in all that I know, and all that you don't know, and we 'd make a big one." The doctor himself was not free from the conceit he delighted to punish in others ; for satire is apt to be a glass, " in which we see every face but our own." He once said, in a miscellaneous company, " England has produced three great classical scholars ; the first was Bentley, the second was Porson, and the third modesty forbids *me* to mention." Occa-sionally egotists will strike rather hard against each other, as in the case of the strutting captain of a militia company, who once, in a fit of temporary condescension, invited a ragged negro to drink negus with him. " Oh ! certainly," rejoined the negro ; ' 'm not proud ; I 'd just

as lieves drink with a militia captain as anybody else.
Dr. Johnson was famous for smashing the thin egg-shells
of conceit which partly concealed the mental impotence
of some of his auditors.   One of them once shook his
head gravely, and said he could not see the force and
application of one of the doctor's remarks.   He was
crushed instantly by the gruff retort — "It is my business, sir, to give you arguments, not to give you brains."

Sometimes the ridiculousness of a remark springs
from the intense superficiality of its conventional conceit,
as in the case of the young lady, who, on being once
asked what she thought of Niagara, answered, that she
never had beheld the falls, but had always heard them
highly spoken of.   Ignorance which deems itself profoundly wise, is also exquisitely ludicrous.   A German
prince once gave his subjects a free constitution; at
which they murmured continually, saying that heretofore they had paid taxes and been saved the trouble of
government, but that now they were not only taxed
but had to govern themselves.   Wit easily unmasks the
hypocrisy and selfishness which underlie loyal and patriotic catchwords.   Parr said that the toast "Church and
King" usually meant a "church without a gospel and a
king above the law;" and Sydney Smith, while lashing
some tory placemen, ebullient with loyalty, observed tha
"God save the King" meant too often, "God save my

pension and my place, God give my sisters an allowance
out of the privy-purse, — make me clerk of the irons, let
me survey the meltings, let me live upon the fruits of
other men's industry, and fatten upon the plunder of the
public."

Again, all snivelling hypocrisy in speculation, such as
that which, when discoursing of the world's evils, de
lights to call Man's sin God's providence, — all boister-
ous noodleism in reform, whose champions would take
society on their knee, as a Yankee takes a stick, and
whittle it into shape ; — to these satire gravitates by a
natural law. The story told by Horace Smith of the
city miss is a good instance of a shock given to affected
and mincing elegance. She had read much of pastoral
life, and once made a visit into the country for the purpose of communing with a real shepherd. She at last
discovered one, with the crook in his hand, the dog by
his side, and the sheep disposed romantically around
him ; but he was without the indispensable musical
accompaniment of all poetic shepherds, the pastoral reed.
" Ah! gentle shepherd," softly inquired she, " tell me
where 's your pipe." The bumpkin scratched his head,
and murmured brokenly, " I left it at home, miss, 'cause
I haint got no baccy ! "

Wit is infinitely ingenious in what Barrow calls " the
quirkish reason," and often pinches hard when it seems

most seriously urbane. Thus a gentleman once warmly
eulogized the constancy of an absent husband in the
presence of his loving wife. "Yes! yes!" assented she
"he writes me letters full of the agony of affection, but
he never remits me any money." — "I can conceive of
that," replied the other, "for I know his love to be unre-
mitting." Byron's defence of the selfish member of Parliament is another pertinent instance :

> "—— has no heart, you say, but I deny it ;
> He has a heart — he gets his speeches by it."

Satire is famous for these quiet side cuts and sympathetic impertinences. An officer of Louis XIV. was
continually pestering him for promotion, and at last
drew from him the peevish exclamation — "You are the
most troublesome man in my army." — "That, please
your majesty, is what your enemies are continually saying," was the reply. When George Wither, the Puritan
poet, was taken prisoner by the Cavaliers, there was a
general disposition displayed to hang him at once ; but
Sir John Denham saved his life by saying to Charles 1.
— "I hope your majesty will not hang poor George
Wither, for as long as he lives it can't be said that I am
the worst poet in England." Sheridan, it is well known,
was never free from pecuniary embarrassments. As he
was one day hacking his face with a dull razor, he
turned to his eldest son, and said, "Tom, if you open

any more oysters with my razor, I 'll cut you off with a shilling." — "Very well, father ' retorted Tom, ' " but where will the shilling come from ?"

Thus into every avenue of life and character Wit darts its porcupine quills, — pinching the pompous, abasing the proud, branding the shameless, knocking out the teeth of Pretension. The foibles and crimes of men, indeed, afford perpetual occasions for wit. As soon as the human being becomes a moral agent, as soon as he has put off the vesture of infancy and been fairly deposited in trowsers, his life becomes a kind of tragi-comical caricature of himself. Tetchy, capricious, wayward, inconsistent, — his ideas sparks of gunpowder which explode at the first touch of fire, — running the gauntlet of experience, and getting cornered at every step, — making love to a Fanny Squeers, thinking her an Imogen, and finding her a Mrs. Caudle, — buffeting and battling his way through countless disappointments and ludicrous surprises, — it is well for him if his misfortunes of one year can constitute his mirth of the next. One thing is certain, that if he cannot laugh as well as rail — if he cannot grow occasionally jubilant over his own verdancy — if he persists pragmatically in referring his failures to the world's injustice instead of his own folly, — he will end in moroseness and egotism, in cant that nivels and misanthropy that mouths. Even genius and

philanthropy are incomplete, without they are accompa-
nied by some sense of the ludicrous ; for an extreme
sensitiveness to the evil and misery of society becomes a
maddening torture if not modified by a feeling of the
humorous, and urges its subjects into morbid exaggerations of life's dark side.   Thus many who, in our day
leap headlong into benevolent reforms, merely caricature
philanthropy.   Blinded by one idea, they miss their
mark, dash themselves insanely against immovable
rocks, and break up the whole stream of their life into
mere sputter and foam.   A man of genius, intolerant of
the world's prose, or incompetent to perceive the humor
which underlies it, cannot represent life without distortion and exaggeration.   Had Shelley possessed humor,
his might have been the third name in English poetry.
The everlasting delight we take in Shakspeare and
Scott comes from the vivid perception they had of both
aspects of life, and their felicitous presentment of them,
as they jog against each other in the world.

As Wit in its practical executive form usually runs
into some of the modifications of satire, so Humor, which
includes Wit, generally blends with sympathetic feeling.
Humor takes no delight in the mere infliction of pain ;
it has no connection with the aggressive or destructive
passions.   In the creation and delineation of comic char
acter it is most delightedly employed, and here " Jona-

than Wild is not too low for it, nor Lord Shaftsbury too nigh ; " it deals with the nicest refinements of the ludi crous, and also with what Sterling calls the " trivial and the bombastic, the drivelling, squinting, sprawling clown- eries of nature, with her worn out stage-properties and rag-fair emblazonments." The man of humor. seeing, at one glance, the majestic and the mean, the serious and the laughable ; indeed, interpreting what is little or ridic- ulous by light derived from its opposite idea ; delineates character as he finds it in life, without any impertinent intrusion of his own indignation or approval. He sees deeply into human nature ; lays open the hidden struc- ture and most complex machinery of the mind, and un- derstands not merely the motives which guide actions, but the processes by which they are concealed from the actors. For instance, life is filled with what is called hypocrisy, — with the assignment of false motives to actions. This is a constant source of the laughable in conduct. Wit, judging simply from the act, treats it as a vice, and holds it up to derision or execration ; but Humor commonly considers it as a weakness, deluding none so much as the actor, and in that self-delusion finds food for its mirth. The character of old John Willett, in Barnaby Rudge, so delicious as a piece of humor, would be but a barren outt in the hands of Wit. Wit cannot treate character. It might, for instance, cluster ir nu-

merable satirical associations around the abstract idea of
gluttony, but it could not picture to the eye such a person as Don Quixote's squire. It cannot create even a
purely witty character, such as Thersites, Benedict or
Beatrice. In Congreve's plays, the characters are not so
much men and women as epigrammatic machines, whose
wit, incessant as a shower of fiery rain, still throws no
light into their heads or hearts. Now Humor will have
nothing to do with abstractions. It dwells snugly in
concrete personal substances, having no toleration either
for the unnaturally low or the factitiously sublime. It
remorselessly brings down Britannia to John Bull, Cale-
donia to Sawney, Hibernia to Paddy, Columbia to Jonathan. It hates all generalities. A benevolent lady, in a
work written to carry on a benevolent enterprise, commended the project to the humanity, the enlightened
liberality, the enlarged Christian feeling, of the British
nation. The roguish and twinkling eye of Sydney
Smith lighted on this paragraph, and he cried out to her
to leave all that, and support her cause with ascertained
facts. "The English," said he, with inimitable humor,
"are a calm, reflecting nation; they will give time and
money when they are convinced; but they love dates,
names and certificates. In the midst of the most heart-
rending narratives, Bull inquires the day of the month,
the year of our Lord, the name of the parish, and the

countersign of three or four respectable householders. After these affecting circumstances have been given, he can no longer hold out; but gives way to the kindness of his nature, — puffs, blubbers, and subscribes !"

There is probably no literature equal to the English in the number and variety of its humorous characters, as we find them in Shakspeare, Jonson, Fletcher, Fielding, Goldsmith, Addison, Scott, and Dickens. There is nothing so well calculated to make us cheerful and charitable, nothing which sinks so liquidly into the mind, and floods it with such a rich sense of mirth and delight, as these comic creations. How they flash upon our inward world of thought, peopling it with forms and faces whose beautiful facetiousness sheds light and warmth over our whole being ! How their eyes twinkle and wink with the very unction of mirth ! How they roll and tumble about in a sea of delicious Fun, unwearied in rogueries, and drolleries, and gamesome absurdities, and wheedling gibes, and loud-ringing extravagant laughter, — revelling and rioting in hilarity, — with countless jests and waggeries running and raining from them in a sun-lit stream of jubilant merriment ! How they flood life with mirth ! How they roll up pomposity and pretence into great balls of caricature, and set them sluggishly in motion before our eyes, to tear the laughter from our lungs ! How Sir Toby Belch, and Sir Andrew

Aguecheek, and Ancient Pistol, and Captain Bobadil
and old Tony Weller, tumble into our sympathies
What a sneaking kindness we have for Richard Swivel
ler, and how deeply we speculate on the potential exist·
ence of Mrs. Gamp's Mrs. Harris ! How we stow away
in some nook or cranny of our brain, some Master Si·
lence, or Starveling the tailor, or Autolychus the rogue,
whom it would not be genteel to exhibit to our Reason
or Conscience ! How we take some Dogberry, or Verges,
or Snug the joiner, tattooed and carbanadoed by the
world's wit, and lay him on the soft couch of our esteem!
How we cuff that imp of mischief, Mr. Bailey, as though
we loved him ! How Peter Peebles, and Baillie Nicol
Jarvie, and Dominie Sampson, and old Andrew Fairser-
vice, push themselves into our imaginations, and imper-
tinently abide there, whether we will or no ! How
Beatrice and Benedict shoot wit at us from their eyes,
as the sun darts beams ! There is Touchstone, "swift
and sententious," bragging that he has "undone three
tailors, had four quarrels, and like to have fought one."
There is Sancho Panza, with his shrewd folly and selfish
chivalry, — his passion for food an argument against the
dogma of the soul's residing in the head, — a pestilent fine
knave and unrighteous good fellow, — tossed about from
generation to generation, an object of perpetual merri
ment. "That man," said King Philip, pointing to one

of his courtiers, rolling on the floor in convulsions of laughter, — "that man must either be mad, or reading Don Quixote."

But what shall we say of Falstaff? — filling up the whole sense of mirth, — his fat body "larding the lean earth," as he walks along, — coward, bully, thief, glutton, all fused and molten in good humor, — his talk one incessant storm of "fiery and delectable shapes" from his forgetive brain! There, too, is Mercutio, the perfection of intellectual spirits, the very soul of gayety, — whose wit seems to go on runners, — the threads of his brain light as gossamer and subtle as steel, — his mirthful sallies tingling and glancing and crinkling, like heat-lightning, on all around him! How his flashing badinage plays with Romeo's love-forlornness! "Romeo is dead! stabbed, — with a white wench's black eye! Shot through the ear with a love-song! The very pin of his heart cleft with the blind bow-boy's butt shaft!" Look, too, at Thersites : — his lithe jests piercing, sharper than Trojan javelins, the brawny Ajax and Agamemnon, and his hard "hits" battering their thick skulls worse than Trojan battle-axes!

If ye like not the sardonic Grecian, then cross from Shakspeare to Scott, and shake hands with that bundle of amiable weaknesses, Baillie Nicol Jarvie. Who can resist the cogent logic by which he defends his free-

booter kinsman, Rob Roy, from the taunts of his brother
magistrates? "I tauld them," said he, "that I would
vindicate nae man's faults; but set apart what Rob had
done again the law, and the misfortune o' some folk
losing life by him, and he was an honester man than
stude on any o' their shanks!"

Look ye now, for one moment, at the deep and delicate humor of Goldsmith. How at his touch the venial
infirmities and simple vanity of the good Vicar of Wake-
field live lovingly before the mind's eye! How we
sympathize with poor Moses in that deep trade of his
for the green spectacles! How all our good wishes for
aspiring rusticity thrill for the showman, who would
let his bear dance only to the genteelest tunes! There,
too, is Fielding. Who can forget the disputes of Square
and Thwackem; the raging, galvanized imbecility of old
Squire Western; the good, simple Parson Adams, who
thought schoolmasters the greatest of men, and himself
the greatest of schoolmasters!

But why proceed in an enumeration of characters
whose name is Legion — who spring up, at the slightest
call, like Rhoderick Dhu's men, from every bush and
brake of memory, and come thronging and crowding into
the brair! There they are, nature's own capricious
offspring — with the unfading rose in their puffed cheeks
with the unfailing glee in their twinkling eyes :

" Age cannot wither, nor custom stale
Their infinite variety ! "

If "time and the hour" would admit, it would not be
out of place to refer to Wit as an auxiliary power in
contests of the intellect; to its influence in detecting
sophisms which elude serious reasoning, such as the substitution, so common among the prejudiced and the igno-
rant, of false causes for striking effects. In Mirth, too,
are often expressed thoughts of the utmost seriousness,
feelings of the greatest depth. Many men are too sensitive to give voice to their most profound or enthusiastic
emotions, except through the language of caricature, or
the grotesque forms of drollery. Tom Hood is an instance. We often meet men whose jests convey truths
plucked from the bitterest personal experience, and whose
very laughter tells of the " secret wounds which bleed
beneath their cloaks." Whenever you find Humor, you
find Pathos close by its side.

Every student of English theological literature knows
that much of its best portions gleams with wit. Five
of the greatest humorists that ever made the world
ring with laughter were priests, — Rabelais, Scarron,
Swift, Sterne, and Sydney Smith. The prose works
of Milton are radiant with satire of the sharpest kind.
Sydney Smith, one of the most benevolent, intelligent
and influential Englishmen of the nineteenth century

a man of the most accurate insight and extensive information, embodied the large stores of his practical wisdom in almost every form of the ludicrous. Many of the most important reforms in England are directly traceable to him. He really laughed his countrymen out of some of their most cherished stupidities of legislation.

And now let us be just to Mirth. Let us be thankful that we have in Wit a power before which the pride of wealth and the insolence of office are abased; which can transfix bigotry and tyranny with arrows of lightning; which can strike its object over thousands of miles of space, across thousands of years of time; and which, through its sway over an universal weakness of man, is an everlasting instrument to make the bad tremble and the foolish wince. Let us be grateful for the social and humanizing influences of Mirth. Amid the sorrow, disappointment, agony and anguish of the world, — over dark thoughts and tempestuous passions, the gloomy exaggerations of self-will, the enfeebling illusions of melancholy, — Wit and Humor, light and lightning, shed their soft radiance, or dart their electric flash. See how life is warmed and illumined by Mirth! See how the beings of the mind, with which it has peopled our imaginations, wrestle with the ills of existence, — feeling their way into the harshest or saddest meditations, with looks that defy calamity; relaxing muscles made rigid with pain hovering o'er the couch of sickness, with sunshine and laughter in their beneficent faces ; softening the austerity of thoughts whose awful shadows dim and darken the brain, — loosening the gripe of Misery as it tugs at the heart-strings ! Let us court the society of these game-some, and genial, and sportive, and sparkling beings, whom Genius has left to us as a priceless bequest ; push them not from the daily walks of the world's life ; let them scatter some humanities in the sullen marts of busi-ness ; let them glide in through the open doors of the heart ; let their glee lighten up the feast, and gladden the fireside of home : —

> " That the night may be filled with music,
>   And the cares that infest the day
> May fold their tents, like the Arabs,
>   And as silently steal away."

THE LUDICROUS SIDE OF LIFE.*

In a lecture on Wit and Humor, which I had the honor of delivering before this society last winter, I attempted an analysis of those qualities, — exhibited the influence of Wit as a political weapon, and alluded to Humor as a creator of comic character. This evening, I desire to ask your attention to another department of the same exhaustless subject, — The Ludicrous Side of Life; that is, those aspects of crime, misery, folly and weakness, under which they appear laughable as well as lamentable. The subject is so philosophical in its nature, presents so many of the more remote and elusive points of character fo analysis, and demands so rigorous a classification of social facts, that the audience must pardon me if the amusement suggested by the title of the lecture is not borne out by a corresponding pleasantry in its treatment.

The ludicrous in life arises from the imperfection o'

* Delivered before the Boston Mercantile Library Association October, 1846.

human nature, from that perpetual contradiction between
our acts and aspirations which makes our ideas everlast-
ng satires on our deeds and institutions. If we consider
only the elements of human nature, we can easily conceive them so harmoniously combined as to constitute
perfection of character; but the moment we pass from
thoughts to facts, we are amazed at the monstrous perversions and misdirections of these elements. Instead
of a reciprocal action of coördinate powers, we find what
appears to be a mad jumble of conflicting opinions and
impulses. We see the seemingly self-centred being, who
goes under the name of Man, whirled continually from
his beckoning ideals by a thousand seductive external
impressions; changing from " half dust, half deity," into
all dust and no deity; and running the dark round of
weakness and wickedness, from the besotted stupidity of
the idiot, to the grinning malignity of the fiend. We
turn, heart-sick and brain-sick, to the past, only to find the
same moral chaos, — a confused mass of folly and crime,
dignified now with the title of expediency, now with that
of glory, — Caligulas and Neros, Cæsars and Napoleons,
James Stuarts and Frederick Williams, each experimenting on the most efficacious way of ruining nations, each
playing off a gigantic game of theft or murder before an
admiring or reverential world. Vice on the throne, virtue on the gibbet, — there you have the two prominen

figures in the grand historical picture painted on the wide canvass of time.

Now, unless there were in the human mind certain powers, by which all this wickedness and wretchedness could be gazed at from a different point of view than that of passion or conscience, there can be no doubt that thought and observation would drive every good man into insanity. We know this from the manner in which excitable spirits all around us rave and fret at the world's evil, even now. We may not say how thin is often the partition which separates the caucus and reform meeting from the strait-jacket and the maniac's cell; and in how many hearts, on fire with an indignant hatred of oppression and hypocrisy, there burns the impatient impulse of the blind giant of old, to pull down the pillars of the social edifice, if by so doing they might crush the Philistines feasting within its walls. But the human mind cannot long live on stilts, and nature therefore has provided two powers by which the asperities of sensibility may be softened, — Imagination and Mirth : Imagination cunningly substituting its own ideals for facts, and smoothly cheering the mind with beautiful illusions; Mirth looking facts right in the face, detecting their ludicrous side, and turning them into objects of genial glee or scornful laughter. By a perception of human faults and follies under the conditions of Humor, we lose our indignant disgust, and regain our humanity; and by seeing crime with the eye of Wit, we find that it is as essentially mean, little and ridiculous, as it is hateful. The serpent, it is true, still retains its form; but its head is no longer raised, its eyes no longer glitter, its fangs no longer dart poison, but it crawls fearfully away to its foul hiding-place, the trample and spurn of every contemptuous heel — and then it becomes our turn to hiss! What, indeed, can be more pitiably ridiculous than the spectacle of a man, endowed at the best or worst with but a small portion of a demon's venom or a demon's power, setting himself up against God and the nature of things! — an insignificant insect in the path of the lightning, sagely bullying the bolt!

Thus the crimes and infirmities of human nature, as manifested in the million diversities of character and peculiarities of action and position, can be made the subjects of merriment as well as moralizing. Change the point of view, and the things which made us shriek will make us laugh. From Lucifer to Jerry Sneak, there is not an aspect of evil, imperfection and littleness, which can elude the light of Humor or the lightning of Wit. It would be impossible, in one or twenty lectures, to show the unnumbered varieties of Mirth, from which these crimes and infirmities may be viewed. I shall confine myself, therefore, to the two extremes of Humor and Wit

the jovial and the bitter; and I cannot better illustrate
them than by a consideration of the two great exponents
of these extremes, Rabelais and Shakspeare's Thersites.

Between these lie unnumbered varieties of mirth. Rabelais is all fun at human weakness; Thersites, all gall
at human depravity. And first, let us look at Rabelais,
the wisest, shrewdest, coarsest, most fertile, most reckless,
of all humorists. Both his life and works were steeped
in fun to the very lips. Fun seemed the condition of his
being; his genius, learning, passions, hopes, faith, all instinctively fashioned themselves into some of the various
oddities of mirth. Hermes shook hands with Momus at
his nativity. The period in which he lived, the first half
of the sixteenth century, was one of amazing licentiousness; and he has portrayed it with a vulgarity as amazing.
The religion of that age seemed to consist in the worship
of two deities from the heathen heaven, Mars and Bac-
chus, and two devils from the Christian pandemonium,
Moloch and Belial. Its enormities were calculated to provoke a shudder rather than a smile. Yet to Rabelais, the
dark intrigues of poisoners and stabbers calling themselves statesmen, and the desolating wars waged by
sceptred highwaymen calling themselves kings, appeared
exquisitely ridiculous. All the actors in that infernal
farce, all who led up the giddy death-dance of the tyrants
and bacchanals, only drew from him roar upon roar o.

elephantine laughter. His humor rushes from him like
an inundation, unfixing the solidest pyramids of human
pride, whelming everything away in a flood of ridicule.
All that was externally dignified in the church and state
of Europe, — kings, queens, nobles, cardinals, — he tum-
bles about like so many mischievous children, and makes
them indulge in the most insane freaks of elvish caprice.
But here we must distinguish between the resistless
mirth of Rabelais, which is compatible with essential
humanity, and the monstrous glee of some base and
detestable tyrants, who have jested with human blood,
and found a demoniacal delight in laughing over deeds
which have consigned them to the execration of posterity.
Such was Nero, who saw in the burning of Rome, set on
fire by himself, only an occasion for exercising his musical talents.   Such was Barrère, that miracle of cruelty
and baseness, who, amid all the horrors of the French
Revolution, never descended into the weakness of pity,
but performed the worst atrocities of oppression and murder with a fiendish glee.   Thus, to please an infamous
companion, he obtained the passage of a law denouncing
the wearing of a certain head-dress as a capital crime
against the state. He never told the story, says his
biographer, without going into convulsions of laughter,
which made his hearers hope he would choke; and
Macaulay adds, that there must have been something

peculiarly tickling and exhilarating, to a mind like his
" in this grotesque combination of the frivolous and the
horrible, — false hair and curling-irons with spouting
arteries and reeking hatchets." Such laughter as this
might indeed make

> " Hell's burning rafters
> Unwillingly reëcho laughters."

But such was not the mirth of Rabelais. He could not
have laughed *with* Nero and Barrère; he could not have
helped laughing *at* them.

From the stories told of Rabelais, he must have been
in life the same strange, wise, sharp, and mirthful imp,
which he appears in his writings. He seems even to
have looked death in the face with a grin on his own.
As his friends were weeping round his bed, he exclaimed,
— " Ah! if I were to die ten times over. I should never
make you cry half so much as I have made you laugh."
Being pressed by some ravenous relations, who thought
him rich, to sign a will leaving them large legacies, he
at last complied, and on being asked where the money
could be found, he answered, " As for that, you must do
like the spaniel, look about and search." As he was
dying, a page entered from the Cardinal du Bellay, to
inquire after his health. The old humorist muttered in
reply, — " Tell my lord in what circumstance you found
me; I am just going to leap into the dark. He is up in

the cock-loft; bid him stay where he is. As for thee, thou 'lt always be a fool. Let down the curtain; the farce is done." Immediately after his death, his relations seized upon a sealed paper, purporting to be his last will and testament, which, on being opened, was found to contain three pithy articles: "I owe much; I have nothing: I leave the rest to the poor."

Many eminent and some virtuous men have left the world with jests on their lips. Augustus Cæsar appealed to the friends round his dying bed, if he had not very well acted the farce of life. Sir Thomas More joked on the scaffold. The wit of Lord Dorset, in his last hours, surprised even Congreve, the wittiest of English comic dramatists. But Rabelais, in life and death, was the most consistent of all the tribe of Democritus. His deepest and subtlest meditations, his most earnest loves and hatreds, were sportively expressed; and when he came to "leap into the dark," it was a jest that lit the way. It would be easy to moralize out the rest of the hour on such a mirthful monstrosity as this; but that is not my business here. There the old wag stands in literary history —a monument of mirth, with his large, unctuous brain, his rosy and roguish face, his fat free-and-easiness; a mad jest lurking in every line of his lawless lips, a wild glee leaping in every glance of his laughing eyes! There is but one Rabelais.

Now Thersites, in Shakspeare's Trolius **and Cres-sida**, is a man of an entirely different make. He repre-sents the class of wits who hate and deride crime from no love of virtue, and belittle greatness merely to glut their waspish spleen. But he is perfect in his way. He talks a whole armory of swords and stilettos. His **words** hurtle through the air like fire-tipped arrows. **They** seem almost to hit the reader, — so keen are they, and sent with such unerring aim. He is the thorniest of all wits. His bitter brilliancy bites into the very core of things. The great-limbed Homeric heroes, Achilles, Ajax, Agamemnon, look small enough in his stabbing sentences. His railing is more executive than their smiting arms; and he tosses them up and down, riddling them with his satire, almost impaling them with his edged scorn. " Hector," he says to Ajax and Achilles, " Hector will have a great catch if he knocks out either of your brains ; 'a were as good crack a fusty nut with no kernel." And then how his sharp malice exults over these examples of " valiant ignorance," these " sodden-witted lords, that wear their tongues in their arms!' His description of Ajax ruminating is perfect. " He oites his lip with a politic regard, as who should say — There were wit in this head an 't would out : and so there is ; but it lies as coldly in him as fire in a flint, which will not show without knocking." Again, he calls him

the ' idol of idiot worshippers," "a full dish of fool," "a
mongrel cur;" and the richly dressed Patroclus he
addresses as — "Thou idle immaterial skein of sleive
silk, thou green sarcenet flap for a sore eye, thou tassel
of a prodigal's purse, thou! Ah! how the poor world is
pestered with such water-flies, diminutives of nature!"
So fares it with "that same dog-fox, Ulysses, and that
stale old mouse-eaten dry cheese, Nestor." Every one
who wishes to know the height and depth of railing
should give his days and nights to Thersites. He accumulates round the objects of his hatred all images of
scorn and contumely; and he hates everybody, not
excluding himself. Everything in him has turned to
spleen; everything that comes from him is dipped in his
gall. His criticism of the persons and events of the
Trojan war, as they pass before his view, takes the heroic
element clean out of them. It is wonderfully edifying to
hear him discourse of Paris and Helen. With one stroke
of his tongue heroes descend into beef-witted bullies,
goddesses dwindle down into silly girls. He buzzes over
the Grecian camp like a hornet, and seizes every favora-
·e moment to dart down and sting. No matter how
much he is beaten by the brawny fist of his master Ajax
·—his tongue revenges every blow n a hail-storm of
scurrilous words. You can hear them patter on the
helmets of the Greeks, like a shower of Trojan stones

Thersites is an everlasting proof of the resistless power of the tongue. He lashes both armies with a whip of words, and leaves his jests sticking in their flesh like so many thorns and thistles. The fine audacity of Shakspeare's world-wide genius could hardly have been more splendidly displayed than thus in placing the bitterest of human satirists side by side with the most poetical of human heroes.

In looking at the laughable side of life, it might be dangerous to depict it *à la* Rabelais or *à la* Thersites. But between these extremes are numberless varieties ; and it is from some half-way station. perhaps, that we may obtain the best view. We have already seen that it is from the inharmoniousness and consequent perversion of the human mind that the ludicrous in human life has its source, and in proportion to the vividness with which we perceive the original laws and principles thus perverted, will be the clearness of our insight into the ridiculousness of the perversions. Now everything morbid, diseased and one-sided, everything out of its due relations, all excess in the development of any one faculty or opinion, go to make up the vast mass of life's bombast and bathos. The slightest glance at society reveals the most contemptible shams strutting under borrowed names Nothing in itself good but is transformed by the cunning alchemy of selfishness into some portentous evil or pitiful deception, transparent to the eye of Mirth, but full of sacredness to the eye of Wonder. There is a great difference, says Coleridge, " between an egg and an eggshell; but at a distance they look remarkably alike." Now, to question these deceptions, to pierce these bubbles with shafts that disclose their emptiness, generally raises the most discordant cackling among the world's geese. Miss Pigeon is so charmed with the attentions of Captain Rook, that she grows amazingly indignant at the voice which forbids the banns. Appearances have so long been confounded with realities, that an attack on the one is too commonly taken as evidence of enmity to the other; and, like the charmed bullet of the hunter, strikes the shepherd, though directed at the wolf. Everybody knows that fanaticism is religion caricatured ; bears, indeed, about the same relation to it that a monkey bears to a man ; yet, with many, contempt of fanaticism is received as a sure sign of hostility to religion. Thus things go moaning up and down for their lost words, and words are perpetually engaged in dodging things; and it becomes exceedingly dangerous for a prudent man to discriminate between a truth and its distortion — between prudence and avarice, acuteness and cunning, sentiment and sentimentality, sanctity and sanctimoniousness, justice and " Revised Statutes," the dignity of human nature and

the Hon. Mr. ——— ; yet it is just in this discrimination that the ludicrous side of life is revealed.

And now let us glance at this heaving sea of human
life, with its pride, its vanity, its hypocrisy, its selfishness
its match-making, its scandal-mongering, its substitution
of the plausible for the true, the respectable for the good,
and pick out a few of its leading falsehoods for comment.
The first quality that strikes us here is human pride, with
its long trains of hypocrisy and selfishness. " This comes
of walking on the earth," said the Spanish hidalgo of
Quevedo, when he fell upon the ground. Alas! that
Tom Moore's bitter pleasantry on the peacock politician
should apply to so large a portion of mankind : —

> " The best speculation that the market holds forth,
>   To any enlightened lover of pelf,
>   Is to buy ——— up at the price he is worth,
>   And sell him at that he puts on himself."

Now this pride, this self-exaggeration, the parent of all
spiritual sins, tracing its long lineage up to Lucifer himself, is as ridiculous as it is malignant. From our well-
bred horror of the Satanic, the devil to us is a sublimely
wicked object ; but I can conceive of Rabelais as rushing
into convulsions of laughter at the folly of Satan, — at
the mere idea of imperfect evil waging its weak war
against omnipotent Good!

What a lesson, indeed, is all history, and all life

to the folly and fruitlessness of pride! The Egyptian kings had their embalmed bodies preserved in
massive pyramids, to obtain an earthly immortality.
In the seventeenth century they were sold as quack
medicines, and now they are burnt for fuel! " The
Egyptian mummies, which Cambyses or Time hath
spared, avarice now consumeth. Mummy is become
merchandise. Mizraim cures wounds, and Pharaoh is
sold for balsams." Pride and vanity have raised those
iron walls of separation between men, that division of
humanity into classes and ranks, which neither benevolence nor religion can leap. The artificial distinctions
of society, the parents of numberless fooleries of bigotry
and prejudice, will probably afford matter of everlasting
moralizing to the preacher, and everlasting merriment to
the wit. " I considered him," said a witness in Thur-
tell's trial, " I considered him a very respectable man."
" What do you mean by respectable ? " — " Why, he kept
a gig ! " Rank, birth, wealth, saith the worldling, thou
shalt have no other gods but these. Genius and virtue
are good only when they are genteel. The brother of
Beethoven was of this creed. He signed his name, to
distinguish himself from his landless brother, " ⸺
Von Beethoven, Land-owner." The immortal composer
retorted by signing his, " Ludwig Von Beethoven, Brain-
owner." We often hear in society the magical death-

warrant pronounced — " He does not belong to our class — she does not belong to our *set*," — as if those words cast out the condemned into another species, — as if the class or set included all in the world we are bound to esteem, all whose rights we are bound to respect. The huntsman, in Joseph Andrews, calls off his hounds from chasing the poor parson, because they would be injured by following *vermin !* The ludicrous bigotries, the stupendous stupidities, which this isolation from the race engenders, are often perfectly amazing instances of human folly. " When a country squire," says Sydney Smith, " hears of an ape, his first impulse is to give it nuts and apples; when he hears of a dissenter, his immediate impulse is to commit it to the county jail, to shave its head, to alter its customary food, and to have it privately whipped." In Christian England the feeling of caste is nearly as potent as in heathen India. The nobleman hardly realizes that he belongs to the same original species, and has part in the same original sin, as the miner and cotton-spinner; — though nothing would seem to be more evident than that

> " From yon blue heaven above us bent,
> The gardener Adam and his wife
> Smile at the claims of long descent."

But we need not cross the Atlantic to discover these division lines between the vulgar little and the vulga great. The weakness of the American people is the absurd importance they attacn to gentility. To gain this, they sacrifice health, strength, comfort, and often honor. As a man here, however, must have power as well as caste, his life oscillates between two ambitions; the ambition to be popular, and the ambition to be genteel. He accordingly puts his "universal brotherhood" into sermons, his patriotism into Fourth of July orations, and his life and soul into "our set." It is curious to see the agency of this gentility in formalizing even love and hatred. "What will Mrs. Grundy say ?"—this pertinent interrogation has sorcery enough to robe malice in smiles, and freeze affection into haughtiness. As there can be no happiness in marriage without station and style, the old worship of Cupid, the god, is transferred to cupidity, the demon ; the test question, not what a person *is*, but what a person *has ;* and the motive, not so much love as an establishment. This has become so common that it is no longer called sin, but prudence. The fact is so glaring that it has even found its way into the weak heads of sentimental novelists. The last result of all this foolery is that kind of intellectual death going under the name of fashionable life ; the declaration that man is not a mysterious compound of body and soul, but of coat and pantaloons ; and the final triumph of dandy nature over human nature. "Nature,' says the coxcomb in Colman's

comedy, to the blooming country girl, "Nature **is very** clever, for she made you; but nature never could **have** made me!"

The two pillars which support this edifice of human pride are impudence and hypocrisy, or shameless pretension and canting pretension. "Words," said a cunning old politician, a few days before his withdrawal from the palace to the tomb, "words were given to conceal, not to express, thought." Of how large a portion of mankind may it be said, that they do not so much live as pretend? Raise the cry of any reform, and crowds of sharpers and dunces rush to pick pockets and talk nonsense under its broad banners, and the satirist stands by to declare, with South, how much of this liberty *of* conscience means liberty *from* conscience, or, with Colton, how much of this freedom *of* thought means freedom *from* thought. Conservatism is a very good thing; but how many conservatives announce principles which might have shocked Dick Turpin, or nonsensicalities flat enough to have raised contempt in Jerry Sneak! "A conservative," says Douglas Jerrold, "is a man who will not look at the new moon, out of respect for that 'ancient institution,' the old one." Radicalism or reform is another very good thing: but, quaintly says old Doctor Fuller, "many hope that the tree will be felled, who hope to gather chips by the fall." When Johnson asserted patriotism to be the la

refuge of the scoundrel, he said something not more than
half true. Would we could aver that he said something
more than half wrong. Philanthropy is another very
good thing, perhaps the best of all good things ; but much
of it which we see is of a cheap kind ; a compounding of
"sins we are inclined to," by condemning those "we
have no mind to ;" an elegant recreation of conscience,
calling for no self-sacrifice, and admitting the union of
noble sentiments with ignoble acts. The English merchant professes to be horror-struck at the atrocities of
southern slavery ; the slaveholder curses England for her
starvation policy to labor ; the Yankee is liberal of
rebukes to both. Now this inexpensive moral indignation
may produce good results ; but shall we throw up our
caps in admiration of the philanthropy of either ? No!
for on the broad and beautiful brow of true philanthropy
is written *self*-denial, *self*-sacrifice. It says, the system
which enriches me harms another, and therefore I repu-
diate it, therefore I will do all in my power to put it
down.

This conscious hypocrisy it is very easy to understand ;
but there is, in a large number of minds, an unconscious
hypocrisy, which presents an almost insoluble problem to
the investigator. In some cases it is self-deceit, resulting
from weakness or ignorance. In others, it indicates the
passage of the hypocrite from being false into falsehood

itself; the quack believing in his own impostures, — the hypocrisy, once on the surface, eating into the very soul of the man, and lying him at last into an organic lie. These two aspects of character can be perceived, but not analyzed. They baffle the metaphysician, only to shine more resplendently on the page of the humorist. What a Leibnitz or Butler could but imperfectly convey, looks out upon us in living forms from the picture-gallery of Cervantes and Shakspeare, of Addison and Steele, of Goldsmith and Dickens. Without recurring to these instances can be readily adduced from every-day life. Benevolence and malignity often coëxist in retailers of scandal; persons, who can be fitly described only in the verbal paradoxes launched by Timon at his "smiling, smooth, detested" parasites, — "courteous destroyers, affable wolves, meek bears." Tears are copiously showered over frailties the discoverer takes a malicious delight in circulating; and thus, all granite on one side of the heart, and all milk on the other, the unsexed scandalmonger hies from house to house, pouring balm from its weeping eyes on the wounds it inflicts with its Stabbing tongue. Again, — you all know, that, a short time since, when a fear was expressed that the Bible would be banished from the public schools, how much horror and indignation thereat emitted itself in the lustiest profane swearing. But perhaps the finest instance of this unconscious hypocrisy is the fact related of the simple southern clergyman. He owned half of a negro slave; and in his prayers, therefore, he prayed that the Lord would preserve his house, his land, his family, and his half of *Pomp.*

It would be impossible to note a thousandth part of the hypocrisies, conscious or unconscious, woven into the very texture of every-day life, and having their source in the desire of men to appear better than they are. Popular as are the realities of avarice, malice, falsehood and chicane, nothing is more unpopular than their appearances. License, therefore, must talk the language of freedom; knavery must stalk on the stilts of philanthropy; public plunder and national degradation must wear the guise of glory and patriotism. Some have almost reached the perfection of South's ideal hypocrite, "who never opens his mouth in earnest, but when he eats or breathes." Everywhere, cant; nowhere, a plain avowal of folly or selfishness. Oliver Cromwell cannot butcher a couple of poor Irish garrisons, without doing it for the glory of God; the Hon. Mr. ——— cannot argue in favor of perpetual slavery, without doing it for the good of the slave. O! never talk of rewarding virtue, for virtue never can be paid in the world's sugar-plums; but if life cannot be carried on without roguery, would it not be well to place a bounty on courageous, uncanting rascality, and, passing by a heap of tongue-virtuous hypocrites, select that man for office who **dares to** acknowledge himself a rogue !

Among the countless deceptions passed off on **our** sham-ridden race, let me direct your attention to **the** deception of dignity, as it is one which includes **many** others.   Among those terms which have long ceased **to** have any vital meaning, the word dignity deserves a **dis**graceful prominence.   No word has fallen so readily **as** this into the designs of cant, imposture and pretence **;** none has played so well the part of verbal scarecrow, **to** frighten children of all ages and both sexes.   It **is at** once the thinnest and most effective of all the **coverings** under which duncedom sneaks and skulks.   Most of **the** men of dignity, who awe or bore their more **genial** brethren, are simply men possessing the art of **passing** off their insensibility for wisdom, their dulness for depth **;** and of concealing imbecility of intellect under **haughti**ness of manner.   Their success in this small game is **one** of the stereotyped satires on mankind.   Once strip **from** these pretenders their stolen garments, once **disconnect** their show of dignity from their real meanness, and **they** would stand shivering and defenceless, objects of the **tears** of pity, or targets for the arrows of scorn.   But it is **the** misfortune of this world's affairs, that offices, fitly **occu** pied only by talent and genius, which despise **pretence** should be filled by respectable stupidity and **dignified**

emptiness to whom pretence is the very soul of life.
Manner triumphs over matter; and throughout society,
politics, letters and science, we are doomed to meet a
swarm of dunces and windbags, disguised as gentlemen,
statesmen and scholars. Coleridge once saw, at a dinner
table, a dignified man with a face wise as the moon's.
The awful charm of his manner was not broken until
the muffins appeared, and then the imp of gluttony forced
from him the exclamation, — " Them 's the jockeys for
me ! " A good number of such dignitarians remain
undiscovered.

It is curious to note how these pompous gentlemen
rule in society and government. How often do history
and the newspapers exhibit to us the spectacle of a
heavy-headed stupiditarian in official station, veiling the
sheerest incompetency in a mysterious sublimity of carriage, solemnly trifling away the interests of the state,
the dupe of his own obstinate ignorance, and engaged,
year after year, in ruining a people after the most dignified fashion ! You have all seen that inscrutable dispen
sation known by the name of the dignified gentleman .
an embodied tediousness, which society is apt not only
to tolerate but worship · a person who announces the
stale commonplaces of conversation with the awful pre-
sision of one bringing down to tne valleys of thought
bright truths plucked on its summits; who is so pro-

foundly deep and painfully solid on the weather, the last
novel, or some other nothing of the day ; who is inex
pressibly shocked if your eternal gratitude does not repay
him for the trite information he consumed your hour in
imparting ; and who, if you insinuate that his calm, contented, imperturbable stupidity is preying upon your
patience, instantly stands upon his dignity, and puts on a
face. Yet this man, with just enough knowledge " to
raise himself from the insignificance of a dunce to the
dignity of a bore," is still in high favor even with those
whose animation he checks and chills, — why? Because
he has, all say, so much of the dignity of a gentleman !
The poor, bright, good-natured man, who has done all in
his power to be agreeable, joins in the cry of praise, and
feelingly regrets that nature has not adorned him, too,
with dulness as a robe, so that he likewise might freeze
the volatile into respect, and be held up as a model spoon
for all dunces to imitate.   This dignity, which so many
view with reverential despair, must have twinned, " two
at a birth," with that ursine vanity mentioned by Coleridge, " which keeps itself alive by sucking the paws of
its own self-importance." The Duke of Somerset was
one of these dignified gentlemen.   His second wife was
the most beautiful woman in England   She once suddenly threw her arms round his neck, and gave him a
kiss which might have gladdened the heart of an empe-

ror. The duke, lifting his heavy head awfully up, and giving his shoulders an aristocratic square, slowly said, "Madam, my first wife was a Howard, and she never would have taken such a liberty."

This absurd importance attached to dignity is a fertile source of bombast in life. It not only exalts the bad or brainless into high position, but it is apt to convert eminent men into embodied hyperboles; for, to fulfil the popular requisitions of greatness, you will sometimes see statesmen descend into this poor deception, and, though giants in action or speculation, condescend to become charlatans in manner. Lord Chatham and Napoleon were as much actors as Garrick or Talma. Now, an imposing air should always be taken as evidence of imposition. Dignity is often a veil between us and the real truth of things. Wit pierces this veil with its glittering shafts, and lets in the "insolent light." Humor carelessly lifts the curtain, swaggers jauntily into the place itself, salutes the amazed wire-pullers with a knowing nod, and ends with slapping Dignity on the back, with a "How are ye, my old boy?"

In truth, the factitious elevation we give to some persons comes from identifying the actual and the ideal, — the imagination cunningly suppressing minor faults, exaggerating certain qualities into colossal size, and calling those qualities by the name of men. The characters

of distinguished personages are generally drawn in this
way.   It is the vice of most biography phies, and gives a
wooden and unnatural aspect to most characters in history   The difference between the truth and deception, in
this regard, is the difference between a character drawn
by Racine and a character drawn by Shakspeare or
Scott.   This factitious dignity cannot stand a moment
the test of ridicule.   One of the most externally awful
and imposing persons in the world is the Speaker of the
House of Commons.   There once happened to be a dead
silence in the house, when its members were all present.
This was broken by a startling hiccough in the gal-
lery, and the voice of a drunken reporter putting the
stunning interrogative, " Mr. Speaker, will you favor us
with a song ? "

The dainty portions of literature are ever liable to
overturn from the shocks of prose.   Not only has life its
udicrous side, but its serious side has its ludicrous
point.   Poetry itself is often an exquisitely ironical
comment upon actual life, but few seem to take the joke.
The original of Goethe's Werther, whose " sorrows "
have become immortal, was a dull fellow, with nothing
in his face indicative of sentiment or intelligence.   A
person who visited him remarked, that nobody would
know he had any brains, if the poet had not informed us
he had blown them out.   Halleck's notion of Wyoming

drawn from observation, is different from Campbell's, drawn from fancy. The Gertrude of Halleck is found 'hoeing corn.' Pastoral life can hardly be found in pastures. All heroism, even, which depends on external costume or form, is ever in danger of being killed by little actualities. "The Iliad," says Sydney Smith, " would never have come down to these times if Agamemnon had given Achilles a box on the ear. We should have trembled for the Æneid if some Trojan nobleman had kicked the pious Æneas in the Fourth Book. Æneas may have deserved it; but he could not have founded the Roman empire after so distressing an accident." And we have all seen how an American general, singed and scarred with the fire of desperately contested battles, came near being extinguished at last, from a slightly increased alacrity in the disposition of his soup.

From this confounding of substance with form, this universal tendency to individual exaggeration and bombast, this stilted way of carrying on life, it has become customary to identify mirth with frivolity. Without insisting upon the depth and wisdom of the great Wits and Humorists of the world, it is evident that the best arguments are often condensed into epigrams, and that good jokes are often comprehensive axioms.

The narrowness of utilitarianism was never made so evident as in the remark, that " we do not estimate the

value of the sun by the amount it saves us in gas.'
Carlyle's whole theory of government is contained in a
quibble, — that nations are not governed by the able
man, but the man able to get appointed. Superstitions
exploded by knowledge, often exist as puns. Thus some
of the ancients, who believed the soul to be made of fire
considered death by drowning to be remediless — water
putting the soul *out*. An epigram often flashes light
into regions where reason shines but dimly. Holmes
disposed of the bigot at once, when he compared his
mind to the pupil of the eye, — "the more light you let
into it, the more it contracts." Nothing better exhibits
the horrors of capricious despotism than the humorous
statement of the King of Candia's habits : "If his tea is
not sweet enough, he impales his footman; and smites
off the head of half a dozen noblemen, if he has a pain
in his own." In this connection, also, it is not inappro-
priate to refer to the importance of a vivid perception of
the ludicrous as a weapon of self-defence. That habit
of instantaneous analysis which we call readiness has
saved thousands from contempt or mortification. The
dexterous leap of thought, by which the mind escapes
from a seemingly hopeless dilemma, is worth all the
vestments of dignity which the world holds. It was
this readiness in repartee which continually saved Vol
taire from social overturn. He once praised anothe

writer very heartily to a third person. "It is very strange," was the reply. "that you speak so well of him, for he says that you are a charlatan." — "O!" replied Voltaire, "I think it very likely that both of us may be mistaken." Again, you must all have heard the anecdote of the young gentleman who was discoursing very dogmatically about the appropriate sphere of woman. "And pray, sir," screamed out an old lady, "what is the appropriate sphere of woman?" — "A celestial sphere, madam!" Robert Hall did not lose his power of retort even in madness. A hypocritical condoler with his misfortunes once visited him in the mad-house, and said, in a whining tone, "What brought you here, Mr. Hall?" Hall significantly touched his brow with his finger, and replied, "What'll never bring you, sir — too much brain!" A rapid change from enthusiasm to nonchalance is often necessary in society. Thus a person once eloquently eulogizing the angelic qualities of Joan of Arc, was suddenly met by the petulant question, — what was Joan of Arc made of? "She was Maid of Orleans." A Yankee is never upset by the astonishing. He walks among the Alps with his hands in his pockets, and the smoke of his cigar is seen among the mists of Niagara. One of this class sauntered into the office of the lightning telegraph, and asked how long it would take to transmit a message to Washington. "Ten minutes," was the reply. "I can't wait," was his rejoinder. Sheridan never was without a reason, never failed to extricate himself in any emergency by his wit. At a country house, where he was once on a visit, an elderly maiden lady desired to be his companion in a walk. He excused himself at first on the ground of the badness of the weather. She soon afterwards, however, intercepted him in an attempt to escape without her. "Well," she said, "it has cleared up, I see." — "Why yes," he answered, "it has cleared up enough for *one*, but not enough for *two*." It was this readiness which made John Randolph so terrible in retort. He was the Thersites of Congress, — a tongue-stabber. No hyperbole of contempt or scorn could be launched against him, but he could overtop it with something more scornful and contemptuous. Opposition only maddened him into more brilliant bitterness. "Is n't it a shame, Mr. President," said he one day in the senate, "that the noble bull-dogs of the administration should be wasting their precious time in worrying the rats of the opposition." Immediately the senate was in an uproar, and he was clamorously called to order. The presiding officer, however sustained him; and, pointing his long, skinny finger at his opponents, Randolph screamed out, "Rats, did I say? — *mice, mice!*"

The ludicrous side of life, like the serious side, has its

.iterature, and it is a literature of untold wealth. **Mirth** is a Proteus, changing its shape and manner with the thousand diversities of individual character, from the most superficial gayety to the deepest, most earnest humor. Thus the wit of the airy, feather-brained Farquhar glances and gleams like heat lightning; that of Milton blasts and burns like the bolt. Let us glance carelessly over this wide field of comic writers, who have drawn new forms of mirthful being from life's ludicrous side, and note, here and there, a wit or humorist. There is the humor of Goethe, like his own summer morning, mirthfully clear; and there is the tough and knotty humor of old Ben Jonson, at times ground down at the edge to a sharp cutting scorn, and occasionally hissing out stinging words, which seem, like his own Mercury's, "steeped in the very brine of conceit, and sparkle like salt in fire." There is the incessant brilliancy of Sheridan, —

> " Whose humor, as gay as the fire-fly's light,
>   Played round every subject, and shone as it played;
>   Whose wit, in the combat as gentle as bright,
>   Ne'er carried a heart-stain away on its blade."

'There is the uncouth mirth, that winds, stutters, wriggles and screams, dark, scornful and savage, among the dislocated joints of Carlyle's spavined sentences. There is the lithe, springy sarcasm, the hilarious *badinage*, the

brilliant careless disdain, which sparkle and scorch **along**
the glistening page of Holmes. There is the sleepy smile
that sometimes lies so benignly on the sweet and serious
diction of old Izaak Walton. There is the mirth **of**
Dickens, twinkling now in some ironical insinuation, —
and anon winking at you with pleasant maliciousness, **its**
distended cheeks fat with suppressed glee, — and then,
again, coming out in broad gushes of humor, overflowing
all banks and bounds of conventional decorum. There
is Sydney Smith, — sly, sleek, swift, subtle, — a moment's motion, and the human mouse is in his paw!
Mark, in contrast with him, the beautiful heedlessness
with which the Ariel-like spirit of Gay pours itself out
in benevolent mockeries of human folly. There, in a
corner, look at that petulant little man, his features
working with thought and pain, his lips wrinkled with a
sardonic smile ; and, see ! the immortal personality *l* as
received its last point and polish in that toiling br in,
and, in a straight, luminous line, with a twang like
Scorn's own arrow, hisses through the air the unerring
shaft of Pope, — to

> " Dasn the proud gamester from his gilded car,"

And,

> " Bare the base heart that lurks beneath a star."

There, a little above Pope, see Dryden, keenly **dissecting**

the inconsistencies of Buckingham's volatile mind, or leisurely crushing out the insect life of Shadwell. —

> " Owned, without dispute,
> Throughout the realms of Nonsense abso.ute."

There, moving gracefully through that carpeted parlor mark that dapper, diminutive Irish gentleman. The moment you look at him, your eyes are dazzled with the whizzing rockets and hissing wheels, streaking the air with a million sparks, from the pyrotechnic brain of Anacreon Moore. Again, cast your eyes from that blinding glare and glitter, to the soft and beautiful brilliancy, the winning grace, the bland banter, the gliding wit, the diffusive humor, which make you in love with all mankind in the charming pages of Washington Irving. And now, for another change, — glance at the jerks and jets of satire, the mirthful audacities, the fretting and teasing mockeries, of that fat, sharp imp, half Mephistopheles, half Falstaff, that cross between Beelzebub and Rabelais, known, in all lands, as the matchless Mr. Punch. No English statesman, however great his power, no English nobleman, however high his rank, but knows that every week he may be pointed at by the scoffing finger of that omnipotent buffoon, and consigned to the ridicule of the world. The pride of intellect, the pride of wealth, the power to oppress — nothing can save the dunce or criminal from being pounced upon by Punch, and held up to

a derision or execration, which shall ring from London to
St. Petersburg, from the Ganges to the Oregon.   From
the vitriol pleasantries of this arch-fiend of Momus, let
us turn to the benevolent mirth of Addison and Steele,
whose glory it was to redeem polite literature from moral
depravity, by showing that wit could chime merrily in
with the voice of virtue, and who smoothly laughed away
many a vice of the national character, by that humor
which tenderly touches the sensitive point with an evan
escent grace and genial glee.   And here let us not forget
Goldsmith, whose delicious mirth is of that rare quality
which lies too deep for laughter, — which melts softly
into the mind, suffusing it with inexpressible delight, and
sending the soul dancing joyously into the eyes, to utter
its merriment in liquid glances, passing all the expression
of tone.   And here, though we cannot do him justice,
let us remember the name of Nathaniel Hawthorne,
deserving a place second to none in that band of humorists whose beautiful depth of cheerful feeling is the very
poetry of mirth.   In ease, grace, delicate sharpness of
satire, — in a felicity of touch which often surpasses the
felicity of Addison, in a subtlety of insight which often
reaches further than the subtlety of Steele, — the humor
of Hawthorne presents traits so fine as to be almost too
excellent for popularity, as, to every one who has attempted their criticism, they are too refined for state

ment. The brilliant atoms flit, hover, and glance before
our minds, but the remote sources of their ethereal light
lie beyond our analysis, —

> "And no speed of ours avails
> To hunt upon their shining trails."

And now let us breathe a benison to these, our mirthful
benefactors, these fine revellers among human weaknesses, these stern, keen satirists of human depravity.
Wherever Humor smiles away the fretting thoughts of
care, or supplies that antidote which cleanses

> "The stuffed bosom of that perilous stuff
> Which weighs upon the heart," —

wherever Wit riddles folly, abases pride, or stings iniqui-
ty, — there glides the cheerful spirit, or glitters the flashing thought, of these bright enemies of stupidity and
gloom. Thanks to them, hearty thanks, for teaching us
that the ludicrous side of life is its wicked side no less
than its foolish ; that, in a lying world, there is still no
mercy for falsehood ; that Guilt, however high it may
lift its brazen front, is never beyond the lightnings of
Scorn ; and that the lesson they teach agrees with the
lesson taught by all experience, — that life in harmony
with reason is the only life safe from laughter, that life
in harmony with virtue is the only life safe from contempt

GENIUS.[*]

———◆———

THERE is one law inwoven into the constitution of things, which declares that force of mind and character must rule the world. This truth glares out upon us from daily life, from history, from science, art, letters, from all the agencies which influence conduct and opinion. The whole existing order of things is one vast monument to the supremacy of mind. The exterior appearance of human life is but the material embodiment, the substantial expression, of thought, — the hieroglyphic writing of the soul. The fixed facts of society, laws, institutions, positive knowledge, were once ideas in a projector's brain — thoughts which have been forced into facts. The scouted hypothesis of the fifteenth century is the time-honored institution of the nineteenth; the heresy of yesterday is the commonplace of to-day. We perceive, in every stage of this great movement, a certain vital force, a spiritual power, to which we give

[*] Delivered before the Boston Mercantile Library Association February, 1848.

the name of Genius. From the period when our present civilized races ran wild and naked in the woods, and dined and supped on each other, to the present time, the generality of mankind have been contented with things as they were. A small number have conceived of something better, or something new. From these come the motion and ferment of life ; to them we owe it that existence is not a bog but a stream. These are men of genius.

There are, therefore, two fields for human thought and action, the actual and the possible, the realized and the real. In the actual, the tangible, the realized, the vast proportion of mankind abide. The great region of the possible, whence all discovery, invention, creation, proceed, and which is to the actual as a universe to a planet, is the chosen region of Genius. As almost everything which is now actual was once only possible, as our present facts and axioms were originally inventions or discoveries, it is, under God, to Genius that we owe our present blessings. In the past, it created the present; in the present, it is creating the future. It builds habitations for us, but its own place is on the vanishing points of human intelligence, —

> " A motion toiling in the gloom,
> The spirit of the years to come,
> Yearning to mix itself with life."

The sphere and the influence of Genius it is easier to

ascertain than to define its nature. What is Genius?
It has been often defined, but each definition has included
but a portion of its phenomena. According to Dr. Johnson, it is general force of mind accidentally directed to a
particular pursuit; but this does not cover the comprehensive genius of Shakspeare, Leibnitz and Goethe;
and, besides, accident, circumstance, do not determine
the direction of narrower minds, but simply furnish the
occasion on which an inward tendency is manifested.
The most popular definition is that of Coleridge, who
calls genius the power of carrying the feelings of childhood into the powers of manhood. Such a power may
indicate the genius of Coleridge and Wordsworth, but
did Napoleon conquer at Austerlitz, Newton discover the
law of gravitation, Shakspeare create Macbeth, by carry
ing the feelings of childhood into the powers of manhood? This mode of defining by individual instances
is like drawing a map of Massachusetts, and calling it the
globe — a thing we are very apt to do.

Indeed, Genius has commonly been incompletely defined, because each definition has been but a description
of some order of genius. A true definition would be a
generalization, made up from many minds, and broad
enough to include all the results of genius in action and
thought. Genius is not a single power, but a combina
tion of great powers. It reasons, but it is not reasoning

t judges, but it is not judgment; it imagines, but it is not imagination; it feels deeply and fiercely, but it is not passion. It is neither, because it is all. It is another name for the perfection of human nature, for Genius is not a fact but an ideal. It is nothing less than the possession of all the powers and impulses of humanity in their greatest possible strength and most harmonious combination; and the genius of any particular man is great in proportion as he approaches this ideal of universal genius. Conceive of a mind in which the powers of Napoleon and Howard, Dante and Newton, Luther and Shakspeare, Kant and Fulton, were so combined as to act in perfect harmony; a mind, vital in every part, conceiving everything with intensity and yet conceiving everything under its due relations, as swift in its volitions as in its thoughts, — conceive of a mind like this, and you will have a definition of genius. As it is, it requires the energies of all men of genius to produce the results of genius. It exists somewhat in fragments. No one human mind comprehends all its elements. The nearest approach to universality of genius in intellect is Shakspeare; in will, Napoleon; in harmony of combination, Washington. It is singular that Washington is not generally classed among men of genius. Lord Brougham declares him to be the greatest man that ever lived, but of moderate talents; — as if being the soul of a revolution and the creator of a country, did not suppose energies equal to those employed in the creation of a poem, — as if there were any other certain test of genius but its influence, any other measure of the power of a cause but the magnitude of its effects!

But to return. Genius, in its highest meaning, being thus an Ideal, which the most powerful natures have but approached, which, while it comprehends all men of genius, is itself comprehended by none, the question still arises, what common quality distinguishes men of genius from other men, in practical life, in science, in letters, in every department of human thought and action? This common quality is vital energy of mind, — inherent, original force of thought and vitality of conception; a quality equally distinguishing the genius of action and meditation, making the mind in which it abides alive, and capable of communicating intellectual and moral life to others. Men in whom this energy glows seem to spurn the limitations of matter; to dive beneath the forms and appearances to the spirit of things; to leap the gulf which separates positive knowledge from discovery the actual from the possible; and, in their grasp of spiritual realities, in their intense life, they seem to demonstrate the immortality of the soul that burns within them. They give palpable evidence of infinite capacity of indefinite power of growth. It seems a mockery to limit their life by years, — to suppose that fiery essence can ever burn out or be extinguished. This life, this energy, this uprising, aspiring flame of thought, —

> "This mind, this spirit, this Promethean spark,
> This lightning of their being," —

has been variously called power of combination, invention, creation, insight; but in the last analysis it is resolved into vital energy of soul, to think and to do.

This quality of genius is sometimes difficult to be distinguished from talent, because high genius includes talent. It is talent and something more. The usual distinction between genius and talent is, that one represents creative thought, the other practical skill; one invents, the other applies. But the truth is, that high genius applies its own inventions better than talent alone can do. A man who has mastered the higher mathematics does not on that account lose his knowledge of arithmetic. Hannibal, Napoleon, Shakspeare, Newton, Scott, Burke, Arkwright, — were they not men of talent as well as men of genius? Because a great man does not always do what many smaller men can often do as well, smaller men must not, therefore, affect to pity him as a visionary, and pretend to lick into shape his formless theories.

But still there doubtless is a marked distinction between men of genius and men simply of talent. Talent

repeats ; Genius creates. Talent is a cistern ; Genius, a
fountain. Talent deals with the actual, with discovered
and realized truths, analyzing, arranging, combining,
applying positive knowledge, and in action looking to
precedents. Genius deals with the possible, creates new
combinations, discovers new laws, and acts from an
insight into principles. Talent jogs to conclusions to
which Genius takes giant leaps. Talent accumulates
knowledge, and has it packed up in the memory ; Genius
assimilates it with its own subctance, grows with every
new accession, and converts knowledge into *power*.
Talent gives out what it has taken in ; Genius, what has
risen from its unsounded wells of living thought. Talent,
in difficult situations, strives to untie knots, which Genius
instantly cuts, with one swift decision. Talent is full of
thoughts ; Genius, of thought : one has definite acquisitions ; the other, indefinite power.

But the most important distinction between the two
qualities is this : — one, in conception, follows mechanical
processes ; the other, vital. Talent feebly conceives objects with the senses and understanding ; Genius, fusing
all its powers together in the alembic of an impassioned
imagination, clutches everything in the conc ete. con
ceives objects as living realities, gives body to spiritue
abstractions and spirit to bodily appearances, and, like

" A gate of steel
Fronting the sun, receives and renders back
His figure and his heat ! "

It is thus the glorious prerogative of Genius to conceive
and to present everything as *alive ;* and here is the secret
of its power. It leads and sways because it communicates living energy, and strikes directly at the soul, —
searching out the very sources of our volitions, bowing
our weak wills before its strong arm, awakening, animating, forcing us along its path of thought, or over its waves
of passion. It commands us because it knows better
than we what is within us. Soul itself, it knows that,
in spite of our contemptible disguises, we too have souls
which must leap up at its voice, and follow whithersoever
it leads. It claims its rightful mastery over our spirits,
by awakening us to a sense of our spiritual existence.
It speaks to us, in our captivity, in the long-forgotten
language of our native land. It sees us wrapped up in
the dead cerements of custom, rusting away in the sep-
ulchre of being, and it cries to us, — " Come forth ! " It
speaks to us, and we hear; it touches us, and we spring
to our feet. A crowd of spirits from the realms of the
deathless come thronging around us ; — from the battle-
field, where Liberty went down under the brutal hoofs
of Power, its immortal image trampled in the dust, —
from the legislative hall, where, amid the collision of

adverse intellects, the orator poured his torrent of fire, ——
from the rack and the stake, where the spirit of man
chanted rapturous hymns in its fierce agonies, and met
death smiling, — from the cell of the thinker, where
mind grappled with tne mysterious unknown, piercing,
with its thought of light, the dark veil of unrealized
knowledge and possible combinations ; — from every
scene where the soul has been really alive, and impatiently tossed aside the material conditions which would
stifle or limit its energies, come the Genii of Thought
and Action, to rouse us from our sleep of death, to tear
aside the thin delusions of our conceit, and to pour into
the shrunken veins of our discrowned spirits the fresh
tides of mental life.   It is this influence of Genius which
has given motion and progress to society ; prevented the
ossification of the human heart and brain ; and though,
in its processes, it may not ever have followed the rules
laid down in primers, it has at least saved history from
being the region of geology, and our present society from
being a collection of fossil remains.

Thus, of the three requisitions of Genius, the first is
soul, and the second, soul, and the third, soul.   We have
already seen that almost all genius is particular, with an
inborn direction to particular pursuits.   The tendency
of its vital force is generally perceived in childhood.
can devote but little space to the youth of genius, though

the subject is tempting, and furnishes numberless anecdotes of the earnestness, the intensity, with which the
great mind early abandons itself to its. irrepressible impulses. Carnot, who, as one of the Committee of Public
Saiety during the French Revolution, directed the operations of fourteen armies, and hurled back the tide of
invasion which came rolling in over the Alps, the Pyre-
nees and the Rhine, was taken, when a child, to the
theatre, where some siege was clumsily represented.
Seeing that the attacking party were so placed as to be
commanded by a battery, he astonished the audience by
demanding that the general should change his position,
and cried out to him that his men were in fire. — The
young genius early exults in the contemplation of power
and beauty. During Scott's childhood, a frightful thun-
der-storm raged at Edinburgh. which made his brothers
and the domestics huddle together in one room, shivering with fear at every peal. Young Walter was found
lying on his back in the garden, the rain pitilessly pelting his face, while he, almost convulsed with delight,
shouted at every flash, " bonnie! bonnie !" Schiller
was found by his father, on a similar occasion, perched
upon a tree; and on being harshly questioned as to his
object, whimpered out that he wanted to see where the
thunder came from Byron's first verses, when a child
of four or five years, displayed the same perverseness

and unbridled vehemence which afterwards flamed out
in Manfred and Cain.   An old lady near his house, who
entertained the belief that on her death her soul would
reside in the moon, bothered him considerably in his
childish pranks.   He revenged himself in four lines : —

> " In Nottingham County there lives, at Swan Green,
> As curst an old lady as ever was seen ;
> And when she does die, *which I hope will be soon,*
> She firmly believes she will go to the moon."

It would be needless to multiply instances, familiar to
everybody, that the man's genius is born with him.
Legislator, reformer, soldier, poet, artist, thinker, — the
child is still " the father of the man."   In some instances,
it must be admitted, the whole man does not grow.   Napoleon's youth prefigured his maturity, and something
else.   The sovereign who crushed the heart of his queen
in his mailed hand, was once a man of sentiment.
When quite young, he fell in love with a young maiden ;
they contrived little meetings ; and he afterwards averred
that their whole happiness then consisted in eating cher-
ries together.

We have seen that genius is vital energy of soul.   In
itself it supposes a harmonious combination of will, intei-
ect and sensibility ; but, as manifested in men of genius
this combination is not perfect.   Hence the division of
powerful natures into men of action and men of medita-

tion, men in whom will predominates, and men in whom thought predominates. In the one case, the vital energy of the mind takes a practical direction, works visibly on society, and produces events. In the other, it takes the direction of meditation, influences society by methods more strictly spiritual, and produces poetry, science, the fine arts, everything that stimulates and gratifies the inward sense of truth, beauty, and power.

And first let us refer to the genius of action, to genius whose thoughts are read in deeds. Men of action may be classed in three divisions : — those who exercise their energies for what they deem the truth ; those who exercise them for personal interest and ambition ; and those in whom selfish and disinterested motives are strangely blended. The greatness of action includes immoral as well as moral greatness, — Cortés and Napoleon, as well as Luther and Washington. Its highest exemplification is where energy of will carries out a great original thought to a practical result, with uprightness of moral intention ; and perhaps the noblest example of this is in Columbus. Its lowest exemplification is where great energies of will are divorced from conscience and humanity ; and perhaps the lowest example of this is in Pizarro. But neither by the side of Columbus nor Pizarro can we place the moral trimmer, without any definite purpose, whose heart is continually aching for the crimes of the bad, but whose will is too infirm to battle bravely for the good. Such a person may shine among well meaning people, but his claims to greatness of any kind are ridic‑ulous. Pizarro was a buccaneer, but he had, at least, ar object, which was to him dearer than life, and to compass it he displayed the valor of a knight and the endurance of a martyr. How strangely does his conduct at the island of Gallo contrast with the tongue-valiant cowardice which characterizes the feebly good! After suffering all that fatigue, famine and pestilence could inflict, short of death, a vessel arrived which offered to carry him and his companions back to Panama. To go was to abandon forever the project of conquering and plundering Peru. Pizarro drew his sword, and traced a line on the sand with it from east to west. Then turning to the south, he said to his band of immortal pirates : — " Friends and comrades ! on that side are toil, hunger, nakedness, the drenching storm, desertion and death ; on this side, ease and pleasure. There lies Peru with its riches ; here, Panama with its poverty. Choose, each man, what best becomes a brave Castilian. For my part, I go to the south." Now, as long as bad men display qualities like these, so long will they rule ; for to qualities like these is given the dominion of the world. Such men, to be checked, are not to be talked about, but to be wrestled with, — to be bravely met by superior force of will, and

overthrown. Never will this be done by the moral bab-
ble of men who wish to serve God, and wish, at the same
time, to live comfortably all their days. Well has the
great Christian poet of the age affirmed, —

> " The law
> By which mankind now suffers is most just
> For, by superior energies, more strict
> Affiance in each other, faith more firm
> In their unhallowed principles, the bad
> Have fairly earned a victory o'er the weak,
> The vacillating, inconsistent good."

The great characteristic of men of active genius is a
sublime self-confidence, springing, not from self-conceit,
but from an intense identification of the man with his
object, which lifts him altogether above the fear of danger and death, which gives to his enterprise a character
of insanity to the common eye, and which communicates
an almost superhuman audacity to his will. Men of this
stamp seem to have a clear and bright vision of what is
hidden from other men, and to push instinctively forward,
through every obstacle, to its attainment. They seem to
hear voices crying to them from the mysterious unknown,
and to answer the call in flashes of supernatural energy.
They ever give the impression of spirits, to whom material obstacles are as flax in the fire. Judge from their
words and their deeds, and you would suppose their

bodies partook, like Milton's angels, of incorporeal substance, which, if pierced or cloven, would instantly re-
unite.   They have no fear of death, because their souls
are thoroughly alive; and the idea of death never occurs
to a live mind.   In following the career of one of these
fierce and flashing intelligences, our astonishment finds
vent in some such words as the heroism of Duke Sophocles forced from Fletcher's honest centurion:

> " By Romulus, he is all soul, I think ;
> He hath no flesh, and spirit cannot be gyved."

Such men, also, dart their souls into vast bodies of men,
become the animating spirit of great enterprises, and
communicate vitality even to those whose submission
they enforce.   Every soldier in the army of Cæsar and
Napoleon, felt the soul of Cæsar or Napoleon glowing
within his own breast.   While obeying another will, new
life seemed poured into his own.   Audacity and a beautiful contempt of death breathe and burn in the words
and deeds of such commanders.   " My lads," said Napoleon to some raw recruits, " you must not fear death ;
when soldiers brave death, they drive him into the
enemy's ranks."   The great Condé, when twice repulsed
with frightful slaughter at Fribourg, led his soldiers up
in person to the mouths of the enemy's cannon, and
hurled his marshal's bâton over the intrenchments
Nothing could resist the impetuosity of French soldiers

after such a spur had oeen given to their energies,
' Follow my plume!" said Henry the Fourth to his
knights;—"you will always find it on the road to victory." "Hang thyself, brave Crillon," said he, in the
same spirit of chivalry; "we have fought at Arques, and
thou wast not there." Speak thus to the higher sentiments of men on great occasions, and you will find their
souls will instinctively mount up to their native region.
When the Spanish Armada threatened England, the
Queen of England spoke to her troops in words warm
from her own lion heart.   She did not tell them that an
invasion would prejudice their interests, or even their
liberties, but she *wondered* that Parma and proud Spain
should *dare* to invade her dominions.   The success of
Luther was in a great degree owing to his indomitable
will,—a will which forced its way through obstacles
which might have daunted armies, and gave to his character that moral intensity, which fitted him to be the
leader in what Guizot calls, "the great insurrection of
human thought against authority."   When advised not
to go to a city, notoriously thronged with his enemies,
he said, "Were there as many devils there as roof-tiles,
I would on!"   This is the feeling of the great reformer
everywhere;—to make life a battle for the truth; to
strike heavier blo vs for the Right than others can for the
Wrong; in one word, to DARE!   This principle has been

repeatedly caricatured by those who have pretended to represent it. It was vilely caricatured in that infernal farce, the French Revolution, in which audacity and mediocrity formed a hideous union. But it is no less the virtue of genius because it is the vice of folly. There is a great difference between the dogmatism of knowledge and the dogmatism of ignorance. Kepler might say, that if God had waited five thousand years before he had raised up a man capable of comprehending His wonderful works, he could wait a thousand for men to comprehend his discoveries; but such language as this is impotent trash, worthy only to be received with a storm of hisses, when uttered by pretentious mediocrity.

This energy and audacity of will characterizes all ruling public men, — statesmen, generals, reformers, orators. In the great orator, especially, it is seen in the condensation, the burning vehemence, the brief, stern strokes, with which he pierces through the reason and through the passions of his audience, directly at their volitions, — upurning, trampling, upon all opposing wills, hurrying the souls whom he has taken captive onward, ever onward, to the insatiable object which impatiently beckons in the distance! Demosthenes, the greatest of orators, is the great master of this intense and rapid *movemen.*. He never repeats; never, says Brougham, comes back upon the ground, "which he has once utterly wasted and

withered up by the tide of fire he has rolled over it."
It was this intense will, this force of being, which chiefly
distinguished the arrogant and ruling genius of Chatham.
He cowed those whom he could neither convince nor
persuade. A country member of Parliament once rose to
accuse him of a palpable inconsistency in his conduct.
He had hardly mumbled a few words before he was
looked down into his seat by the steady scorn which
blazed upon him from Chatham's eye. It was this force
which gave such audacity to his bursts of blended opinion
and passion — as in that well-known exclamation in the
House of Lords, — " They tell me that America has
resisted. I am rejoiced to hear it !" " Sugar, my
lords," said he, on another occasion, in his deep, grave
voice. A well-bred sneer instantly smiled on the lips of
his noble auditors, at the disparity between the term and
the tone. Chatham saw it, kindled at the insult, and
repeated sugar three times, in his fiercest tones and with
his most violent gesticulations, until he awed them into
putting on civil faces. He then asked, derisively, " Who
will laugh at sugar now ?" We sometimes see this
power exercised in private life, and controversies settled
by force of will, instead of force of argument. Dr. Johnson wielded it with admirable energy. The records of
Robert Hall's conversation boil over with an audacity of
expression, which cuts clean through the ' linen decen-

ties" of polite life. "Mr. Hall," said one of his parish-
ioners, "I understand you are going to marry Miss
————." — " I marry Miss ————! I would as soon
marry Beelzebub's eldest daughter, and go home and live
with the old folks." Again, speaking of Dr. Ryland, he
exclaimed, " Why, sir, Dr. Ryland 's all piety; all piety
together, sir. If there were not room in heaven, God
would turn out an archangel for him." His proposal to
his housekeeper had a similar wildness. " Betty, do you
love the Lord Jesus ? " — " Yes, sir." — " And Betty, do
you love me ? "— " Yes, sir." They were married at once.

Perhaps the most wonderful example of this audacity
in a mind at once vast and flexible, intense and comprehensive, is in Cæsar, — a man to whose commanding
genius empire seemed but another term for action.
Compared with him, Alexander seems but a hot-headed
boy, and even Napoleon " pales his uneffectual fire."
The amazing strength of his mind is not so remarkable
as its plastic character — the ease with which it accom-
modated itself to every emergency — its wonderful fusion
of will, intelligence and passion. It never hardened in
any part, and all its powers were thus capable of instantaneous concentration. Though his determinations were
as sure as they were swift, we still never speak of his
iron will, feeling that such a term would not express its
ethereal strength, and its felicity of adaptation to every

occasion. The acts of Cæsar affect us like unexpected flashes of imagination in a great poem. At the age of seventeen, in flying from the power of Sylla, he fell into the clutches of pirates. They fixed his ransom at twenty talents. "It is too little," he said; "you shall have fifty; but once free, I will crucify every one of you;" and he did it. When his favorite legion mutinied, he abandoned them before they could abandon him, and they followed him like spaniels, suing for forgiveness. In Spain, his legions would obey neither his entreaties nor commands to attack the vast army opposed to them. But they knew not the resources of their commander. Seizing a shield, he cried, "I will die here!" and rushed singly upon the Spanish ranks. Two hundred arrows flew against him, when within ten paces of the enemy, — and his soldiers could not but charge in his support. At Rome, when he heard of plots to assassinate him, he proudly dismissed his guards, and ever afterwards walked through the streets alone and unarmed. Well might his "honorable murderers" have wondered, as that withered frame lay before them, pierced with twenty stabs, that a body so worn and weak could have contained so vast and vehement a soul. In all history we have no other instance of a mind of such ethereal make, divorced from moral principle. The Romans thought him a god, and to all posterity he will be the great, bad man of the world.

ınterpenetrate the will of Luther, the benevolence of Howard, the religion of Fenelon, with the mind of Goethe, and you would have a man as resistless for duty as Cæsar was for glory. But, you may say, this military courage is not spiritual, but physical. Let us hear the testimony of one qualified to speak to this point, — of one who was both warrior and writer, — the testimony of the great tragic poet of Greece. How run the lines written by himself to serve for his own epitaph?

> "Athenian Æschylus, Eurphorian's son,
>   Buried in Geta's fields, these words declare;
>   His deeds are registered at Marathon,
>   Known to tne deep-haired Mede who met him there."

Have we not here the same stern, fiery, invulnerable *soul*, which clothed in verse of such imperishable grandeur the awful agonies of the chained Prometheus?

But to return: Brutus has been placed above Cæsar in greatness by those who write books for children. Now, Brutus had no genius; was simply a proud, inflexible, hard-minded and narrow-minded patrician whose notion of liberty was below that of Russia's autocrat, and whose notion of virtue was worse than his notion of liberty. "Virtue," said he, just before his leath, — "vain word, futile shadow, slave of chance Alas! I believed in thee!"—Here a heroical soul! Here a great moral genius! Why, Cæsar would not have saiı

such a thing even of vice! No man who had vitally conceived virtue, as a living reality, — ever identified himself with it, — could thus have mocked its awful immortality with his peevish atheism. He called virtue a word, because to him it was a barren proposition *about* virtue, to which his understanding assented, — not a living realization *of* virtue, which his whole nature adored. How mean does such a man appear by the side of such a woman as Joan of Arc, the saint of France! How much more force dwelt in the little peasant maiden than in Rome's proud patrician! She, in the might and the simplicity of her nature, identified herself with duty, and, armed in her intelligence and faith, was, in her sphere, as resistless as Cæsar, — because her mind was as vital. From the time her soul first caught the sound of the cathedral bells, chiming above her cottage home, to the period when she fell into the gripe of the grim English wolves, her life was one expression of holiness, purity and action. Viewed in connection with the Satanic passions of that dark period, she seems to descend upon her age as a heavenly visitant, with celestial beauty and celestial strength. France has no nobler boast than her heroic genius; England no fouler stain than her brutal murder. She is among the greatest of the great of action. It is almost needless to say that in English history she appears variously as witch wanton,

sorceress and fanatic, — not as the wisest, purest, ablest
intelligence of her time.

We have seen, so far, that vital energy of soul is the
great characteristic of the genius of action. It is not
less so of the genius of meditation. We call the one
force of character; the other, force of mind: but vital
thought is at heart of both. True depth and strength
of character is in proportion to the living spiritual principle within the man. Force, power, dominion, are
traced in letters of fire on the brow of the thinker, as on
the crown of the actor. From both come those kindling,
quickening influences, which move the world. But to
the thinker, the range of the man of action is all too narrow to satisfy the creative energy of his intellect. The
reformer, the soldier, the patriot, each commonly over-
estimates the importance of his special object, from not
vitally conceiving its relations as well as itself. Shakspeare cannot do the work of Luther, because he is on
an eminence where Luther's work falls into its right
relations to other possible reforms, which Luther feebly
conceives or fiercely underestimates. To Luther it is
the thing to be done; to Shakspeare, only *one* thing to
be done. Shakspeare, again, would not expend his energies for the objects of Napoleon, because he sees further
and deeper than Napoleon into their nature. Yet w
are not from this to conclude that the force exercised in

the region whence events indirectly spring, is not as great as that exercised in the region whence events directly spring. Influence is the measure of power ; and he must be a dealer in hardy assertions who shall say that the influence on mankind of men of action has been greater than men of thought. In truth, action is influential, as meditation is influential, just in proportion to the vital thought it embodies and represents.

It may be as well here to mention a common prejudice against genius, that it is a quality of idle, lazy men; of clever vagabonds, who have a knack of seizing some things by intuition which others obtain by logic ; of men. who spontaneously perceive what others laboriously investigate. If a child flouts at parental authority, abhors study, investigates the condition of hen-roosts, and practically illustrates new views of property, his sloth, trickery and thieving, are apt to be laid to his genius. All miserable pretenders, poetasters, quacks, ranters, — disciples of disorder everywhere, — are considered to be fools and vagabonds in virtue of their genius. The general feeling is well expressed in an anecdote told of Mason. Some person brought him a subscription paper for the poems of Ann Yearsley, the inspired milk-maid, describing her as a heaven-born genius. He gave four-and-sixpence, — "four shillings," he said, "for charity, and the odd sixpence for her heaven-born genius." The work-house,

the jail, the penitentiary, are considered to be full of men of genius. The quality is held to be naturally opposed to order, to common-sense, and to worldly success Even where a man like Burns, or Otway, or Cowper, filled a nation with his fame, it is still remembered that Otway starved to death, that Burns died drunk, that Cowper died mad. " There 's small choice," cries Mediocrity, " in rotten apples." People therefore consider genius, at the best, a doubtful benefit : —

> " The booby father craves a booby son,
> And by Heaven's blessing thinks himself undone."

Now, admitting that Genius, working in bad organizations, and exposed to a continual conflict with surrounding malignity and stupidity, may end in " despondency and madness," — may seem, as Rousseau's did to Byron,

> " A tree
> On fire with lightning, with ethereal flame
> Kindled and blasted," —

yet the fault is not in having too much genius, but in not having genius enough. Take Milton, the invincible; that adamantine strength of will which made such wild work among the sensualists and renegades of his time, — was not that a portion of his genius ? When a great man sinks into despondency, or fear, or inaction his genius slumbers or has departed. He is an Achilles dozing in luxurious sloth, while the plains are ringing with war; and to him should be addressed the trumpet call of Patroc.us : —

> " Sweet,
> Rouse thyself; and the weak, wanton Cupid
> Shall from your neck unloose his amorous fold,
> And, like a dew-drop from the lion's mane,
> Be shook to air! "

Indeed, genius in thought supposes energy of will to rouse energies of intellect, and is the exact opposite of laziness or indulgence. It is self-directed power; energy, which, if it do not come spontaneously, must be induced. As far as it is genius it is labor, the hardest work that man can do, and its discoveries and combinations are earned by the very sweat of the brain. It is true, thoughts seem sometimes to fall into the mind of the poet, like stray birds of paradise; but be sure they have been lured thither by the poet's potent spells. Again, in the external activity of men of genius there are great differences, from the physical inertia of Thomson, lazily biting the ripe side of a peach on the tree, his hands thrust immovably in his pockets, to the harricane movement of Byron, who had, if we may believe Mr. Gilfillan, "the activity of a scalded fiend;" yet the Seasons were as much the result of inward energy as Childe Harold. But the thought of genius, you may say, comes spontaneously,

·— swift as lightning. Yes; but that gathering together
of forces, which precedes and causes the lightning,— what
is that ? The thought of the law of gravitation flashed
across the mind of Newton ; but the mental labor which
for years preceded it, the millions of thoughts which
came from that exhaustless fountain before the right one
flashed, — there was the work of a giant. The mind of
genius, being vital, grows with exercise; assimilates
knowledge into the very life-blood of thought, every new
acquisition becoming additional power ; and though the
last result may seem simple, the processes by which it is
mastered are complex and mighty. In view of the diffi-
culties to be overcome, and the annoyances to be tossed
aside, by the original thinker, Buffon defined genius as
patience. In the power of patient labor, Newton mod-
estly saw the difference between himself and other men.
He did not consider that this *power* of patient labor was
his genius ; that continuity and concentration of thought
are in proportion to the size and vitality of the thinking
principle. Let those who prate about indolent genius
conceive of the energy of Scott. At the age of fifty-six
he resolutely braced up his energies of mind to pay a
debt of six or seven hundred thousand dollars, by literature. In three years he produced thirty volumes. His
frame began to break down. Dr. Abercrombie implored
him to desist from writing. "I tell you what it is, doc

tor," said Scott, "when Molly puts the kettle on, you might as well say, don't boil!"

This living energy of mind, it is hard to kindle. How many go down to the grave without having known, during a long life, what thought is! How many abide in miserable superstitions, victims of every quack in religion, politics and literature, their minds mere collections of chips and hearsays, feeling their degradation, yet preferring it to the labor of mental effort! This slavery of the soul, these chains clanking upon every utterance of opinion, can only be broken by the strength within the man. It is a comparatively easy task to induce men to sacrifice comfort and wealth, to be fanatics, and very brave fanatics, for any cruel nonsense which has obtained in the world, — but to induce them to think, — oh! that is requiring too much for the energies of mortal man! And yet, forsooth, the world is becoming too intellectual! We educate the intellect too much! "My friends," said Dr. Johnson, "clear your minds of cant!"

Indeed, education can hardly be too intellectual, unless by intellectual you mean parrot knowledge, and other modes of mind-slaughter. No education deserves the name, unless it develops thought, — unless it pierces down to the mysterious spiritual principle of mind, and starts that into activity and growth. There, all educa tion, intellectual, moral, religious, begins; for morality, religion, intelligence, have all one foundation in vital thought; — that is, in thought which conceives all objects with which it deals, whether temporal or eternal visible or invisible, as living realities, not as barren propositions. Here is the vital principle of all growth in learning, in virtue, in intelligence, in holiness. If this fail, there is no hope:

> " The pillared firmament is rottenness,
> And earth's base built on stubble."

Thus force of being, to labor, to create, to pluck out the heart of nature's mystery, — this is the law of genius. It would be impossible here to follow this live and life-giving thought of man in its invasion of the possible and the unknown. Its result is human knowledge, — the sciences of mind and matter, poetry and the plastic arts, with their myriad untraceable influences upon society and individual character. Genius, mental power, wherever you look, you see the radiant footprints of its victorious progress. It has surrounded your homes with comfort; it has given you the command of the blind forces ·f matter; it has exalted and consecrated your affections; it has brought God's immeasurable universe nearer to ﹄our hearts and imaginations; it has made flowers of paradise spring up even in poor men's gardens. And above all, it is never stationary; its course being eve onward to new triumphs, its repose but harmonious ac ivity, its acquisitions but stimulants to discoveries. Answering to nothing but the soul's illimitable energies, it is always the preacher of hope, and brave endeavor, and unwearied, elastic effort. It is hard to rouse in their might these energies of thought; but when once roused, when felt tingling along every nerve of sensation, the whole inward being thrilling with their enkindling inspiration,

"And all the God comes rushing on the soul,"

there seem to be no limits to their capacity, and obstacles shrivel into ashes in their fiery path. This deep feeling of power and joy, this ecstasy of the living soul, this untamed and untamable energy of Genius, — you cannot check its victorious career as it leaps exultingly from discovery to discovery, new truths ever beckoning imploringly in the dim distance, a universe ever opening and expanding before it, and above all a Voice still crying, On! on! — On! though the clay fall from the soul's struggling powers! — On! though the spirit burn through its garment of flesh, as the sun through mist' — On! on!

"Along the line of limitless desires.'

INTELLECTUAL HEALTH AND DISEASE.*

A PROMINENT characteristic of the present day, and in many respects an admirable one, is the universal attention given to the subject of bodily health ; but, like many other movements founded on half-truths, it has been pushed by fanaticism into ludicrous perversions. Physiology has been systematized into a kind of popular gospel, in whose doctrines the soul seems of little importance in comparison with the gastric juice. Physic having become a fashion, a valetudinary air is now the sign of your true coxcomb; and every idle person has his pet complaint, which he nurses in some genteel infirmary. There is an universal cant about health ; every city and hamlet is beleaguered by the hosts of Hippocrates, the floods of Hydropathy, and the animalculæ of Homeopathy ; and no person can venture into the street without being assaulted by some Hygeian highwayman, wh

* Delivered before the Literary Societies of Dartmouth College July 25, 1849.

presents a phial to his head, and demands his patience or his purse. Now, the practical consequence of this deification of the body and worship of dietetics, is to bring men under the dominion of a sickly selfishness and a craven cowardice, while pretending to teach them the physical laws of their being. Man obeys the highest law of his being when he takes his life in his hand, and boldly ventures it for something he values more than self. Life cast away for truth or duty, even for fame or knowledge, is better than life saved for the sake of living. But your true disciple of physiological religion, with his morbid consciousness of that collection of veins, bones, muscles and appetites, which he calls himself, would consider it a monstrous violation of the physical laws of his being to obey a benevolent impulse which endangered a blood-vessel, or to purchase the discovery of a new truth at the expense of deranged digestion : and he would survey with lazy wonder the strange ignorance of Howard, penetrating into pestilential prisons ; of Washington, exposing his person to a storm of bullets ; of Ridley, serenely yielding his frame to that baptism of fire which enrolled him forever in the glorious army of martyrs. Such acts as these were doubtless violations of physical laws, and prove that heroes are not framed on accurate physiological principles.

Indeed health and disease, in their highest meaning,

refer more to the mind than to the body. A **code of** ethics built on physical laws can but inculcate a selfish **superficial** prudence; and prudence, except in weaklings will not restrain self-indulgence, and ought not to restrair self-sacrifice. There are no duties, therefore, which art not resolvable into moral duties; no vices which have not their scorpion nest in the heart. Do you suppose that any knowing prattle about the breathing or digesting apparatus will still the hoarse clamor of gluttony and sensuality? Will it relax the grasp of Satanic pride? In truth, you will find that prudence without conscience holds but a rein of flax on the wild war-horses of passion. But it is a characteristic weakness of the day to super-ficialize evil; to spread a little cold cream over Pande-monium, erect a nice little earthly paradise upon it, and then to rush into misanthropy because the thin structure instantly melts. Indeed, it is at the very core of the mind that we must search for the principles of health and disease, — in the mysteries of will, intelligence, senti-nent and passion, rather than in the organs which are their instruments or victims. Besides, bodily maladies may be badges of disgrace, or titles of honor; your drunkard and your philosopher may both take their " leap into the dark" from apoplexy; and there is a great dif-ference between Milton, sacrificing his eyesight from the love of liberty, and Byron, sacrificing his digestion from the love of gin.

The subject, therefore, to which 1 would call your attention, is intellectual health and disease, as it exists in individuals and in nations. To one who reflects on the nature and capacity of the human mind, there is something inconceivably awful in its perversions. Look at it as it comes, fresh and plastic, *from* its Maker; look at it as it returns, stained and hardened, *to* its Maker. Conceive of a mind, a living soul, with the germs of faculties which infinity cannot exhaust, as it first beams upon you in its glad morning of existence; quivering with life and joy; exulting in the bounding sense of its developing energies; beautiful, and brave, and generous, and joyous, and free, — the clear, pure spirit bathed in the auroral light of its unconscious immortality: and then follow it, in its dark passage through life, as it stifles and kills, one by one, every inspiration and aspiration of its being, until it becomes but a dead soul entombed in a living frame It may be that a selfish frivolity has sunk it into contented worldliness, or given it the vapid air of complacent imbecility. It may be that it is marred and disfigured by the hoof-prints of appetite, its humanity extinguished in the mad tyranny of animal ferocities. It may be that pride has stamped the scowl of hatred upon its front; that avarice and revenge, set on fire of hell, have blasted and

blackened its unselfish affections. The warm sensibility
gushing spontaneously out in world-wide sympathies, —
the bright and strong intellect, eager for action and
thirsting for truth, — the rapturous devotion, mounting
upwards in a pillar of flame to God, — all gone, and
only remembered as childish enthusiasm, to point the
sneer of the shrewd, and the scoff of the brutal! Where,
in this hard mass of animated clay, wrinkled by cunning
or brutalized by selfishness, are the power and joy proph-
esied in the aspirations of youth?

> " Whither hath fled the visionary gleam?
> Where is it now, the glory and the dream?"

To give the philosophy of this mental disease, to subject the mind to that scrutiny which shall account for its
perversions, we must pass behind its ordinary operations
of understanding, sensibility and imagination, and attempt
to clutch its inmost spirit and essence. Now, an analysis
of our consciousness, or rather a contemplation of the
mysterious processes of our inward life, reveals no faculties and no impulses which can be disconnected from
our personality. The mind is no collection of self-acting
powers and passions, but a vital, indissoluble unit and
person, capable, it is true, of great variety of manifesta
tion, but still in its nature a unit, not an aggregate
For the purposes of science, or verbal convenience
e may call its various operations by different names

according as it perceives, feels, understands or imag·
ines ; but the moment science breaks it up into a
series of disconnected parts, and considers each part
oy itself as a separate power, that moment the living
principle of mind is lost, and the result is an anarchy of faculties. Fortunately, however, we cannot free
ourselves, by any craft of analysis, from personal pro-
nouns. A man who speaks or acts, instinctively men-
tions it as — *I* said, *I* did. We do not say that Milton's
imagination wrote Paradise Lost, but that Milton wrote
it. There is no mental operation in which the whole
mind is not present; nothing produced but by the joint
action of all its faculties, under the direction of its central
personality. This central principle of mind is spiritual
force, — capacity to cause, to create, to assimilate, to be.
This underlies all faculties ; interpenetrates, fuses, directs
all faculties. This thinks, this feels, this imagines, this
worships ; this is what glows with health, this is what is
enfeebled and corrupted by disease. Call it what you
please, — will, personality, individuality, character, force
of being ; but recognize it as the true spiritual power
which constitutes a living soul. This is the only pecu·
liarity which separates the impersonal *existence* of a
vegetable from the personal *life* of a man. The material
universe is instinct with spiritual existence, but only in
man is it individualized into spiritual life.

Now, there is no such thing as faculty which has not its root in this personal force. Without this, thought is but insanity, and action, fate. Men do not stumble, and blunder, and happen into Iliads, and Æneids, and Divina Commedias, and Othellos, in a drunken dream of poetic inspiration, but work and grow up to them. It is common, I know, to point to some lazy gentleman, and say that there is a protuberance on his forehead or temple sufficiently large to produce a Hamlet or a Principia, if he only had an active temperament. But the thing which produces Hamlets and Principias is not physical temperament, but spiritual power. What a man does is the real test of what a man is; and to declare that he has great capacity but nothing great to set his capacity in motion, is an absurdity in terms.

This mind, this free spiritual force, cannot grow, cannot even exist, by itself. It can only grow by assimilating something external to itself, the very condition of mental life being the exercise of power within on objects without. The form and superficial qualities of objects it perceives; their life and spirit it conceives. Only what the mind conceives, it assimilates and draws into its own life; — intellectual conception indicating a penetrating vision into the heart of things, through a fierce, firm exertion of vital creative force. In this distinction between perception and conception, we have a principle which accounts for the limited degree in which so many persons grow in intelligence and character, in grace and gracelessness. Here, also, is the distinction between assent and faith, theory and practice. In the one case, opinions lie on the surface of the mind, mere objects, the truth of which it perceives, out which do not influence its will; in the other, ideas penetrate into the very substance of the mind, become one with it, and are springs of living thought and action. For instance, you may cram whole folios of morality and divinity into the heads of Dick Turpin and Captain Kidd, and both will cordially assent to their truth ; but the captives of Dick's blunderbuss will still have to give up their purses, and the prisoners of Kidd's piracy will still have to walk the plank. On the other hand, you may pour all varieties of immoral opinions and images into the understanding of a pure and high nature, and there they will remain, unassimilated, uncorrupting; his mind, like that of Ion,

> " Though shapes of ill
> May hover round its surface, glides in light,
> And takes no shadow from them."

In accordance with the same principle, all knowledge, however imposing in its appearance, is but superficial knowledge, if it be merely the mind's furniture, not the mind's nutriment. It must be transmuted into mind, as food is into blood, to become wisdom and power. There

‚s many a human parrot and memory-monger, **whe** has read and who recollects more history than Webster · but in Webster, history has become judgment, foresight executive force, mind. That seemingly instinctive sa. gacity, by which an able man does exactly the right thing at the right moment, is nothing but a collection of facts thus assimilated into thought. This power of instanta- neous action without reflection is the only thing which saves men in great emergencies; but far from being inde- pendent of knowledge and experience, it is their noblest result. Many of the generals opposed to Napoleon understood military science as well as he did; but he beat them on every occasion where victory depended on a wise movement made at a moment's thought, because science had been transfused into his mind, while it was only attached to theirs. Every truly practical man, whether he be merchant, mechanic, or agriculturalist, thus transmutes his experience into intelligence, until his will operates with the celerity of instinct. In the order of intellectual development, intuition does not precede observation and reflection, but is their last perfection First, slow steps, cautious examination, comparison, rea soning; then, thought and action, swift, sharp and sure as the lightning.

If the mind thus grows by assimilating externa **objects,** it is plain that the character of the objects **i** assimilates will determine the form of its development, and its health or disease. Mental health consists in the self-direction of mental power, in the capacity to perceive its own relations to objects and the relations of objects to each other, and to choose those which will conduce to its enlargement and elevation. Disease occurs both when it loses its self-direction, and its self-distrust. When it loses its self-direction, it surrenders itself to every outward impression; when it loses its self-distrust, it surrenders itself to every inward whim. In the one case, it loses all moral and intellectual character, becomes unstrung, sentimental, dissolute, with feebleness at the very heart of its being; in the other, it perversely misconceives and discolors external things, views every object as a mirror of self, and, having no reverence for aught above itself, subsides into a poisonous mass of egotism, conceit, and falsehood. Thus disease occurs both when the mind loses itself in objects, and when objects are lost in it, — when it parts with will, and when it becomes wilful. The last consequence of will submerged is sensuality, brutality slavishness; the last consequence of will perverted is Satanic pride. Now, it is an almost universal law, that the diseased weak, the men of unrestrained appetites, shall become the victims and slaves of the diseased strong, the men of unrestrained wills, and that the result of this relation shall be misery, decay and death, to both. Here

ıs the principle of all slavery, political, intellectual, and
religious, in individuals and in communities.

Thus if the primitive principle of mind be simply the
capacity to assimilate external objects, and if objects in
this process become mind and character, it is obvious
that self-direction, — the power to choose, to resist, to act
in reference to law, and not from the impulse of desire, —
is the condition of health and enduring strength. Let
us now consider how these objects, — which may be
included under the general terms of nature and other
minds, — influence for evil or good the individual soul,
according as their impulse is blindly followed, wilfully
perverted, or genially assimilated.

The objects which have the most power over the mind
are probably those in visible nature which refer to appetite and passion. These are continually striving to draw
the mind into themselves, to weaken the force at its cen-
re and soul, to reduce it into mere perception and sensation, and to destroy its individual life. The emotion
which accompanies this yielding of the mind to death
has, with a bitterness of irony never excelled by man or
demon, been called pleasure. Now, it is a mistake which
ıs apt to vitiate theology, to confound will with wilfulness, and to make destruction of will the condition of
ısing to God. But will weakened, or will destroyed
ver goes downwards. It delivers itself to sensuality, — o

to fanaticism, which is the sensuality of the religious sentiment, — not to spirituality, not to Deity. A being placed like man among strong and captivating visible objects, becomes, the moment he loses self-direction, a slave, in the most terribly comprehensive meaning of that all-annihilating word ; and I believe the doctrine runs not that we are slaves, but children of God.

Will is also often confounded with wilfulness in the metaphysics of that æsthetic criticism which deals with the grandest creations of genius. The highest mood of the mind is declared to be that where it loses its individuality in the objects it contemplates ; where it becomes objective and healthy, in distinction from subjective or morbid. This objectiveness is confounded with self-abandonment, and thus causative force is absurdly denied while treating of the soul's creative acts. But it is not by self-abandonment that the far-darting, all-assimilating intellect of Genius identifies itself for the moment with its conceptions ; it is rather by the sublimest exercise of will and central force. Let us take, in illustration, three poets, in an ascending scale of intellectual precedence ; — Keats, the representative of sensitiveness ; Byron, of wilfulness ; Shakspeare, of self-direction. Now, in Keats, — a mind of immense spontaneous fruitfulness, — a certain class of objects take his intellect captive, melt and merge his individual being in themselves, are

stronger than he, and hold him in a state of soft diffu
sion in their own nature. The impression left on the
imagination is of sensuous beauty, but spiritual weakness. Then Byron, arrogant, domineering, egotistic,
diseased, — viewing nature and man altogether in relation
to himself, and spurning the objective laws of things, —
forces objects, with autocratic insolence, into the shape
of his own morbid nature, stamps them with his mark,
and leaves the impression of intense, narrow, wilful
energy. But Shakspeare, the strongest of creative intellects, and comprehensive because he was strong, passes,
by the gigantic force of his will, into the heart of other
natures; is sensuous, impassioned, witty, beautiful, sublime, and terrible, at pleasure; rises by the same force
with which he stoops; in his most prodigious exertions
of energy ever observes laws instead of obeying caprice;
comprehends all his creations without being comprehended by them; and comes out at the end, not Falstaff, or Faulconbridge, or Hamlet, or Timon, or Lear,
or Perdita, but Shakspeare, the beneficent and august
intellect which includes them all. The difference between him and other poets is, that, in virtue of passing
into another life by force of will, not by being drawn in
by force of the object, he could escape from it with ease
and proceed to animate other existences, thus keeping
his mind constantly assimilating and working with

nature. Keats was drawn into his particular class of objects, and could not get out. Byron drew objects into himself, and then poisoned them by capriciously distorting and discoloring their essential character. Keats would have stayed with Perdita; Byron, with Timon.

Let us next consider, in further illustration of our theme, those potent forces which come, through history, through literature, and through social communion, from other minds, and from whose action a continual stream of influences is pouring in upon the individual soul. Those which proceed from society, to benefit or corrupt, are so obvious that it is needless to emphasize their power. Look around any community, and you find it dotted over with men, marked and ticketed as not belonging to themselves, but to some other man, from whom they take their literature, their politics, their religion. They are willing captives of a stronger nature; feed on his life as though it were miraculous manna rained from heaven; complacently parade his name as an adjective 'o point out their own; and give wonderful pertinence to that nursery rhyme, whose esoteric depth irradiates even its exoteric expression: —

> Whose dog are you ?
> I am Billy Patton's dog,
> Whose dog are *you* ? "

This social servility, as seen in its annual harvest of

dwindled souls, abject in everything, from the tie of a
neckcloth to the points of a creed, is a sufficiently strong
indication of the tyranny which a few forcible persons
can establish in any of our "free and enlightened" communities; but perhaps a more subtle influence than that
which proceeds from social relations, comes from that
abstract and epitome of the whole mind of the whole
world, which we find in history and literature. Here the
thought and action of the race are brought home to the
individual intelligence; and the danger is, that we make
what should be our emancipation an instrument of servi-
tude, fall a victim to one author or one age, and lose the
power of learning from many minds, by sinking into the
contented vassal of one; and end, at last, in an intellectual
resemblance to that gentleman who only knew two tunes,
"one of which," he said, "was Old Hundred, and the
other — was n't." The danger to individuality, in reading,
is not that we repeat an author's opinions or expressions
but that we be magnetized by his spirit to the extent of
being drawn into his stronger life, and losing our particular being. Now, no man is benefited by being conquered; and the most modest might say to the mightiest
— to Homer, to Dante, to Milton, to Goethe, — "Keep
off, gentlemen, — not so near, if you please; you can de
me vast service, provided you do not swallow me up; my
personal being is small, but allow me to say of it, as

Touchstone said of Audrey, his wife, ' A poor thing, sir, but mine own.' "

Indeed, we can never fully realize and reverence a great nature, never grow through a reception of his spirit, unless we keep our individuality distinct from his.   In the case of a large and diseased mind, the caution becomes more important.   The most popular poet of the present century is so in consequence of the weakness of his readers, who are not so much his pupils as his slaves. Byron, in virtue of his superior force, breaks into their natures, so to speak, — passes into the very core of their moral and intellectual being, — makes them live, in thought, his life, — *Byronizes* them : and the result of the conquest is a horde of minor Byrons, with their thin dilutions of misanthropy and licentiousness, not half so good as the original Peter and John they have delivered up.   " It was nae great head in itsell," said the old Scotchwoman as that of Duke Hamilton rolled from the block, " but it was a sair loss to him." — In view of the enfeebling and corrupting influence exercised by a morbid nature, one is reminded of the anecdote told of Whitefield, the preacher.   A drunkard once reeled up to him, with the remark, — " Mr. Whitefield, I am one of your converts." — " I think it very likely," was the reply, " for I am sure you are none of God's."

The truth probably is, that the fallacies on this subject

of will and personality, in matters pertaining both to intellect and morals, have their source in man's hatred to work, to the independent exercise of power; accordingly he tries, cunningly enough, to ignore the fact that work is the law by which the mind grows, and affects reverie the opium-eating of the intellect, and calls it thinking Theology and philosophy are both apt to be pervaded by a kind of pantheism, in which the perfection of our nature is represented to consist in merging the soul in universal being, and its heaven a state where it loses itself in a sea of delicious sensations. It is needless to add that many realize a tolerable heaven of their kind — on earth.

Passing from the individual to the community, let us now survey the two forms of mental disease, self-worship and self-abandonment, as expressed in the history of states. A nation is no more a mere collection of individuals, than an individual is a mere collection of faculties. It has a national life, more or less peculiar in its features, and subject to disease and decay ; and of this national life its form of civilization is the embodiment. Now, in the earlier ages of the world, in the childhood of humanity, the characteristic form of mental disease is feebleness of personal being, and the consequent absorption of the individual in surrounding objects. He deifies and worships every form and expression of external power, perceiving a god, audible or visible, in every out

ward force. He is, of course, the natural prey of craft,
ferocity, and tyranny, and his weakness is perverted into
a besotted superstition, and a worship even of beasts and
inanimate idols. Such were the myriads of that dark
Egypt, which looms so gloomily up above the clouds of
oblivion, the very image of disease and death. The
civilization of India had the same inherent weakness ; —
the popular mythology, a medley of picturesque brutali-
ties; the learned philosophy, a dreamy pantheism, wasting and withering the primitive springs of action, its first
principle the immersion of the individual soul in the Infinite. India fell by a law as certain as gravitation before
the fe ocity of Mahometan conquest, and the Mahometan
conquerors as certainly before the energy of England.

The civilization of the Asiatics, indeed, was a systematized anarchy of wretchedness and rapine, — a
monstrous agglomeration, representing a despot, a priest-
hood, and a huddled mass of human creatures with slave
written upon and burnt into their inmost being. The
vices of the tyrant are caprice, self-exaggeration, defiance
of restraint; the vices of the slave are falsehood, pol-
troonery, and sensuality : and a national life composed of
such elements, demoniacal vices on the one hand, and
abject vices on the other, must sink into imbecility, and
totter to the tomb.

In passing from the simple forms of Asiatic life to the

complex civilization of Greece, a more difficult problem
presents itself. The Greek Mind, with its combination
of energy and objectiveness, its open sense to all the
influences of nature, its wonderful adaptation to philosophy, and art, and arms, — where, it may be asked, can
you detect disease in that? The answer to this question is fortunately partly contained in the statement of a
fact. Greek civilization is dead; the Greek mind died
out more than two thousand years ago; a race of heroes
declined into a race of sycophants, sophists. and slaves;
and no galvanic action of modern sympathy has ever yet
convulsed it into even a resemblance of its old life. Now,
if it died, it must have died of disease; for nothing else
has power to kill a nation. In considering the causes of
the decay of a national mind so orderly, comprehensive
and creative as the Greek, we must keep steadily
prominent the fact that it began in Satanic energy,
and that it is an universal law that this energy in the
end consumes itself. Perhaps the history of the Greek
Mind is best read in the characteristics of its three
great dramatists, — sublime and wilful in Æschylus,
beautiful in Sophocles, sentimental in Euripides. The
Greek deified Man, first as an object of religion, then as
an object of art. Now, as it is a consequence of high
culture, that a superstition, having its source in human
passions, shall subside from a religion into an art, the

Greek became atheistical as he grew intelligent. He had, so to speak, a taste for divinities, but no belief in them. He acknowledged nothing higher than his own mind; waxed measurelessly proud and conceited; worshipped, in fact, himself. He had opinions on morals, but he assimilated no moral ideas. Now, the moment he became an atheist, the moment he ceased to rise above himself, he began to decay. The strength at the heart of a nation, which keeps it alive, must either grow or dwindle; and, after a certain stage in its progress, it can only grow by assimilating moral and religious truth. Moral corruption, which is the result of wilful energy, eats into the very substance and core of intellectual life Energy, it is true, is requisite to all greatness of soul; but the energy of health, while it has the strength and fearlessness of Prometheus chained to the rock, or Satan buffeting the billows of fire, is also meek, aspiring and reverential. Its spirit is that of the stout old martyr, who told the trembling brethren of the faith who clustered around his funeral pyre, that if his soul was serene in its last struggle with death, he would lift up his hands to them as a sign. They watched, with tremulous eagerness, the fierce element, as it swept along and over his withered frame, and, in the awful agonies of that moment when he was encircled with fire, and wholly hidden from their view, two thin hands quivered up above fagot **and** flame, and closed in the form of prayer.

In the Greek mind, the wilful element took the **form** of conceit rather than pride, and it is therefore in the civilization of Rome that we must seek for the best expression of the power and the weakness of Satanic passion. The myth, which declares its founders to have been suckled by a wolf, aptly symbolizes that base of ferocity and iron will on which its colossal dominion was raised. The Roman mind, if we look at it in relation to its all-conquering courage and intelligence, had many sublime qualities; but pride, hard, fierce, remorseless, invulnerable pride and contempt of right, was its ruling characteristic. It existed just as long as it had power to crush opposition. But avarice, licentiousness, effeminacy, the whole brood of the abject vices, are sure at last to fasten on the conqueror, humbling his proud will, and turning his strength into weakness. The heart of that vast empire was ulcerated long before it fell. The sensuality of a Mark Antony is a more frightful thing than the sensuality of a savage; and when self-abandonment thus succeeds to self-worship, and men are literally given over to their lusts, a state of society exists which in its demoniacal contempt of restraint, sets all descrip tion at defiance. The irruption of barbarian energy **into that** worn-out empire, — the fierce horde of **savages**

that swept in a devouring flame over its plains and cities, — we view with something of the grim satisfaction with which an old Hebrew might have surveyed the engulfing of Pharaoh and his host in the waters of the Red Sea.

In the dark ages which succeeded the overthrow of the Roman empire, modern civilization had its birth; and with those ages it is still connected by an organic bond. This civilization is the most complex that ever existed. If we pass back to its youth, we find in it two grand leading principles of order and disorder, of health and disease, whose contact, collision and union, almost constitute its history. These are, the Feudal System and the Christian Church. Now, feudalism is the embodiment of Satanic pride. Its will is its law. It does everything it has power to do, without regard to the judgment of heaven or earth. It plants its iron heel firm upon the weak, and lifts its iron front firm upon the strong, and says, in its pitiless valor, — " What I obtained by force take by force, if you can." I speak not of the feudalism of romance, but of history ; not as we find it in Miss Porter's novels, but as we find it in the pages of Froissart and Monstrelet, of Michelet and Thierry. Feudalism, as a fact, was a cruel and remorseless oligarchy, in which a horde of independent barons, acknowledging allegiance to a central power in the state, but

nullifying the decisions of that power at their own pleasure, wielded a merciless dominion over a nation of serfs.
Now, this relation of master and slave, this division of
tyranny into many parts, and making each man a tyran
in his own domain, is the devil's own contrivance for
ruining both the oppressor and the oppressed. It cor-
rupts, corrodes, and consumes the inmost principle of
national life. Accordingly, the chronicles of the middle
ages teem with crimes, which almost realize a good-
natured man's idea of the bottomless pit. Hatred, rapine
revenge, lust, blasphemy, — all those ferocious and suici-
dal vices which slowly consume the vigor whence they
spring, — rage and revel there, with that peculiar demoniacal scorn of restraint, which characterizes the brutali-
ties of a spiritual being. The popular insurrections of the
period reveal, as by a flash of lightning, the condition of
that vaunted society where capital owns labor. For a
moment you see the serf burst his bonds, pass from the
brute into the maniac, and rush into the insanest excesses
of licentiousness ; and then comes the mailed baron, cool,
collected, ruthless in his ferocity, trampling him down
again with the diabolical malignity of inhuman strength.
But hatred indulged to inferiors eventually generates
hatred to equals, and poisons at last the domestic rela
tion itself. The unnatural crimes which blacken the
annals of so many families, ironically styled noble, —

father arrayed against son, brother against brother, and murder staining the very hearth-stones of the baronial castle, — are but the final results of pampered self-will conducting us into the black depths of minds, in whom hatred and moody pride have extinguished the last instinct to which reverence can cling.

Still, you may contend, in these old barons there dwelt a tremendous force. True : but was it durable ? Who are their descendants ? Mere weaklings in comparison with the descendants of their former serfs. Where is their system ? Why, its fossil remains blew up not eighteen months ago, and a wondering people, who had long been scared by its frowning looks, found it to be a mere miserable shell and sham, its life and substance all eaten away, — " self-fed and self-consumed."

But side by side with this Feudalism was established the Christian Church. Thus Pandemonium and Heaven were both, so to speak, organized on earth ; acted and reäcted on each other, and passed into each other's life. The consequence of this mixture of principles was, that the church was corrupted, and feudalism improved, eventually to be destroyed. There was at least the recognition of something higher than man, something which the soul might reverence. This was the salvation of modern society, as it continually poured into veins, shrunken and withered by moral evil, some rills of moral life. The leading characteristic, however, of religion, at the **period** ɔf which we are speaking, consisted in its ɔeing **an** opinion or a fanaticism. The feudal baron would have been shocked had you called him an atheist, even wɧ:!e performing acts and pampering passions which are **the** essence of atheism, for he held to Christianity as **an** opinion; and when some overpowering calamity broke down his stubborn will, and Remorse fixed its fangs upon his heart, he was as liable as the most slavish of his serfs to be swept away in a torrent of fanaticism.   But this fanaticism, though itself a disease, and representing **a** will in ruins rather than a character built up, is still **a** reäction against pride, and limits the ravages of moral evil, as physical suffering limits unbridled appetites.

Now, if we examine modern history with a view **to** observe the working of the religious element in its events, — watching this element as it mingles with the harsher qualities of that mass of humanity of whose life it forms a part, — we cannot fail to notice its agency in every great social convulsion which has saved modern civiliza tıon from the death of the ancient, and saved it by toppling down the institutions in which its social disease had come to a head.   But we shall also see that eacḫ reform and revolution has partaken of the corruption **of** the community in which it originated; has been but **an** **ınadequ**ate expression of moral force; and has **exhibiteɑ** unmistakable signs of the Satanic element blended with its beneficent purpose. In short, modern civilization, in regard to its life, is a corrupted Christianity. It has opinions more or less true, but it has imperfectly assimilated truth. It assents to perfect doctrines, but it lives a kind of Christian diabolism. Consequently, all the great movements of the European mind have been but fits of splendid fanaticism, followed by reäctions towards apathy; and have indicated little more than the desperate moral disease they partially eradicated. The Crusades, the Reformation, the English Revolutions of 1640 and 1688, the French Revolutions of 1789 and 1848, all prove that a community cannot lift itself by a convulsive throe above the high water mark of its practical life. Its contortions are signs of vitality, but of vitality struggling with death. There has been progress in European society, if we reckon it not by years but centuries; but it has been a progress marked by jerks rather than by steps. It has not yet arrived at that degree of spiritual force, that momentum of moral energy, which is the condition of healthy motion, — of steady, temperate, determined, onward, ever onward movement. At the present time it presents no spectacle of order, but rather of disorder after stagnation. Peace it does not deserve, and peace it will not obtain. Repose is harmonious activity, the top and crown of the highest force, leaning for support on eternal

laws ; not that sultry and sluggish apathy which **lazily**
welters in fleeting expedients.   The legitimist, **who**
would establish apathy under the forms of monarchy; **the**
agrarian, who would establish apathy under the forms **of**
communism ; are both mistaking immobility **for order**
and seeking material happiness through **intellectual**
death.   Comfort is the god of this world, but comfort **it**
will never obtain by making it an object.

In considering the national life of our own country, **I**
would wish to treat it neither in the style of a Jeremiad
nor in the style of a Fourth of July oration.   Our **national**
life is peculiar, not only as a composite formed from an
imperfect fusion of different races, but it is open to influences from all ages and all times.   Though a civilization may die, it leaves imperishable records of itself in
history and in literature, and these, after the nation
itself is dead, become living and active agents in mould-
ing the natures of all with whom they come in contact.
Accordingly, as everybody here reads or listens, India,
Greece, and Rome, as well as Germany, France, and
England, rush into our national life through a thousand
conductors, — their diseased as well as healthy elements
becoming objects which we assimilate, and which palpably affect our conduct.   The conceit of Greece, the pride
of Rome, the arrogance of feudal Europe, speak and **act**
in America to-day, from the lips and in the lives **of dem-**

ocrat and moneycrat, of philanthropist and misanthrope
The national life, in short, is to a certain extent diseased,
and our people more or less believe in the capital error
that they can thrive by selfishness, injustice, and energy
unregulated by law.

This wilful element is so modified by institutions, that
in the northerner it appears as conceit, in the southerner
as pride.   Both doubtless possess great virtues, but as
ooth are sufficiently well acquainted with that fact, let
us here dwell ungraciously on the vices of each.   The
leading defect of the Yankee consists in the gulf which
separates his moral opinions from his moral principles.
His talk about virtue in the abstract would pass as sound
in a nation of saints, but he still contrives that his interests shall not suffer by the rigidity of his maxims.   He
goes, so to speak, for the linen decencies of sin ; and the
Evil One, being an accommodating personage, will as
readily appear in satin slippers as in cloven hoofs.   Your
true Yankee, indeed, has a spruce, clean, Pecksniffian
way of doing a wrong, which is inimitable.   He passes
resolutions declaring himself the most moral and religious man in the land, and then, with the solemn strut of
an Alsatian hero, proceeds to the practical business of
life.   Believing, after a certain fashion, in justice and
retribution, he still thinks that a sly, shrewd, keen, supple gentleman like himself, can dodge, in a quiet way,

the moral laws of the universe, without any particular pother be ng made about it. He is a self-admiration society in one. He will never be first in a scheme of rapine ; but, once drawn in, to him, as to Macbeth, returning is as tedious as go on. If you ask his opinion about a recent war, he will put on a moral face, declare bloodshed to be an exceedingly naughty business, and roll off a series of resounding schoolboy commonplaces, as though he expected a choir of descending angels had paused in mid air to hear and be edified ; but then, he adds, with a compromising chuckle, that it was an amazingly bright thing though, that whipping of the Mexicans ! Here it fs, — he really believes in whipping the weak. He loves energy in itself, apart from the purposes which make energy beneficent; and as he is apt to deem his intelligence appropriately employed in preying on those who have less, his practical philosophy has sometimes found vent in that profound and elegant maxim, — " Every one for himself, and Satan catch the hindmost." True, Satan does catch the hindmost, but all history teaches that in the end he catches the foremost also.

But, I think I hear you ask, what say you of our philanthropy ? Certainly nothing here as to its beneficent action, but a word as to its diseased aspect. It is to be feared that our benevolence is more opinion than life and, accordingly, it is apt to degenerate into sentiment ality or malice · to be mere inoffensively neffective primer morality and elegant recreation of conscience, or morose, snappish and snarling invective ; in other words, to lack will, or to be wilful. In a community whose life is in any way diseased, it is difficult for the best men to escape the ruling contagion ; to oppose an evil without catching it ; to war with the devil without using the devil's own weapons.

But perhaps the chief Satanic element in our national life comes from the south. There, in the "full tide" of unsuccessful "experiment," is a feudal system, modified by modern humanity, but modified also by modern thrift. The feudal baron did not sell his serfs. Now, this peculiar institution has one vital evil which alone would ruin any country outside of Adam's paradise, — it makes labor disreputable. But it is bad in every respect, corrupting the life both of master and slave ; and it will inevitably end, if allowed to work out its own damnation, in a storm of fire and blood, or in mental and moral sterility and death. Looking at it, not sentimentally or shrewishly, much less with any mean feeling of local exultation, but simply with the eye of reason, — what is it but a rude and shallow system of government, which has been tried over and over again, and exploded over and over again, the mere cast-off nonsense of extinct civilizations, bearing on its front the sign of being a more stupid blunder than it is a crime? Now, we can sympathize with a person who has had the gout transmitted to him, the only legacy of a loving father; but that a man should go deliberately to work, bottle in hand, to establish the gout in his own system, is an absurdity which touches the Quixotic in diabolism. Yet this, or something like to this, has been gravely proposed, and some of our southern brethren have requested us to aid in the ludicrously iniquitous work. No; we should say to these gentlemen, — If you have a taste for the ingenuities of mischief, plant, if you will, on your new territory, small-pox and typhus fever, plant plague, cholera and pestilence, but refrain, if not from common honesty, at least from common intelligence, from planting a moral disease infinitely more destructive, and which will make the world shake with laughter or execrations, according as men consider the madness of its folly, or the brazen impudence of its guilt.

In these remarks on Intellectual Disease, I have referred all along, negatively at least, to Intellectual Health. We have seen that this health consists neither in the self-abandonment of the sensitively weak, nor the self-worship of the wilfully strong. A few words more, to guard against some possible misconceptions. Self-direc tion of mental power, which has been assumed as the condition of healthy mind, is the only possible means of self-devotion, of self-sacrifice, of rising above self. I indicates a mind serene, cheerful, hopeful, courageous, ever active, ever aspiring, with reverence for all above itself, and genial love, not bitter contempt, for all below. But I might well be accused of shallow philosophy, did I leave the subject here. Mind, it is true, is free spiritual force, but it is inscrutably dependent on the Force which created it. It is a cause, but a limited cause ; a power, constituted such by an Infinite Power ; and it grows mightier as it ascends to its Source. In this connection, let me not presume to speak, but call witnesses from the mountain peaks and pinnacles of intellect, — beings who rose thither in virtue of an amazing force directed upwards, — that they may testify to their deep sense of this mysterious dependence. Thus Newton closes the greatest work of pure science which ever came from the mind of man, with an affecting thanksgiving to that Infinite Intelligence who bestowed the power which produced it. Thus Spenser, with his exhaustless opulence of fanciful creation, and burning sense of the loveliness of things, can still find in the world of nature and the world of imagination no fit symbols of the Vision which haunts his soul, until it is lifted up in a " Hymn to Heavenly Beauty." Thus Milton, in whom glowed a spirit that braved every storm of fortune and spurned every touch of fear, from whose brow glanced harmless the thunders of dominant hierarchies, and who opposed to unnatural persecution adamantine will, still never " soared in the nigh reason of his fancies, with his garland and singing robes about him," without first, in his own divine words, ' pouring out his soul in devout prayer to that Eternal Spirit, who can enrich with all utterance and knowledge, and sends out His Seraphim, with the hallowed fire of His altar. to touch and purify the lips of whom He pleases." And from one of England's most curious and not least sceptical of intellects, a deep and prying inquirer into the mysteries of his consciousness, comes that burst of mournful rapture, which has awed and thrilled every soul in which it has entered, that " there is a common spirit which plays within us yet makes no part of us, the Spirit of God, the fire and scintillation of that noble and mighty essence which is the life and radical heat of all minds ; and," he adds, " whosoever feels not the warm breath and gentle ventilation of this spirit, (though I feel his pulse,) I cannot say he lives · for, truly, without this, to me there is no heat under the tropic, and no light, though I dwelt in the very body of the sun."

USE AND MISUSE OF WORDS.*

WE congratulate that large, respectable, inexpressive, and unexpressed class of thinkers, who are continually complaining of the barrenness of their vocabulary as compared with the affluence of their ideas, on the appearance of Dr. Roget's volume. If it does nothing else, it will bring a popular theory of verbal expression to the test; and if that theory be correct, we count upon witnessing a mob of previously mute Miltons and Bacons, and speechless Chathams and Burkes, crowding and tramping into print. Dr. Roget, for a moderate fee, prescribes the verbal medicine which will relieve the congestion of their thoughts. All the tools and

* Thesaurus of English Words, so classified and arranged as to facilitate the Expression of Ideas and assist in Literary Composition. By Peter Mark Roget, late Secretary of the Royal Society, Author of the Bridgewater Treatise on Animal and Vegetable Physiology, etc. Revised and edited, with a List of Foreign Words, defined in English, and other Additions, by Barnas Sears, D. D., Secretary of the Massachusetts Board of Education. Boston : Gould and Lincoln. 12mo. pp. 468.

implements employed by all the poets and philosophers
of England can be obtained at his shop. The idea being
given, he guarantees in every case to supply the word.
Dr. Sears, the American editor, has, it is true, deemed
it his duty to retrench the exuberance of the original
in the phraseology of slang, and has thus made it a useless book to a numerous and constantly increasing class
of *beaux-esprits*, whose conceptions and passions would
find no adequate vent in any dialect milder and clean-
lier than that which derives its force and flavor from
Billingsgate and Wapping ; but for all ordinary purposes, either of copiousness or condensation, of elegance
or energy, Dr. Roget's volume, as weeded by Dr. Sears,
will be found to be amply sufficient.   Indeed, if the apt
use of words be a mechanical exercise, we cannot doubt
that this immense mass of the raw material of expression will be rapidly manufactured into history, philosophy, poetry, and eloquence.

Seriously, we consider this book as one of the best
of a numerous class, whose aim is to secure the results
without imposing the tasks of labor, to arrive at ends
by a dexterous dodging of means, to accelerate the
tongue without accelerating the faculties.   It is an outside remedy for an inward defect.   In our opinion, the
work mistakes the whole process by which living thought
makes its way into living words, and it might be thor-

oughly mastered without conveying any real power or facility of expression. In saying this, we do not mean that the knack of mechanical rhetoric may not be more readily caught, and that fluency in the use of words may not be increased, by its study. But rhetoric is not a knack, and fluency is not expression. The crop of ready writers, of correct writers, of elegant writers, of writers capable of using words in every mode but the right one, is already sufficiently large to meet the current demand for intellectual husk, chaff, and stubble. The tendency of the time to divorce the body of words from the soul of expression, and to shrivel up language into a mummy of thought, would seem to need the rein rather than the whip. The most cursory glance over much of the "literature" of the day, so called, will indicate the peculiar form of marasmus under which the life of language is in danger of being slowly consumed. The most hopeless characteristic of this literature is its complacent exhibition of distressing excellences, — its evident incapacity to rise into promising faults. The terms are such as are employed by the best writers, the grammar is good, the morality excellent, the information accurate, the reflections sensible, yet the whole composition neither contains nor can communicate intellectual or moral life ; and a critical eulogium on its merits sounds like the certificate of a

schoolmaster as to the negative virtues of his pupils.
This fluent debility, which never stumbles into ideas
nor stutters into passion, which calls its commonplace
comprehensiveness, and styles its sedate languor repose,
would, if put upon a short allowance of words, and
compelled to purchase language at the expense of conquering obstacles, be likely to evince some spasms of
genuine expression ; but it is hardly reasonable to expect
such verbal abstemiousness at a period when the whole
wealth of the English tongue is placed at the disposal
of the puniest whipsters of rhetoric, — when the art of
writing is avowedly taught on the principle of imitating
the "best models," — when words are worked into the
ears of the young in the hope that something will be
found answering to them in their brains, — and when
Dr. Peter Mark Roget, who never happened on a verbal
felicity or uttered a "thought-executing" word in the
course of his long and useful life, rushes about, book in
hand, to tempt unthinking and unimpassioned mediocrity into the delusion, that its disconnected glimpses of
truths never fairly grasped, and its faint movements of
embryo aspirations which never broke their shell, can
be worded by his specifics into creative thought and
passion.   The bill of fare is indeed immense ; what a
pity that the absence of such insignificant elements as
mouths, stomachs, and the appetite of hunger may pre-
clude the possibility of a feast !

Far, therefore, from being disposed to increase the vocabulary of such writers, and students of the art of writing, by books like this " Thesaurus," we grudge them the words they have already pressed into their service. They have not earned the right to use their words by exercising any inward energy of thought on the things to which they relate. The first condition of true expression is an effort of mind, which restrains rather than stimulates fluency. The ease with which accredited maxims derived through the ear can be attached to words which have been decoyed through the same populous thoroughfare, offers a desperate temptation to avoid the trouble equally of thinking and expressing. The ears write. Take, for example, the truths of morality and religion, which unrealizing minds and rapid pens have so hardened into truisms, that it has become a mark of genius to restore and re-vivify their original freshness and power. Now there are few creatures so pitiable as to need information on these topics, and few writers so stupid as to be unable to give it. What is required is, not information, but inspiration. The maxims and doctrines are the commonest furniture of the commonest minds. The office, therefore, of the moralist is to impart, not moral truisms, but moral life. The office of the preacher is, not to communicate the forms of religious doctrine, but to

infuse the substance of religious vitality. All moralizing and all preaching are ineffective which do not
thus strike through the understanding directly at the
will, and purify and invigorate the sources of moral and
religious action.   But to do this requires a face-to-face
knowledge of the truths to be driven home, — vivid inward experience poured out in living, breathing, palpi-
tating words.   The man who eliminates from these
universal principles their divine significance and awful
beauty, and prattles about them as truisms, soon becomes as dull, dry, and feeble as his topics, and his
poverty of soul is just as evident when his diction is
elegant and copious as when it is mean and pinched.
The treasures of language, poured into such a mind,
are " like money dropped into a dead man's hand."

What is really wanted, therefore, " to facilitate the
expression of ideas," is something which will facilitate
the conception of ideas.   What is really wanted " to
assist in literary composition," is a true philosophy of
expression, founded on a knowledge of the nature and
operations of the mind, and of the vital processes by
which thought incarnates itself in words.   Expression
is a purely mental act, the work of the same blended
force and insight, will and intelligence, that thinks.   Its
power and clearness answer to the power and clearness
of the mind whence it proceeds.   Its peculiarities cor

respond to the peculiarities of the individual nature it
represents. Its perfection consists in identifying words
with things, — in bending language to the form, and
pervading it with the vitality, of the thought it aims to
arrest and embody. In those cases where thought
transcends the sensuous capacities of language to utter
its conceptions, the expression will still magically suggest the idea or mood it cannot directly convey, just as
a more than earthly beauty looks out from the beautiful
faces of Raphael's Madonnas, indicating the subtile passage into form of a soul and sentiment which no mere
form could express. There are no more simple words
than " green," " sweetness," and " rest," yet what depth
and intensity of significance shines in Chaucer's "green,"
— what a still ecstasy of religious bliss irradiates
" sweetness," as it drops from the pen of Jonathan Ed-
wards, — what celestial repose beams from " rest " as
it lies on the page of Barrow ! The moods seem to
transcend the resources of language, yet they are expressed in common words, transfigured, sanctified, im-
paradised, by the spiritual vitality which streams through
them. The words are among the cheapest articles in
Dr. Roget's voluminous catalogue ; but where is the
cunning rhetorician who can obtain them there ?

Expression, then, whether direct or suggestive, is
thought *in* the words or *through* the words, and not

15

thought *and* the words. Thought implies two elements, the subject thinking and the object thought. When the process of thinking reaches that degree of intensity in which the object of thought is seen in clear vision, — when the thinking mind comes into direct contact with the objective thing or idea it has " felt after " and found, — the words which it then weaves into the visible garment of its mingled emotion and conception are words surcharged and flooded with life, — words which are living things, endowed with the power, not only to communicate ideas, but to convey, as by spiritual conductors, the shock and thrill which attended their conception. Instead of being mere barren signs of abstract notions, they become media through which the life of one mind is radiated into other minds. They inspire as well as inform ; invigorate as well as enlighten. Such language is the spiritual body of the thinker, which never dies or grows old, but has a relative immortality on earth, and makes him a contemporary with all succeeding generations ; for in such language not only are thoughts embodied, but words are ensouled.

The fact that expression like this is beyond the power of ordinary minds does not affect its value as a guiding principle of rhetorical education. The difficulty is that the principle is not generally admitted. It is supposed that the development and the discipline of thought are to be conducted apart from the development and discipline of the power of expressing thought. Fill your head with words, and when you get an idea fit it to them, — this is the current mode, prolific in famished intellects and starveling expressions. Hence the prevailing lack of intellectual conscientiousness, or closeness of expression to the thing, — a palpable interval between them being revealed at the first probe of analysis. Words and things having thus no vital principle of union, being, in fact, attached or tied together, they can be easily detached or unbound, and the expression accordingly bears but the similitude of life.

But it is honorable to human nature that men hate to write unless inspired to write. As soon as rhetoric becomes a mechanical exercise it becomes a joyless drudgery, and drudgery ends in a mental disgust which impairs even the power to drudge. There is consequently a continual tendency to rebel against commonplace, even among those engaged in its service. But the passage from this intellectual apathy to intellectual character commonly lies through intellectual anarchy. The literature of facts connected by truisms, and the literature of things connected by principles, are divided by a wide, chaotic domain, appropriated to the literature of desperation; and generally the first token that a writer has become disgusted with the truisms of the under-

standing is his ostentatious parade of the paradoxes of
sensibility.   He begins to rave the moment he ceases
to repeat.

Now the vital processes of thought and expression are
processes of no single faculty or impulse, but of a whole
nature, and mere sensibility, or mere understanding, or
mere imagination, or mere will, can never of itself produce the effects of that collected, concentrated, personal
power, in which will, intellect, and sensibility are all
consolidated in one individuality.   The utmost strain
and stir of the impulses can but mimic strength, when
they are disconnected from character.   Passion, in the
minds of the anarchists of letters, instead of being poured
through the intellect to stimulate intelligence into power,
frets and foams into mere passionateness.   It does not
condense the faculty in which it inheres, but diffuses
the faculty to which it coheres.   It makes especial claim
to force ; but the force of simple sensibility is a pretentious force, evincing no general might of nature, no
innate, original, self-centred energy.   It blusters furi-
ously about its personal vigor, and lays a bullying emphasis on the " ME," but its self-assertion is without
self-poise or self-might.   The grand object of its tempestuous conceit is to make a little nature, split into
fragmentary faculties and impulses, look like a great
nature, stirred by strong passions, illumined by positive

ideas, and directed to definite ends. And it must be admitted that, so far as the public is concerned, it often succeeds in the deception. Commonplace, though crazed into strange shapes by the *delirium tremens* of sensibility, and uttering itself in strange shrieks and screams, is essentially commonplace still; but it often passes for the fine frenzy and upward, rocket-like rush of impassioned imagination. The writer, therefore, who is enabled, by a felicitous deformity of nature, to indulge in it, contrives to make many sensible people guilty of the blasphemy of calling him a genius; if he have the knack of rhyming, and can set to music his agonies of weakness and ecstasies of imbecility, he is puffed as a great poet, superior to all the restraints of artistic law; and he is allowed to huddle together appetite and aspiration, earth and heaven, man and God, in a truculent fashion peculiarly his own. Hence such "popular" poems as Mr. Bailey's "Festus" and Mr. Robert Montgomery's "Satan."

The misuse of words in this literature of ungoverned or ungovernable sensibility has become so general as to threaten the validity of all definitions. The connection between sign and thing signified has been so severed that it resembles the logic of that eminent master of argumentation, of whom it was said, "that his premises might be afflicted with the confluent small-pox without his conclusion being in any danger of catching it." Objects are distorted, relations disturbed, language put upon the rack to torment it into intensity, and the whole composition seems, like Tennyson's organ, to be " groaning for power," yet the result both of the mental and verbal bombast is simply a feverish feebleness, equally infecting thought and style. Big and passionate as are the words, and terrible as has been their execution in competent hands, they resolutely refuse to do the work of dunces and maniacs. The spirits are called, but they decline to come.

Yet this resounding emptiness of diction is not without popularity and influence, though its popularity has no deep roots and its influence is shallow. Its superficial effectiveness is indicated, not more by the success of the passionate men who fall naturally into it, than by the success of the shrewd men who coldly imitate it. Thus Sheridan, who of all orators had the least sensibility and the most wit and cunning, adopted in many of his speeches a style as bloated as his own face, full of fustian deliberately manufactured, and rant betraying the most painful elaboration. Our own legislative eloquence is singularly rich in speeches whose diction is a happy compound of politic wrath and flimsy fancies, glowing with rage worthy of Counsellor Phillips's philippics, and spangled with flowers that might have been

gathered in the garden of Mr. Hervey's " Meditations."
But we should do great injustice to these orators if we
supposed them as foolish as they try to make themselves
appear in their eloquence ; and it is safe to impute more
than ordinary reptile sagacity, and more than ordinary
skill in party management, to those politicians who indulge in more than ordinary nonsense in their declama-
tions. The incapacity to feel, which their bombast
evinces, proves they are in no danger of being whirled
into imprudences by the mad emotions they affect.
Such oratory, however, has a brassy taint and ring in-
expressibly distasteful both to the physical and intellectual sense, and its deliberate hypocrisy of feeling is a
sure sign of profligacy of mind.

It is only, however, when sensibility is genuine and
predominant, that it produces that anarchy of the intellect in which the literature of desperation, as contrasted
with the literature of inspiration, has its source. The
chief characteristic of this literature is absence of restraint. Its law is lawlessness. It is developed according to no interior principle of growth ; it adapts itself
to no exterior principle of art. In view of this, it is
somewhat singular that so large a portion of its products
should be characterized by such essential mediocrity,
since it might be supposed that an ordinary nature,
disordered by passion, and unrestrained by law, with a

brain made irritable, if not sensitive, by internal rage, would exhibit some hysteric bursts of genius. But a sharp inspection reveals, in a majority of cases, that it is the old commonplace galvanized. Its heat is not that of fire, but of hot water, and no fusing power is perceptible in its weltering expanse. We are reluctantly compelled to admit that chaos cannot create, and that a great display of fussiness may be consistent with a lamentable lack of force.

Even in those writers in whom this sensibility is connected with some genius, and the elements of whose minds exhibit marks of spontaneous power, we are continually impressed with the impotence of anarchy to create, or combine, or portray. They never present the thing itself about which they rave, but only their feelings about the thing. They project into nature and life the same confusion of objects and relations which exists in their own minds, and stir without satisfying. That misrepresentation is a mental as well as moral offence, and that no intellect is sound unless it be conscientiously close to the truth of things in perception and expression, are maxims which they scorn to allow as checks on their freedom of impulse. But with all their bluster, they cannot conceal the limitation of their natures in the impudence of their claims.

And this brings us to the consideration of words as

media for the emission and transpiration of character,
— as expressions, not simply of thoughts or emotions,
but of natures, — as modes by which literature is pervaded with vitality and peopled with men, so that a
criticism on styles is resolved into an exposition of
persons. This function of language seems to us its
noblest, because its honestest function. Words, to be
sure, never really lie, though appearances are sometimes
strongly against them. The truth leaks out from the
most hypocritical sentences; and we have repeatedly
read books, manufactured on Dr. Roget's pattern, in
which the words seemed to feel degraded by the drudgery they were engaged in; to a practised ear audibly
grumbled at being turned from " nimble servitors " into
stupid slaves; and every moment eagerly gave in evidence against their taskmasters. Again, it is undoubtedly true, that a good portion of the sensuality, vulgarity, misanthropy, malignity, and littleness of soul, which
take a literary form, is communicated in the phrases and
images of their opposites, but communicated almost as
effectively as if the words were drawn from the fish-
market, instead of being drawn from the Bible. Indeed,
if there be any animating life behind or within a composition, that peculiar life, and no other, will escape
into the consciousness of the reader, without regard to
the nature of the opinions or the language in which

they are clothed.   A Satanic drop in the blood makes a clergyman preach diabolism from scriptural texts, and a philanthropist inculcate misanthropy from the rostrum of reform.   It is all love in words, all hatred in spirit; and the Devil is content.   An oversight of this obvious principle converts criticism into a mere gibberish.   Take, for instance, such writers as P. J. Bailey and Alexander Smith, two of the most hopeful desperadoes of "young literature," quick in apprehension, fertile in fancy, ravenous in impulse, and whose sad baggage of a muse has been loudly hailed as the true celestial maiden on the sole evidence of her robes.   Doubtless, through the crack in their heads split by passion, we have a view of quite a splendid anarchy of faculties and sensibilities, — doubtless they are adorned with some of the most gorgeous trappings of poetry, — but still they are not essentially poets.   They give us, not poetry, but a poetic debauch.   They evince an appetite for the ideal, rather than a sentiment for it, and whether it pleases them to soar into heaven or dive into hell, whether they take us among saints or sinners, a predominant animalism, penetrating every shining phrase and image, is the impression they stamp upon the mind. The thing does not taste well in the mouth, — gives no ideal pleasure or satisfaction; and, for our own part, we confess a preference for Dante, Milton, and Goethe on the same themes, though we cheerfully admit their inferiority in intellectual topsy-turviness and the blaze of words. Were the powers and passions of these desperate gentlemen harmonized into unity, we should see at once how moderate is the real size and weight of natures, which appear of such astounding dimensions and force in their shattered state. By this compression, however, they might dwindle into — poets, — poets of the second class, it is true, but still poets, which they are altogether too splendid and sublime to be at present.

If the latent nature of a writer thus struggles through his words, and hypocrisy, conscious or unconscious, in his mode of writing, fails to conceal his disposition, — if mental anarchy, though wielding all the external resources of language, can still express only itself, — there would seem to be very strong inducements in literature for authors to be honest. Many a poor wight, who struts in the purple and fine linen of verbiage, a target for criticism, would be an interesting object if he were content with the homely suits which exactly fit his conceptions. Every writer whose aim is not to appear, but to be, and who directs his powers to the expression of what he really is, succeeds, at least, in making himself readable; for such a writer urges no opinions which have not been domesticated in his own understanding, testifies to no facts which are not realities to his own consciousness, and uses no words which he has not earned the right to use by testing their conformity to his own impressions or insight.   And it is curious how flexible language becomes when a writer's vocabulary is thus limited by his intellectual character, and with what ease a few words do the whole business of expression.   A presiding personality, indeed, acts as a magnet; all related words come tripping to it, as if eager and glad to leave their limbo of generality and to form part of a new organism; to feel through their shrunken veins the flow and throb of fresh, warm blood, and to partake in the rapture of individual existence. Then language really becomes alive, and thus, too, books attain the power to live.   All others, after a few convulsive efforts, die and are forgotten, or are known only to the antiquary who prowls among the cemeteries of letters, reading inscriptions on tombstones.

We do not, of course, mean to assert that all individualities that take a literary form become conspicuous in becoming genuine.   The compositions which embody poverty and littleness of individual being must exist in the obscurity in which they were born; but they still exist.   The benevolent literary historian who visits them in their dingy paper hovels always finds them in a wretched condition, but always finds them alive.

Perhaps the lowest form of what we call intellectual character is visible in the pamphlets of those political hacks, who, from Walpole's time to that of Lord Chatham, were employed by booksellers and statesmen to enlighten the British public on national affairs, — in other words, to do the dirty work of politics. These men undoubtedly exhibit singular littleness of nature, and singular feebleness of vitality ; but still their minds act as units, and every sentence is steeped in the meanness and malevolence in which their whole life seems to have been absorbed. We are afraid that a dispassionate criticism must give them the appellation of ragamuffins and sneaks; but yet it is due to them to say that they are not ashamed of their characters, whether they were natural from their cradles, or acquired in the garrets of Osborne and Mist. They are most assuredly stupid, very stupid ; but then their stupidity is a positive, and not a negative quality. Throughout their writings we observe quite a laudable persistence in kind and fidelity to type, without any eccentric rhetorical deviations into brilliancy or decency. As we read them, even at this late day, their natures appear to ooze or dribble out in the vapid emphasis of every italicized word, in the sly venom of every insinuated scandal, in the limping movement of every dismal witticism, in the lowness of all the lying statements, in the impotence of all the toothless sarcasms, in the vagabond disorder of all the rags of rhetoric. But then it is pleasant occasionally to be in the company of dunces who are so complacent in their duncery, who are stirred by no fretful aspiration to be fine writers, who are so thoroughly content with the puddle in which they live, and who, as true artists of the little and the low, would disdain to borrow the snapping terseness of Pope's verse, or the flowing richness of Bolingbroke's prose, or the manner of any other " eminent hands " and " persons of honor," in order to give their lean thoughts and reptile dispositions a more splendid verbal raiment than the characteristic one supplied from their own wardrobes. These writers, too, are by far the most honest of their kind. Minds as small and natures as mean as theirs have since addressed themselves to similar tasks without displaying similar frankness. From the time of Junius and Burke, the tomtits of English politics have sported the beaks and talons, and arrayed themselves in the plumage, of the vultures and the eagles. The feeblest rancor aspires to wear the aspect of ravenous malignity, and the weakest pugnacity would tower and scream in the regions of imaginative passion.

The next form of intellectual character, whose verbal expression rewards analysis, is found in those men who deal with obvious facts and principles, but really grasp and handle them. Their sense is common sense, but common sense as character, not as hearsay. All their notions are organized into abilities and written out in their lives; truisms from their lips have the effect of original perceptions; and old saws and proverbs, worn to shreds by constant repetition, startle the ear like brilliant fancies, when uttered by men whose dispositions they have formed and whose actions they have guided. Such persons are commonly narrow and bigoted, and profess great contempt for everything that lies beyond the range of their vision. They delight, indeed, to call their opinions "views," in order, it would seem, to suggest the test of sight to which they have been subjected; and they give them additional emphasis by putting them in the possessive case. They are not general "views," but "my views." These opinions have not been argued into their heads, and history and experience afford no instance of their having been ever argued out of them. Solidified as they are into muscle and bone, their hard tenacity of hold, impregnable to the syllogism, would almost resist the axe or the battering-ram. To change the "views" of such minds is a task resembling the boring of tunnels or the blasting of rocks. Their phraseology, when its organic pith and substance are uncorrupted by the schoolmaster, is, of course, singularly close, compact, and vital, indicating an interior perception of, and familiar acquaintance with, the matters about which they talk.   In English literature, these thinkers and rhetoricians of humble life are contemptuously referred to as "the vulgar," and young students are pathetically adjured not to catch the infection of their speech ; but it seems to us that they hint the true philosophy of rhetoric better than Dr. Campbell directly teaches it ; for their words are always things, and the aim of the loftiest creative thinker is, in expression, to give solidity to spiritual facts.   Even in the use of tropes they evince a more subtile knowledge of the vital processes of figurative expression than most of the poëtasters who sniff at them.   "That horse of yours," said a friend of ours to a farmer, "is very handsome."   "Yes," was the drawling reply, "but he is — as — slow — as — cold molasses."   We doubt if an analyst could find, out of the great poets, a better example than this on which to exercise his skill in giving the genesis of an imaginative analogy.   The idea, as Bacon would say, is thoroughly "immersed in matter." The authors who have studied the modes of thinking and expression characteristic of "the vulgar," have always exercised a wide influence ; for in that school they learned to think in the concrete, and to give to thoughts the form and significance of visible realities. The reserved power always underlying the sparse speech of ordinary men, imparts tenfold meaning and force to their words and images. Sir Edward Coke, a man of prodigious ability and acquirement, but still essentially commonplace in his intellect and prejudices, was once goaded by rage and hatred into an imagination in which his whole massive nature seemed to emit itself in a Titanic stutter of passion. We refer, of course, to his calling Sir Walter Raleigh a "spider of hell," — an image in which loathing became executive, and palpably smit its object on the cheek. It was from the fact that imagination was so small an element in his general power, and required the utmost depth of passion to be pushed into prominence, that it acted so like a bolt when it did flame fiercely out. The image may be a small matter in itself, but it becomes tremendous when we see the whole roused might of Sir Edward Coke glare terribly through it. The spider, indeed, appears to be a favorite symbol of ordinary fancies to express spite. Thus Henry Fox, in a hot attack on Lord Chancellor Hardwicke, who was supposed to have no desire to reform the many abuses of his office, exclaimed : " Touch but a cobweb in Westminster Hall, and *the old spider of the Law* is out upon you, with all his vermin at his heels." This image makes the flesh creep.

Common sense, as embodied in character, has a downright directness of expression often offensively

16

dogmatic, though the dogmatism is not without justification in the evident certainty — the iron clutch — of its
hold upon things. But in men of coarse strength of
nature, endowed with broad perceptions on low levels
of thought, this practical sagacity is apt to wax into
conceit with itself, to be developed in connection with
pride and self-will, and gradually to degenerate into a
bearish arrogance of self-assertion, in which a good
portion of its original clearness of view is obscured.
The moment this divorce between force and insight
occurs, will is pampered at the expense of understanding, and the result is a wilfulness, whose expression is
marked by an overbearing dogmatism, hateful to all
who delight in the dominion of reason over animal
vigor and effrontery. Men of this stamp often preserve
more than an ordinary degree of intellect; but intellect
is still a tool to be used, not a torch to guide. Both in
literature and in life, they are the swashbucklers, bullies,
and bravos of speech, unscrupulous, despotic, wrong-
headed, ambitious to conquer rather than anxious to
convince, and indisposed, indeed, to give any reasons
for saying or doing a thing, so long as they can "bid
their will avouch it." They are often very effective as
writers, orators, statesmen, theologians, from their war-
like attitude and tactics, — using words as bullets,
throwing off statements and arguments like successive

discharges of cannon, and thoroughly understanding
the art of rapidly concentrating the heaviest mass of
invective on the weakest point of resistance. Lord
Chancellor Thurlow is a shining example of the method
by which opponents may be cowed or scattered by
abuse, and offices of trust and honor taken by assault.
By sheer strength of imperious, indomitable impudence,
he pushed himself into high station, and, what is more,
did what he pleased after he attained it. He was not
content to rule ; he was unhappy unless he could
domineer. During the time that he hung, " like a low,
black cloud," over the House of Lords, the proudest
peers were abashed by the scowl of his shaggy brow,
the ominous growl of his voice, " like thunder heard
remote," and the impending lightnings which seemed
ready to dart from his eyes at the slightest touch of
provocation. His means of success were immense
confidence in himself, immense assumed contempt for
others, and the favor of his Most Wilful Majesty,
George III., who was attracted to him by a kindred
spirit. He would have his own way. He unhesitat-
ingly plotted against administrations of which he was
himself a member, hectored statesmen of his own party,
gave judgments in chancery without condescending to
state reasons for them, and fairly bullied his contemporaries into the opinion that he was a great statesman

and a great jurist. There was a fascination in his towering effrontery. George III. and his queen were eminently moral people, yet Thurlow was a favorite of both, though he openly defied moral restraints. When Chancellor, he was "keeper of the King's conscience" and of a mistress, paraded his illegitimate children in public, and swore more terribly than ever did "our army in Flanders." At one time, when the King was threatened with insanity, and was palpably incompetent to understand the acts which the Chancellor carried to him for his approval, Thurlow became impatient at the demands of his Majesty to have their purport explained to him. "It's all —— nonsense," said the gruff Chancellor, "to try to make your Majesty understand them, and you had better consent to them at once." He sometimes employed Mr. Justice Buller, a judge in every respect his superior, to sit for him in the Court of Chancery, and praised his decisions publicly; but on its being said to him that it was remarkable that a Common Law judge should be so familiar with Equity, Thurlow exclaimed, "Equity! he knows no more of it than a horse; but he disposes somehow of the cases, and I seldom hear of them again." When Mr. Pitt's death was announced to him, he remarked, "A —— good hand at turning a period!" This insolent assumption of superiority is stamped on all his speeches, public and private ; but it must be admitted that he had completely mastered the art of individualizing language, and of making words perform the office of blows and stabs.

There are many people who cannot recognize the presence of a powerful personality, except it be thus exhibited in salient personal traits.   But personal force, in its healthy development, purifies itself from obtrusive individualities in proportion to the singleness and vigor of its aim and purpose ; and in works of simple statement and argumentation we often feel the presence of character as a moving power, when it fails to be visible in obstructive singularities.   It is character that states and reasons, though character broadened into understanding, and seemingly as impersonal as the facts and principles it grasps and expounds.   Dr. Samuel Clarke, John Stuart Mill, Sir William Hamilton, and Daniel Webster are instances in point.   In the language of these men we observe an austere conscientiousness of phrase, as if every word had been severely tested and kept subordinate to the thought which it is used to convey.   The sober and solid tramp of their style reflects the movement of intellects that palpably respect the relations and dimensions of things, and to which exaggeration would be immorality.   We should hesitate to call them creative thinkers, and equally to place them in point of greatness below any but creative thinkers of the first class. It is indeed with a sigh of regret, that a critic who has studied Sir William Hamilton is compelled to station him not even abreast of Hobbes and Locke.

In passing from intellectual character of this testing and reasoning, but not especially originating, species to creative power, we do not at first ascend. Natures comparatively little often exhibit faculties which are fine in kind, though limited in degree, and exhibit them also as centred in character. In their expression there is none of the hardness which distinguishes the tough vitality and vigor of men in whom understanding predominates. The little there is in them melts, flows, fuses, shines. They can create and combine, though their creations and combinations be petty and of small account; and they leave the permanent print of their natures in those sly corners and crevices of the literature of a language, which the omnivorous general reader delights to explore. Colley Cibber, for instance, is a small creature enough, but still an indissoluble unit and representative of flippant character, endowed with a delightful little imagination exactly answering to the demands of his little nature, and fertile in little creations and bright and shallow gossip, always meaning well and never meaning much. Horace Walpole, a higher example of the same flippancy, built up, through an assimilation of all the frippery of literature and all the frippery of fashionable life, a character perfect in its kind, and within its sphere undoubtedly creative. The affectation of his style has its roots in the affectation of his nature, and it is an admirable style for him. The sarcastic pertness of his diction, in which wit and observation tend to crystallize in words, and become brittle as they grow sparkling, shows a nature not so fluid as Cibber's, and acting more by starts and flings of fanciful inspiration. His wit is unmistakably original, sometimes in kind. An old and pious lady, into whose hands some of Lord Rochester's licentious letters came, burned them, — "for which," Walpole petulantly says, "she is now burning in — heaven." Occasionally a single word does the work of a paragraph. "Lady ——," he remarks in one of his letters, "looks ghastly and *going.*"

Geniality is a finishing grace to intellectual character, and we especially feel its sweetness in natures of great reach and depth ; but in minds whose endowments are by no means extraordinary, it sometimes amounts to a weakness. Leigh Hunt is an example of what we should call a fondling character, and a great master of its verbal expression. Language in his hands is the most flexible of instruments to convey dainty and

pleasant sensations. His self-content is so great that
it flows out in content with all the world. He fon-
dles everything and everybody. Shakespeare, Spenser,
Shelley, Coleridge, he dandles on his knee, as if they
were babies, paws them, and would fill their dear little
mouths with sugared epithets of eulogy. This he seems
to think is genial criticism. Even divine things cannot
escape his all-tolerating kindliness; for, whatever sects
and churches may say, he knows that the world was
made after the image of Leigh Hunt. The Deity with
him is not so much Infinite Goodness as infinite good-
nature, and we believe he published a devotional book
to inculcate that doctrine. He talks very cosily about
Dante, and appeals to the readers whom he conducts
through the " Inferno," if they really can believe that
such fine fellows as they there behold in torments ought
to be treated in that way. Throughout his writings,
indeed, he seems to think that the wax taper, which he
holds so jauntily, can light up all the gloom and dark-
ness of the moral universe. This foppery is of a different kind from Walpole's, and is much more delightful;
but it is still foppery, though the foppery of philanthropy.

We have, doubtless, said more than enough respecting
words as media for the transpiration of character, and
it would be a waste of illustration to trace the working

of the principle through other forms of personality, such as the sentimental, the Satanic, the eccentric, the religious, and the heroic. In all of these, however, language is moulded into the organic body of thought, and the organisms stand out in literature with the distinctness and the diversity of organic forms in nature. The words are veined, and full of the lifeblood of the creative individualities projected into them with unwithholding energy. In criticising such works we soon discover that what we at first call faults of style are in reality faults of character. But such individualities are more or less narrow and peculiar; and it is only when we arrive at those rare natures, with sensibility, reason, fancy, wit, humor, imagination, all included in the operations of one mighty, spiritual force, which we feel to be greater than one or all of the faculties and passions, that we compass the full meaning of intellectual character in apprehending its highest form. Such men — Shakespeare, for example — appear to be impersonal simply because their personality is so broad. They are impersonal relatively, not positively. Capable of discerning, interpreting, representing, the actual and possible peculiarities of human character, they seem to have few peculiarities of their own. They have no leading idea, because they have so many ideas; no master passion, because they have so many passions; no hobby, great or little, sublime or mean, because they possess a vital conception of relations, as well as a vital conception of things and persons. But they never really pass, as creative minds, beyond the limits of their characters; for it is always men that create, not some vagrant faculty of men.

It is sometimes doubted if the style of such writers can be taken as the measure of their power and variety of power. Now there is in the smallest individual intelligence an abstract possibility which is never realized in any mode of expression while he is in the body, and this limitation is especially felt when we read the works of the greatest individualized intelligences. So far, and only so far, are we inclined to concede that the great masters and creators of language find in words but a partial expression of their natures. What is directly conveyed in words and images, according to their literal interpretation, is, of course, inadequate to fix and embody a mind like Shakespeare's; but then the marvel of Shakespeare's diction is its immense suggestiveness, — his power of radiating through new verbal combinations or through single expressions a life and meaning which they do not retain in their removal to dictionaries. When the thought is so subtile, or the emotion so evanescent, or the imagination so remote, that it cannot be flashed upon the " inward eye," it is hinted to the inward ear by some exquisite variation of tone. These irradiations and melodies of thought and feeling are seen and heard only by those who think into the words, but they are nevertheless there, whether perceived or not. An American essayist on Shakespeare, Mr. Emerson, in speaking of the impossibility of acting or reciting his plays, refers to this magical suggestiveness in a sentence almost as remarkable as the thing it describes. "The recitation," he says, "begins: one golden word leaps out immortal from all this painted pedantry, *and sweetly torments us with invitations to its own inaccessible homes!*" He who has not felt this witchery in Shakespeare's style has never read him. He may have looked *at* the words, but has never looked *into* them.

We have been able, in these hasty observations on the use and misuse of words, to touch upon only a few topics connected with our theme. There are many others that would repay investigation, which we have hardly named, such as the intimate connection between clearness and freshness of expression, — the sources of the pleasure we take in style apart from the importance of the matter it conveys, — the difference between an author's expressing an idea to himself and expressing it to others, — the power of words, as wielded by a man of genius, to create or evoke in

another mind the thought or emotion they embody, —
the peculiar vitality and the amazing mystical signifi‹
cance of language when used as the organ for expressing the phenomena of rapture and ecstasy, — and the
interior laws which regulate the construction and movement of style, according as the purpose is to narrate,
describe, reason, or invent.   But we have not space at
present to consider these topics with the attention they
deserve.   In the somewhat extended remark into
which we have been provoked by the publication of
Dr. Roget's "Thesaurus," we have confined ourselves
to a few obvious principles, and have labored to show
the hopelessness of all attempts to make language really
express anything finer, deeper, higher, or more forcible
than what lives in the mind and character of the writer
who uses it.   Especially in all that relates to strength
of diction, we think it will be found that the utmost
affluence in energetic terms will, of itself, fail to impress
on style any vital energy of soul ; for this energy,
whether it work like lightning or like light, whether it
smite and blast, or illumine and invigorate, ever comes
from the presence of the man in the words.

WORDSWORTH.*

---◆---

THE death of this eminent poet, after an honorable
and useful life, prolonged to eighty years, will doubtless provoke a new conflict of opinions regarding the
nature and influence of his great and peculiar mind.
The universal feeling among all lovers of what is deep
and delicate and genuine in poetry must be,

> " That there has passed away a glory from the earth ";

and not until literature receives an original impulse
from a nature equally profound and powerful will it be
called upon to mourn such a departure.   His death was
worthy of an earthly career consecrated by devout and
beautiful meditations to a life beyond life, — his soul,
so long the serene guest of his mortal frame, meekly
withdrawing itself at the end to a world not unfamiliar
to his raised vision here below.

We confess, at the outset, to an admiration for
Wordsworth's genius bordering on veneration, but we

---

* Written when the news came of his death.

trust that we can speak of it without substituting
hyperbole for analysis, without burying the essential
facts of his mental constitution under a load of panegyric. It appears to us that these facts alone convict
his depreciating critics of malice or ignorance ; that
the kind of criticism to which he was originally subjected, and which even now occasionally reappears
with something of the sting of its old flippancy, is
essentially superficial and untenable, failing to cover
the ground it pretends to occupy, and disguising nonsense under a garb of shrewdness and discrimination.
The opinion of a man of ability on subjects which he
understands, and on objects he really discerns, is entitled to respect, and we do not deny that Jeffrey's
opinions on many important matters are sound and
valuable ; but, in relation to Wordsworth, whom he
perversely misunderstood, he appears presumptuously
incompetent and undiscerning throughout his much
vaunted criticisms ; in every case missing the peculiarities which constituted Wordsworth's originality, and
satirizing himself in almost every sarcasm he launched
at the poet. The usual defence set up for such a critic
is, that he judges by the rules of common sense ; but
every poet who deserves the name is to be judged by
the common sense of the creative imagination, not by
the common sense of the practical understanding ; and

mere police of letters, we imagine that Wordsworth will readily assume his place as the greatest of English poets since Milton.

In claiming for him a position in that line of English poets which contains no other names than those of Chaucer, Spenser, Shakespeare, and Milton, we imply that he is not only great as an individual writer, but that he is the head and founder of a new school of poets; that he is the point from which the future historian of English letters will consider the poetry of the age; that he introduced into English literature new elements, whose inspiration has not yet spent itself, but continues to influence almost every poet of the day; that

> " Thither, as to their fountain, other stars
> Repairing, in their golden urns draw light."

This fact can be chronologically proved. In the " Lines on Revisiting Tinturn Abbey," written as far back as 1798, and in which we have the key-note of Wordsworth's whole system of viewing nature and man, we perceive not only a new element of thought added to English poetry, but an element which appeared afterward in Shelley and Byron — modified, of course, by their individuality — and still appears, with decreasing force, in Tennyson and Browning. Plato and Lord Bacon are not more decidedly originators of new scientific methods than Wordsworth is the originator of a new poetical method. Even if we dislike him, and neglect his poetry, we cannot emancipate ourselves from his influence, as long as we are thrilled by the most magnificent and ethereal passages in Shelley and Byron. We may be offended at the man, but we cannot escape from his method, unless our reading of the poets stops with Goldsmith and Cowper.

The vital poems of Wordsworth — those which are really inspired with his spirit and life, and not mere accretions attached to his works — form a complete whole pervaded by one living soul, and, amid all their variety of subject, related to one leading idea, namely, the marriage of the soul of man to the external universe, whose "spousal hymn" the poet chants. They constitute together the spiritual body of his mind, exhibiting it as it grew into beautiful and melodious form through thirty years of intense contemplation. To a person who has studied his works with sufficient care to obtain a conception of the author's personality, every little lyric is alive with his spirit, and is organically connected with the long narrative and didactive poems. This body of verse is, we think, a new creation in literature, differing from others not only in degree but in kind; an organism, having its own interior laws, growing

from one central principle, and differing from Spenser
and Milton as a swan differs from an eagle, or a rose
from a lily.

We need hardly say that the central power and
principle of this organic body of verse is Wordsworth
himself. He is at its heart and circumference, and
through all its veins and arteries, as the vivifying and
organizing force, — coloring everything with his peculiar individuality, representing man and nature through
the medium of his own original and originating genius,
and creating, as it were, a new world of forms and
beings, idealized from hints given by the actual appearances of things. This world is not so various as that
of Shakespeare or Scott, nor so supernatural as that
of Milton; but it is still Wordsworth's world, a world
conceived by himself, and in which he lived and moved
and had his being. A true criticism of his works,
therefore, should be a biography of his mind, exhibiting
the vital processes of its growth, and indicating the
necessary connection between its gradual interior development and the imaginative forms in which it was
expressed. This we cannot pretend to do, having
neither the insight nor the materials for such a task,
and we shall be content with attempting a faint outline
of his mental character, with especial reference to those
qualities which dwelt near the heart of his being, and

17

which seem to have been woven into the texture of his mind at birth.

Wordsworth was born in April, 1770, of parents sufficiently rich to give him the advantages of the usual school and collegiate education of English youth. He early manifested a love for study, but it may be inferred that his studies were such as mostly ministered to the imagination, as he displayed, from his earliest years, a passion for poetry, and never seems to have had a thought of choosing a profession. At the University of Cambridge he appears to have read the classics with the divining eye and assimilating mind of a poet, and if he did not attain the first position as a classical scholar, he certainly drank in beyond all his fellows the spirit of the great writers of Greece and Rome. In a mind so observing, studious, thoughtful, imaginative, and steadfast as his, the power of which consisted more in concentration of view than rapidity of movement, the images of classical poetry must have been firmly held and lovingly contemplated; and to his collegiate culture we doubtless owe the exquisite poems of Dion and Laodamia, the grand interpretative, uplifting mythological passage in The Excursion, and the general felicity of the classical allusions and images throughout his works. He probably wrote much as well as meditated deeply at college, but very few of his juvenile pieces have been preserved, and those which are preserved seem little more than exercises in expression. On leaving college he formed the determination of educating his poetical faculty by a communion with the forms of nature, as others study law and theology. He resided for some time in the West of England, and at about the age of twenty made the tour of France, Italy, Switzerland, and Germany, travelling mostly on foot, diving into forests, lingering by lakes, penetrating into the cottages of Italian peasants and German boors, and alternating the whole by a residence in the great European cities. This seems to have occupied nearly two years of his life; its immediate, but not its only result, was the publication of his " Descriptive Sketches in Verse," indicating accurate observation rather than shaping imagination, and undistinguished by any marked peculiarities of thought or diction. We next hear of him at Bristol, the companion of Coleridge and Southey, and discussing with those eager and daring spirits the essential falsehood of current poetry as a representation of nature. The sensible conclusion of all three was this: that the worn-out epithets and images then in vogue among the rhymers were meaningless; that poetry was to be sought in nature and man; and that the language of poetry was not a tinsel rhetoric, but an impassioned utterance of thoughts and emotions awakened by a direct contact of the mind with the objects it described. Of these propositions, the last was one of primary importance, and in a mind so grave, deep, and contemplative as Wordsworth's, with an instinctive ambition to be one of " Nature's Privy Council," and dive into the secrets of those visible forms which had ever thrilled his soul with a vague and aching rapture, the mere critical opinion passed into a motive and an inspiration.

" The Lyrical Ballads," published in 1798, and to which Southey and Coleridge contributed, were the first poems which indicated Wordsworth's peculiar powers and passions, giving the first hints of his poetical philosophy, and the first startling shock to the tastes of the day. They were mostly written at Allfoxden, near the Bristol Channel, in one of the deepest solitudes in England, amid woods, glens, streams, and hills. Here Wordsworth had retired with his sister ; and Coleridge was only five miles distant at Stowey. Cottle relates some amusing anecdotes of the ignorance of the country people in regard to them, and to poets and lovers of the picturesque generally. Southey, Coleridge and his wife, Lamb, and the two Wedgewoods, visited Wordsworth in his retirement, and the whole company used to wander about the woods, and by the sea, to the great wonder of all the honest people they met. As they

were often out at night, it was supposed they led a
dissolute life; and it is said that there are respectable
people in Bristol who believe now that Mrs. Coleridge
and Miss Wordsworth were disreputable women, from
a remembrance of the scandalous tattle circulating then.
Cottle asserts that Wordsworth was driven from the
place by the suspicions which his habits provoked,
being refused a continuance of his lease of the Allfoxden house by the good man who had the letting of it,
on the ground that he was a criminal in the disguise of
an idler.   One of the villagers said, " that he had seen
him wander about at night *and look rather strangely at
the moon!*   And then he roamed over the hills like
a partridge."   Another testified " he had heard him
mutter, as he walked, in some outlandish brogue, that
nobody could understand."   This last, we suppose, is
the rustic version of the poet's own statement, —

> " He murmurs near the running brooks
> A music sweeter than their own."

Others, however, took a different view of his habits, as
little flattering to his morals as the other view to his
sense.   One wiseacre remarked confidently : " I know
what he is.   We have all met him tramping away
toward the sea.   Would any man in his senses take all
that trouble to look at a parcel of water ?   I think he

carries on a snug business in the smuggling line, and, in these journeys, is on the lookout for some *wet* cargo." Another, carrying out this bright idea, added, " I know he has got a private still in his cellar ; for I once passed his house at a little better than a hundred yards' distance, and I could smell the spirits as plain as an ashen fagot at Christmas." But the charge which probably had the most weight in those times was the last. " I know," said one, " that he is surely a desperd French Jacobin ; for he is so silent and dark that no one ever heard him say one word about politics." The result of all these various rumors and scandals was the removal of Wordsworth from the village. It is curious that, with such an experience of English country-people, Wordsworth should never have looked at them dramatically, and represented them as vulgar and prejudiced human beings as well as immortal souls. It proves that humor did not enter at all into the constitution of his nature ; that man interested him more than men ; and that his spiritual affections, connecting humanity constantly with its divine origin, shed over the simplest villager a light and atmosphere not of earth.

While the ludicrous tattle to which we have referred was sounding all around him, he was meditating Peter Bell and the Lyrical Ballads, in the depths of the Allfoxden woods, and consecrating the rustics who

were scandalizing him. The great Poet of the Poor,
who has made the peasant a grander object of contemplation than the peer, and who saw through vulgar
externals and humble occupations to the inmost soul of
the man, had sufficient provocations to be the satirist of
those he idealized.

In these Lyrical Ballads, and in the poems written at
the same period of their publication, we perceive both
the greatness and the limitations of Wordsworth, the
vital and the mechanical elements in his poetry. As
far as his theory of poetic diction was unimaginative, as
far as its application was wilful, it became a mere matter of the understanding, productive of little else than
shocks to the poetic sense, and indicating the perversity
of a powerful intellect, pushing preconceived theories to
the violation of ideal laws, rather than the rapt inspiration of the bard, flooding common words and objects
with new life and divine meanings. It is useless to
say that the passages to which we object would not
provoke a smile if read in the spirit of the author.
They are ludicrous in themselves, and would have
made the author himself laugh had he possessed a moderate sense of the humorous. But the gravest objection
against them is, that they do not harmonize with the
poems in which they appear, — are not vitally connected
with them, but stand as excrescences plastered *on* them,

— and instantly suggest the theorizer expressing his scorn of an opposite vice of expression, by deliberately substituting for affected elegance a simplicity just as much tainted with affectation. Wordsworth's true simplicity, the simplicity which was the natural vehicle of his grand and solemn thoughts, the simplicity which came from writing close to the truth of things, and making the word rise out of the idea conceived, cannot be too much commended ; but in respect to his false simplicity, his simplicity for the sake of being simple, we can only say that it has given some point to the sarcasm, " that Chaucer writes like a child, but Wordsworth writes childishly." * These objectionable passages, however, are very few ; they stand apart from his works and apart from what was essential in him ; and they are to be pardoned, as we pardon the occasional caprices of other great poets.

Another objection to the Lyrical Ballads, and to Wordsworth's poems generally, is an objection which relates to his noblest creations. He never appears to have thoroughly realized that other men were not Wordsworths, and accordingly he not infrequently violates the law of expression, — which we take to be the expression of a man to others, not the expression of a

---

* Thackeray, insensible to his real genius, always called him " Daddy Wordsworth."

man to himself. He speaks, as it were, too much to his own ear, and having associated certain words with subtile thoughts and moods peculiar to himself, he does not seem aware that the words may not of themselves convey his meaning to minds differently constituted, and accustomed to take the expressions at their lexicon value. In this he differs from Coleridge, whose words and music have more instantaneous power in evoking the mood addressed, and thread with more force and certainty all the mental labyrinths of other minds, and act with a tingling and inevitable touch on the finest nerves of spiritual perception. The Ancient Mariner and Christobel almost create the moods in which they are to be read, and surprise the reader with a revelation of the strange and preternatural elements lying far back in his own consciousness. Wordsworth has much of this wondrous wizard power, but it operates with less direct energy, and is not felt in all its witchery until we have thought into his mind, become enveloped in its atmosphere, and been initiated into the " suggestive sorcery " of his language. Then, it appears to us, he is even more satisfying than Coleridge, moving as he does in the transcendental region of thought with a calmer and more assured step, and giving evidence of having steadily gazed on those spiritual realities which Coleridge seems to have casually seen by flashes of lightning. His language consequently is more temperate, as befits a man observing objects familiar to his mind by frequent contemplation ; but, to common readers, it would be more effective if it had the suddenness and startling energy coming from the first bright vision of supernatural objects. As it is, however, his style proves that his mind had grown up to those heights of contemplation to which the mind of Coleridge only occasionally darted, under the winged impulses of imagination ; and therefore Wordsworth gives more serene and permanent delight, more " sober certainty of waking bliss," than Coleridge, however much the latter may excel in instantaneousness of effect.

The originality of the Lyrical Ballads consisted not so much in an accurate observation of Nature as in an absolute communion with her, and interpretation of the spirit of her forms. They combine in a remarkable degree ecstasy with reflection, and are marvellously refined both in their perception of the life of nature and the subtile workings of human affections. Those elusive emotions which flit dimly before ordinary imaginations and then instantly disappear, Wordsworth arrests and embodies ; and the remotest shades of feeling and thought, which play on the vanishing edges of conception, he connects with familiar objects, and brings home to our common contemplations. In the sphere of the affections he is confessedly great. The still, simple, searching pathos of "We are Seven"; the mysterious, tragic interest gathered around "The Thorn"; and the evanescent touch of an elusive mood in "The Anecdote for Fathers," indicate a vision into the deepest sources of emotion. The poems entitled, "Expostulation and Reply," "The Tables Turned," "Lines Written in Early Spring," "To My Sister," and several others, referring to this period of 1798, evince many of the peculiar qualities of his philosophy, and combine depth of insight with a most exquisite simplicity of phrase. The following extracts contain hints of his whole system of thought, expressing that belief in the life of nature, and the mode by which that life is communicated to the mind, which reappear, variously modified, throughout his writings : —

> Nor less I deem that there are Powers
> Which of themselves our minds impress;
> That we can feel this mind of ours
> *In a wise passiveness.*

—

> And hark ! how blithe the throstle sings!
> He, too, is no mean preacher :
> Come forth into the light of things,
> Let Nature be your teacher.

> She has a world of ready wealth,
> Our minds and hearts to bless, —

Spontaneous wisdom breathed by health,
  Truth breathed by cheerfulness.

One impulse from a vernal wood
  May teach you more of man,
Of moral evil and of good
  Than all the sages can.

Sweet is the lore which Nature brings;
  Our meddling intellect
Misshapes the beauteous forms of things,·
  We murder to dissect.

Enough of Science and of Art;
  Close up those barren leaves;
Come forth and bring with you a heart
  That watches and receives.

———

I heard a thousand blended notes,
  While in a grove I sat reclined,
In that sweet mood when pleasant thoughts
  Bring sad thoughts to the mind.

———

Through primrose tufts in that sweet bower,
  The periwinkle trailed its wreaths;
And 't is my faith that every flower
  Enjoys the air it breathes.

———

There is a blessing in the air
  Which seems a sense of joy to yield
To the bare trees, and mountains bare,
  And grass in the green field.

———

One moment now may give us more
  Than years of toiling reason:

> Our minds shall drink at every pore
> The spirit of the season.
>
> *Some silent laws our hearts will wake,*
> *Which they shall long obey:*
> We for the year to come may take
> Our temper from to-day.

But the most remarkable poem written at this period of Wordsworth's life is that on Tintern Abbey, " Lines composed on Revisiting the Banks of the Wye." We have here that spiritualization of nature, that mysterious sense of the Being pervading the whole universe of mattter and mind, that feeling of the vital connection between all the various forms and kinds of creation, and that marriage of the soul of man with the visible universe, which constitute the depth and the charm of Wordsworth's " divine philosophy." After describing the landscape which he now revisits, he proceeds to develop the influence it has exerted on his spirit : —

> These beauteous forms,
> Through a long absence, have not been to me,
> As is a landscape to a blind man's eye :
> But oft in lonely rooms, and 'mid the din
> Of towns and cities, I have owed to them,
> In hours of weariness, sensations sweet,
> *Felt in the blood, and felt along the heart,*
> And passing even into my purer mind
> With tranquil restoration ; feelings, too,
> Of unremembered pleasure ; such, perhaps,

As have no slight and trivial influence
On that best portion of a good man's life,
His little nameless, unremembered acts
Of kindness and of love. Nor less, I trust,
To them I may have owed another gift
Of aspect more sublime ; that blessed mood,
In which the burthen of the mystery,
In which the heavy and the weary weight
Of all this unintelligible world,
Is lightened ; *that serene and blessed mood,*
In which the affections gently lead us on,
Until the breath of this corporeal frame,
And even the motion of our human blood
Almost suspended, we are laid asleep
In body, and become a living soul;
While with an eye made quiet by the power
Of harmony, and the deep power of joy,
We see into the life of things.

He then proceeds to describe the passionate fascination which Nature exerted over his youth, and the
change which had come over him by a deeper and
more thoughtful communion with her spirit. When we
consider that Wordsworth, at this time, was only twenty-
eight, and that even the emotions described in the first
part of our extract had no existence in contemporary
poetry, we can form some idea of his giant leap in
advance of his age, as indicated by the unspeakable
beauty and novelty of the concluding portion. The
reader will notice that although the style becomes

almost transfigured by the intense and brooding imagination which permeates it, the diction is still as simple as prose.

> I cannot paint
> What then I was.   The sounding cataract
> Haunted me like a passion ; the tall rock,
> The mountain, and the deep and gloomy wood,
> Their colors and their forms, were then to me
> An appetite, a feeling, and a love,
> That had no need of a remoter charm,
> By thought supplied, nor any interest
> Unborrowed from the eye.   That time is past,
> And all its aching joys are now no more,
> And all its dizzy raptures.   Not for this
> Faint I, nor mourn, nor murmur ; other gifts
> Have followed; for such loss, I would believe,
> Abundant recompense.   For I have learned
> To look on nature, not as in the hour
> Of thoughtless youth; but hearing oftentimes
> The still, sad music of humanity,
> Nor harsh nor grating, though of ample power
> To chasten and subdue.   And I have felt
> A presence that disturbs me with the joy
> Of elevated thoughts; *a sense sublime*
> *Of something still more deeply interfused,*
> Whose dwelling is the light of setting suns.
> And the round ocean and the living air,
> And the blue sky, and in the mind of man;
> A motion and a spirit, that impels
> All living things, all objects of all thought,
> And rolls through all things.   Therefore am I still

> A lover of the meadows and the woods,
> And mountains ; and of all that we behold
> From this green earth; of all the mighty world
> Of eye and ear — both what they half create
> And what perceive; well pleased to recognize
> In nature and the language of the sense,
> The anchor of my purest thoughts, the muse,
> The guide, the guardian of my heart, and soul
> Of all my moral being.

It is this "sense sublime of something still more deeply interfused" that gives to a well-known passage in the concluding portion of the poem its particular significance.

> Nature never did betray
> The heart that loved her; 't is her privilege,
> Through all the years of this our life, to lead
> From joy to joy; *for she can so inform*
> *The mind that is within us, so impress*
> *With quietness and beauty, and so feed*
> *With lofty thoughts,* that neither evil tongues,
> Rash judgments, nor the sneers of selfish men,
> Nor greetings where no kindness is, nor all
> The dreary intercourse of daily life,
> Shall e'er prevail against us, or disturb
> Our cheerful faith, that all which we behold
> Is full of blessings.

In Wordsworth's use of the word Nature, it must always be borne in mind that he means, to use his own phrase, —

> The Original of human art,
> *Heaven-prompted* Nature.

This poem, the seed-thought of all the poetry of the first half of the nineteenth century, enables us to understand the process by which so peculiar a nature as Wordsworth's grew to its spiritual stature. It was by placing his mind in direct contact with natural objects, passively receiving their impressions in the still hours of contemplation, and bringing his own soul into such sweet relations to the soul of nature as to " see into the life of things "; or, as he expresses it, in another connection, " his soul had *sight* " of those spiritual realities, of which visible forms and hues are but the embodiment and symbolical language. Nature to him was therefore always *alive*, spiritually as well as visibly *existing ;* and he felt the correspondence between his own life and her life, from perceiving that one spirit penetrated both. Not only did he perceive this, but he mastered the secret alphabet by which man converses with nature, and to his soul she spoke an audible language. Indeed, his mind's ear was even more acute than his mind's eye; and no poet has excelled him in the subtle perception of the most remote relations of tone. Often, when he is on the peaks of spiritual contemplation, he hears voices when he cannot see shapes, and mutters mystically of his whereabouts in words which suggest

18

rather than embody meaning. He grew in spiritual strength and height by assimilating the life of nature, as bodies grow by assimilating her grosser elements; and this process was little disturbed by communion with other minds, either through books or society. He took nothing at second-hand; and his Nature is not the Nature of Homer, or Dante, or Shakespeare, or Milton, or Scott, but essentially the Nature of Wordsworth, the Nature which he saw with his own eyes, and shaped with his own imagination. His humanity sprang from this insight, for not until he became impressed with the spirit of Nature, and divined its perfect adaptation to nourish and elevate the human mind, did he perceive the worth and dignity of Man. Then simple humanity assumed in his mind a mysterious grandeur, and humble life was spiritualized by his consecrating and affectionate imagination. He might then say, with something of a proud content, —

> The moving accident is not my trade;
> To freeze the blood I have no ready arts;
> 'T is my delight alone in summer shade,
> To pipe a simple song for thinking hearts.

The passages in which this thoughtful humanity and far-sighted spiritual vision appear in beautiful union are too numerous for quotation, or even for reference. We will give but two, and extract them as hints of his spiritual biography and the growth of his mind.

Love he had found in huts where poor men lie;
His daily teachers had been woods and rills,
The silence that is in the starry sky,
The sleep that is among the lonely hills.

—

But who is He with modest looks,
And clad in homely russet brown?
He murmurs near the running brooks
A music sweeter than their own.

He is retired as noontide dew,
Or fountain in a noonday grove;
And you must love him, ere to you
He will seem worthy of your love.

The outward shows of sky and earth,
Of hill and valley, he had viewed;
And impulses of deeper birth
Had come to him in solitude.

In common things that round us lie
Some random truths he can impart, —
The harvest of a quiet eye
That sleeps and broods on his own heart.

We shall give but one more extract; illustrative of
the moral wisdom which the poetic recluse had drunk in
from Nature, and incorporated with his own character.
It was written at the age of twenty-five.

If thou be one whose heart the holy forms
Of young imagination have kept pure,
Stranger! henceforth be warned; and know that pride,
Howe'er disguised in its own majesty,

Is littleness ; that he who feels contempt
For any living thing, hath faculties
Which he has never used; that thought with him
Is in its infancy.   The man whose eye
Is ever on himself doth look on one,
The least of nature's works, one who might move
The wise man to that scorn which wisdom holds
Unlawful, ever.   O be wiser, Thou!
Instructed that true knowledge leads to love;
True dignity abides with him alone
Who, in the silent hour of inward thought,
Can still suspect, and still revere himself,
In lowliness of heart.

We have dwelt thus long on Wordsworth's first characteristic publication, because it expresses so well the nature of his own mind, and because it gave an original impulse to poetical literature. These Lyrical Ballads were published in the summer of 1798, and though they attracted no general attention corresponding to their original merit, they exercised great influence upon all the young minds who were afterwards to influence the age.   In September, 1798, in company with Coleridge, he visited Germany, and on his return he settled at Grasmere, in Westmoreland ; a spot well known to all readers of his poetry, and where he continued to reside for fifteen years.   In 1803 he married a Miss Mary Hutchinson, of Penrith. Neither was wealthy, their joint income being but £100 a year.

Of his wife we know little, except that she was of small stature and gentle manners, and was loved by her husband with that still, deep devotion characteristic of his affections. He refers to her, in a poem written in his old age, as

> She who dwells with me, whom I have loved
> With such communion, that no place on earth
> Can ever be a solitude to me.

Between 1803 and 1807, when a second volume of Lyrical Ballads was published, he wrote many of the most beautiful and sublime poems in his whole works. To this period belong " The Memorials of a Tour in Scotland" (1803), containing " The Solitary Reaper," " The Highland Girl," " Ellen Irwin," " Rob Roy's Grave," and other exquisite and glowing impersonations, — his grand sonnets dedicated to " National Independence and Liberty," — " The Horn of Egremont Castle," " Heart-Leap Well," " Character of a Happy Warrior," " A Poet's Epitaph," " Vandracour and Julia," the " Ode to Duty," and, above all, the sublime " Ode on the Intimations of Immortality from the Recollections of Childhood,"* which appears not to have been struck off at one heat, but to have been composed at various periods between the years 1803 and 1806.

---

* In the opinion of Mr. Emerson, " the high-water mark which the intellect has reached in this age."

There are no events, in the common acceptation of
the term, in Wordsworth's life after the period of his
marriage, except the publication of his various works,
and the pertinacious war waged against them by the
influential critics. Though his means were at first limited, he soon, through the friendship of the Earl of Lons-
dale, received the appointment of Distributor of Stamps
for the counties of Westmoreland and Cumberland, a
sinecure office, the duties of which were done by clerks,
but which seems to have given him an income sufficient
for his wants. In 1809 he published a prose work on
the " Convention of Cintra," which, though designed as
a popular appeal in favor of the oppressed Spaniards,
was little read at the time, and is now forgotten.
Southey, whose mind was on fire with sympathy for the
Spanish cause, says of this pamphlet, in a letter to
Scott: " Wordsworth's pamphlet will fail of producing
any general effect, because the sentences are long and
involved ; and his friend, De Quincey, who corrected
the press, has rendered them more obscure by an
unsound system of punctuation. This fault will out-
weigh all its merits. The public never can like anything which they feel it difficult to understand. I
impute Wordsworth's want of perspicuity to two causes,
— his admiration of Milton's prose, and his habit of
dictating instead of writing : if he were his own scribe
his eye would tell him where to stop."

But the great work to which Wordsworth was devoting the best years of his life, was his long philosophical poem of "The Recluse," designed to give an account of the growth of his own mind, and to develop all the peculiarities, poetical, ethical, and religious, of his system of thought. A large portion of this remains unpublished, but the second part was issued in quarto, in 1814, under the title of "The Excursion," and was immediately seized upon by all the wit-snappers and critics of the old school, and mercilessly " probed, vexed, and criticised." Jeffrey, who began his celebrated review of it in the Edinburgh with the sentence, " This will never do," was successful in ridiculing some of its weak points, but made the mistake of stigmatizing its sublimest passages as " unintelligible ravings." The choice of a pedler as the hero of a philosophical poem, though it was based on facts coming within the author's knowledge, was a violation of ideal laws, because it had not sufficient general truth to justify the selection. A pedler may be a poet, moralist, and metaphysician, but such examples are for biography rather than poetry, and indicate singularity more than originality in the poet who chooses them. Allowing for this error, subtracting some puerile lines, and protesting against the tendency to diffusion in the style, "The Excursion" still remains as a noble work, rich in description, in narrative, in sentiment, fancy, and imagination, and replete with some of the highest and rarest attributes of poetry. To one who has been an attentive reader of it, grand and inspiring passages crowd into the memory at the mere mention of its title. It is, more perhaps than any other of Wordsworth's works, enveloped in the atmosphere of his soul, and vital with his individual life ; and in all sympathetic minds, in all minds formed to feel its solemn thoughts and holy raptures, it feeds

" A calm, a beautiful, and silent fire."

" The Excursion " was followed, in 1815, by the " White Doe of Rylstone," a narrative poem, which Jeffrey said deserved the distinction of being the worst poem ever printed in a quarto volume, and which appears to us one of the very best. We do not believe the " White Doe " is much read, and its exceeding beauty, its subtle grace, its profound significance, are not perceived in a hasty perusal. It is instinct with the most refined and ethereal imagination, and could have risen from the depths of no mind in which moral beauty had not been organized into moral character. Its tenderness, tempered by " thoughts whose sternness makes them sweet," pierces into the very core of the heart. The purpose of the poem is to exhibit suffering as a purifier of character, and the ministry of sympathies,

> " Aloft ascending, and descending quite
> Even unto inferior kinds,"

in allaying suffering ; and this is done by a story sufficiently interesting of itself to engage the attention,
apart from its indwelling soul of holiness. In the representation of the Nortons we have the best specimens
of Wordsworth's power of characterization, a power
in which he is generally deficient, but which he here
exhibits with almost dramatic force and objectiveness.

" Peter Bell " and " The Wagoner," which appeared
in 1819, were executed in a spirit very different from
that which animates the " White Doe. " They were
originally written to illustrate a system, and seem to
have been published, at this period, to furnish the
enemies of Wordsworth some plausible excuse for attacking his growing reputation. " Peter Bell " was conceived and composed as far back as 1798, and though
it exhibits much power and refinement of imagination, the treatment of the story is essentially ludicrous.
But still it contains passages of description which are
eminently Wordsworthian, and which the most accomplished of Wordsworth's defamers never equalled.
With what depth, delicacy, sweetness, and simplicity
are the following verses, for instance, conceived and
expressed : —

He roved among the vales and streams,
  In the green wood and hollow dell;
They were his dwellings night and day, —
But Nature ne'er could find the way
  Into the heart of Peter Bell.

In vain, through every changeful year,
  Did Nature lead him as before;
A primrose by the river's brim
A yellow primrose was to him,
  And it was nothing more.

—

At noon, when by the forest's edge
  He lay beneath the branches high,
The soft blue sky did never melt
Into his heart; *he never felt*
  The witchery of the soft blue sky.

On a fair prospect some have looked
  And felt, as I have heard them say,
As if the moving time had been
A thing as steadfast as the scene
  On which they gazed themselves away.

—

There was a hardness in his cheek,
  There was a hardness in his eye,
As if the man had fixed his face,
In many a solitary place,
  Against the wind and open sky.

"The Wagoner" is altogether unworthy of Wordsworth's genius. It is an attempt of a poet without
humor to be gay and jocular, and very dismal gayety it

is. But even this poem is not to be dismissed **without** a reference to its one exquisite passage, — that in which he describes the obligation upon him to write it : —

> Nor is it I who play the part,
> But a *shy spirit* in my heart,
> That comes and goes — will sometimes leap
> From hiding-places ten years deep;
> Or haunts me with familiar face,
> Returning, like a ghost unlaid,
> Until the debt I owe be paid.

The next volume of Wordsworth was a series of sonnets, under the general title of " The River Duddon," published in 1820, and singularly pure in style and fresh in conception. This was followed, in 1821, by " Itinerary Sonnets," chronicling a journey to the Continent; " Ecclesiastical Sonnets," in 1822, celebrating events and characters in the history of the English church; and " Yarrow Revisited, and other Poems," in 1834. In old age he still preserved his young love for Nature, and lost none of his power of interpreting her teachings. In a poem entitled " Devotional Incitements," written at the age of sixty-two, and distinguished for the delicate keenness of its insight, no less than its lyric rapture, it will be perceived that natural objects were still visible and audible to his heart and imagination. " Where," he exclaims, —

Where will they stop, those breathing powers,
The *spirits* of the new-born flowers?
They wander with the breeze, they wind
Where'er the streams a passage find;
Up from their native ground they rise
In mute aerial harmonies;
From humble violet — modest thyme —
Exhaled, the *essential odors* climb,
As if no space below the sky
Their subtle flight could satisfy:
Heaven will not tax our thoughts with pride —
If like ambition be *their* guide.

Roused by the kindliest of May-showers,
The spirit quickener of the flowers,
That with moist virtue softly cleaves
The buds, and freshens the young leaves,
The birds pour forth their souls in notes
Of rapture from a thousand throats —
Here checked by too impetuous haste,
While there the music runs to waste,
With bounty more and more enlarged
Till the whole air is overcharged.
Give ear, O man, to their appeal,
And thirst for no inferior zeal,
Thou, who canst *think* as well as *feel.*

—

Alas ! the sanctities combined
By art to unsensualize the mind,
Decay and languish ; or, as creeds
And humors change, are spurned like weeds:
And priests are from their altars thrust;
Temples are levelled with the dust ;

And solemn rites and awful forms
Founder amid fanatic storms,
Yet evermore, through years renewed
In undisturbed vicissitude,
Of seasons balancing their flight
On the swift wings of day and night,
Kind Nature keeps a heavenly door
Wide open for the scattered Poor,
Where flower-breathed incense to the skies
Is wafted in mute harmonies;
And ground fresh cloven by the plough
Is fragrant with a humbler vow;
Where birds and brooks from leafy dells
Chime forth unwearied canticles,
And vapors magnify and spread
The glory of the sun's bright head —
Still constant in her worship, still
Conforming to the eternal Will,
Whether men sow or reap the fields
Divine monition Nature yields,
That not by bread alone we live,
Or what a hand of flesh can give;
That every day should leave some part
Free for a sabbath of the heart.

On the death of Southey, Wordsworth was appointed Poet Laureate. The latter years of his life were passed in undisturbed serenity, and he appears to have retained his faculties to the last. His old age, like his youth and mature manhood, illustrated the truth of his poetic teachings, and proves that poetry had taught him

the true theory of life.   One cannot contemplate him
during the last ten years of his existence, without being
forcibly impressed with his own doctrine regarding the
lover of nature : —

> Thy thoughts and feelings shall not die,
> Nor leave thee when old age is nigh
>   A melancholy slave ;
> *But an old age serene and bright,*
> *And lovely as a Lapland night,*
>   *Shall lead thee to thy grave.*

The predominating characteristic of Wordsworth's
poetry is thoughtfulness, a thoughtfulness in which every
faculty of his mind and every disposition of his heart
meet and mingle ; and the result is an atmosphere of
thought, giving a softening charm to all the objects it
surrounds and permeates.   This atmosphere is sometimes sparkingly clear, as if the airs and dews and sunshine of a May morning had found a home in his imagination ; but, in his philosophical poems, where he
penetrates into a region of thought above the ken of
ordinary mortals, this atmosphere is touched by an ideal
radiance which slightly obscures as well as consecrates
the objects seen through it, and occasionally it thickens
into mystical obscurity.   No person can thoroughly
enjoy Wordsworth who does not feel the subtle effect
of this atmosphere of thought, as it communicates an

· **air** of freshness and originality even to the commonplaces of his thinking, and apparels his loftier conceptions in celestial light, —

> " The gleam,
> The light that never was on sea or land,
> The consecration and the poet's dream."

The first and grandest exercise, therefore, of his
imagination is the creation of this harmonizing atmosphere, enveloping as it does the world of his creation
with that peculiar light and air, indescribable but unmistakable, which enable us at once to recognize and to
class a poem by Wordsworth. We do not hesitate to
say that, in its peculiarity, there is nothing identical
with it in literature, — that it constitutes an absolutely
new kind of poetry, in the Platonic sense of the word
"kind." An imagination which can thus fuse all the faculties and emotions into one individuality, so that all the
vital products of that individuality are characterized by
unity of effect, is an imagination of the highest *kind*.
The next question to be considered is the variety which
this unity includes : for Shakespeare himself, the most
comprehensively creative of human beings, never goes
beyond the unity of his individuality, his multifarious
variety always answering to the breadth of his personality. He is like the banyan-tree in the marvellous
fertility of his creativeness, and the province of human-

ity he covers; but the fertility all comes from one root and trunk, and indicates simply the greatness of the *kind,* as compared with other *kinds* of trees. The variety in the operation of Wordsworth's imagination we will consider first in its emotional, and second in its intellectual, manifestation, — of course, using these words as terms of distinction, not of division, because when we employ the word "imagination" we desire to imply a fusion of the whole nature of the man into one living power. In the emotional operation of Wordsworth's imagination we discern his Sentiment. No term has been more misused than this, its common acceptation being a weak affectionateness; and, at best, it is considered as an instinct of the sensibility, as a simple, indivisible element of humanity. The truth is that sentiment is a complex thing, the issue of sensibility and imagination; and without imagination sentiment is impossible. We often meet excellent and intelligent people, whose affections are warm, whose judgments are accurate, and whose lives are irreproachable, but who lack in their religion, morality, and affections an elusive something which is felt to be the last grace of character. The solution of the problem is found in their want of Sentiment, — in their want of that attribute by which past scenes and events, and absent faces, and remote spiritual realities, affect the mind like objects which are visibly present. Now, without this Sentiment no man can be a poet, either in feeling or faculty; and Wordsworth has it in a transcendent degree. In him it is revealed, not only in his idealizing whatever in nature or life had passed into his memory, but in his religious feeling and in his creative art. Scenes which he had viewed years before, he tells us, still

> *Flash* upon that *inward eye*,
> Which is the bliss of solitude.

Thus Sentiment is that operation of imagination which recalls, in a more vivid light, things absent from the bodily eye, and makes them act upon the will with more force and inspiration than they originally exerted in their first passionate or thoughtful perception; and from its power of extracting the essence and heightening the beauty of what has passed away from the senses and passed into memory, it gives the impulse which sends the creative imagination far beyond the boundaries of actual life into the regions of the ideal, to see what is most beautiful here

> Imaged there
> In happier beauty; more pellucid streams,
> An ampler ether, a diviner air,
> And fields invested with purpureal gleams,
> Climes, which the sun, who sheds the brightest day
> Earth knows, *is all unworthy* to survey.

19

It is needless to adduce passages to prove the depth
and delicacy of Wordsworth's sentiment, sanctifying as
it does natural objects and the humblest life, and lend-
ing to his religious faith a mysterious, ineffable beauty
and holiness. In our view of the quality it must
necessarily be the limitation of a poet's creativeness,
for the imagination cannot represent or create objects
to which it does not tend by a sentiment; and Wordsworth, while he has a sentiment for visible nature, a
religious sentiment, a sentiment of humanity, is still
confined to the serious side of things, and has no sentiment of humor. If he had humor as a sentiment, he,
dowered as he is with imagination, would have it as a
creative faculty, for humor is simply the imagination
inspired by the sentiment of mirth.

Let us now survey the power and scope of Wordsworth's imagination, considered in its intellectual manifestation. Here nothing bounds its activity but its
sentiments. It is descriptive, pictorial, reflective, shaping, creative, and ecstatic; it can body forth abstract
ideas in sensible imagery; it can organize, as in the
"White Doe," a whole poem around one central idea;
it can make audible in the melody of words shades of
feeling and thought which elude the grasp of imagery;
it can fuse and diffuse itself at pleasure, animating, coloring, vitalizing everything it touches. In description

it approaches near absolute perfection, giving not only the scene as it lies upon the clear mirror of the perceptive imagination, but representing it in its life and motion as well as form. The following, from " The Night Piece," is one out of a multitude of instances : —

> He looks up — the clouds are split
> Asunder — and above his head he sees
> The clear Moon, and the glory of the heavens
> There, in a black blue vault she sails along,
> Followed by multitudes of stars, that, small
> And sharp and bright, along the dark abyss
> Drive as she drives.

In the description of the appearance of the " White Doe," we have not only form, hue, and motion, but the feeling of wonder that the fair creature excites, and the rhythm which musically expresses the supernatural character of the visitant, — all embodied in one vivid picture : —

> The only voice that you can hear
> Is the river murmuring near.
> — When soft ! — the dusky trees between,
> And down the path through the open green,
> Where is no living thing to be seen;
> And through yon gateway, where is found,
> Beneath the arch with ivy bound,
> Free entrance to the church-yard ground —
> *Comes gliding in with lovely gleam,*
> *Comes gliding in serene and slow.*

Soft and silent as a dream,
A solitary Doe!
White she is as lily of June,
And beauteous as the silver moon
When out of sight the clouds are driven
And she is left alone in heaven;
Or like a ship, some gentle day,
In sunshine sailing far away,
A glittering ship that hath the plain
Of ocean for her own domain.

In the following we have a mental description, so subtle and so sweet as to make the "sense of satisfaction ache" with its felicity : —

And she has smiles to earth unknown,
Smiles that, with motion of their own,
Do spread and sink and rise;
That come and go, with endless play,
And ever as they pass away,
Are hidden in her eyes.

This is from the little poem to "Louisa." It is curious that Wordsworth, in the octavo edition of his works, published when he was seventy-seven years old, omits this stanza. It was so refined that he had probably lost the power to perceive its delicate beauty, and dismissed it as meaningless.

In describing Nature, as connected with, and embodied in human thoughts and sentiments, Wordsworth's descriptive power rises with the complexity of the theme. Thus, in the poem of Ruth, we have an example of the perversion of her energizing power : —

> The wind, the tempest roaring high,
> The tumult of a tropic sky,
>   Might well be dangerous food
> For him, a youth to whom was given
> So much of earth — so much of heaven,
>   And such impetuous blood.
>
> Whatever in those climes he found
> Irregular in sight or sound,
>   Did to his mind impart
> A kindred impulse, seemed allied
> To his own powers, and justified
>   The workings of his heart.
>
> Nor less, to feed voluptuous thought,
> The beauteous forms of nature wrought,
>   Fair trees and gorgeous flowers;
> The breezes their own languor lent;
> *The stars had feelings*, which they sent
>   Into those favored bowers.

In another poem, we have an opposite and purer representation of Nature's vital work, in an ideal impersonation which has nothing like it in the language : —

> Three years she grew in sun and shower,
> Then Nature said, a lovelier flower
>   On earth was never sown;
> This child I to myself will take;

> She shall be mine, and I will make
>   A lady of my own.
>
> Myself will to my darling be
>   th law and impulse; and with me
>   The girl in rock and plain,
> In earth and heaven, in glade and bower,
> Shall feel an overseeing power
>   *To kindle or restrain.*
>
> She shall be sportive as the fawn,
> That wild with glee across the lawn,
>   Or up the mountain springs;
>   *nd hers shall be the breathing balm,*
>   *id hers the silence and the calm*
>   *Of mute insensate things.*
>
> The floating clouds their state shall lend
> To her; for her the willow bend;
>   Nor shall she fail to see
> Even in the motions of the Storm,
> Grace that shall mould the maiden's form
>   By silent sympathy.
>
> The stars of midnight shall be dear
> To her; and she shall lean her ear
>   In many a secret place
> Where rivulets dance their wayward round,
> *And beauty born of murmuring sound*
>   *Shall pass into her face.*

But the most common exercise of Wordsworth's imagination is what we may call its meditative action, —

its still, calm, searching insight into spiritual truth, and
into the spirit of Nature. In these, analysis and reflection become imaginative, and the "more than reasoning mind" of the poet overleaps the boundaries of
positive knowledge, and, steadying itself on the vanishing points of human intelligence, scans the "life of
things." In the poems in which meditation predominates, there is a beautiful union of tender feeling with
austere principles, and this austerity prevents his tenderness from ever becoming morbid. As his meditative
poems more especially relate to practice, and contain
his theory of life, they grow upon a studious reader's
mind with each new perusal. In them the Christian
virtues and graces are represented in something of their
own celestial beauty and power, and the poet's "vision
and faculty divine" are tasked to the utmost in giving
them vivid and melodious expression. He is not, in
this meditative mood, a mere moralizing dreamer, a
vague and puerile rhapsodist, as some have maliciously
asserted, but a true poetic philosopher, whose wisdom
is alive with the throbs of holy passion; and

> Beauty — a living Presence of the earth —
> Surpassing the most fair ideal Forms
> Which craft of delicate spirits hath composed
> From earth's materials — waits upon his steps;
> Pitches her tents before him as he moves,
> An hourly neighbor.

But though these poems are essentially meditative in spirit, they are continually verging on two forms of the highest poetic expression, abstract imagination and ecstasy; and the clear, serene, intense vision which is their ordinary characteristic, is the appropriate mood out of which such forms of imagination naturally proceed. Let us first give a specimen of the creativeness of his imagination in its calmly contemplative mood, and we will select one of his many hundred sonnets : —

> Tranquillity ! the sovereign aim wert thou
>   In heathen schools of philosophic lore;
>   Heart-stricken by stern destiny of yore
> The Tragic Muse thee served with thoughtful vow;
> And what of hope Elysium could allow
>   Was fondly seized by Sculpture to restore
>   Peace to the Mourner. *But when He who wore*
> *The crown of thorns around his bleeding brow*
>   *Warmed our sad being with celestial light,*
> Then Arts, which still had drawn a softening grace
>   From shadowy fountains of the Infinite,
> Communed with that Idea face to face:
> And move around it now as planets run,
> Each in its orbit round the central sun.

We will not stop to comment on the wealth of thought contained in this sonnet, or the lingering suggestiveness of that wonderful line, —

> " Warmed our *sad* being with celestial light,"

but proceed to give another example, fragrant with the deepest spirit of meditation : —

More sweet than odors caught by him who sails
Near spicy shores of Araby the blest,
A thousand times more exquisitely sweet,
The freight of holy feeling which we meet
In thoughtful moments, wafted by the gales
From fields where good men walk, and bowers wherein they rest.

The following sonnet may be commended to warriors and statesmen, as containing a wisdom as practical in its application as it is lofty in its conception : —

I grieved for Bonaparté with a vain
And an unthinking grief!   The tenderest mood
Of that man's mind — what can it be ?   What food
Fed his first hopes?   What knowledge could *he* gain?
'T is not in battles that from youth we train
The Governor who must be wise and good,
And temper with the sternness of the brain
Thoughts motherly and meek as womanhood.
Wisdom doth live with children round her knees;
Books, leisure, perfect freedom, and the talk
Man holds with week-day man in the hourly walk
Of the mind's business; these are the degrees
By which true sway doth mount; this is the stalk
True Power doth grow on; and her rights are these.

We will now extract a magnificent example of abstract imagination, growing out of the meditative imagination, and penetrated by it.   It is the " Thought of a

Briton on the Subjugation of Switzerland "; the " two voices" are England and Switzerland.

> Two Voices are there; one is of the sea,
> One of the mountains; each a mighty Voice:
> In both from age to age thou didst rejoice,
> They were thy chosen music, Liberty !
> There came a Tyrant, and with holy glee
> Thou fought'st against him; but hast vainly striven:
> Thou from thy Alpine holds at length art driven,
> Where not a torrent murmurs, heard by thee
> Of one deep bliss thine ear hath been bereft:
> Then cleave, O cleave to that which still is left;
> For, high-souled Maid, what sorrow would it be
> That mountain Floods should thunder as before,
> And Ocean bellow from his rocky shore,
> And neither awful Voice be heard by thee!

Of the ecstatic movement of Wordsworth's imagination, we might extract numberless instances, rushing up, as it does, from the level of his meditations, throughout his poetry. Take the following, from the " Ode to Duty " : —

> Stern Lawgiver! yet thou dost wear
>   The Godhead's most benignant grace;
> Nor know we anything so fair
>   As is the smile upon thy face;
> *Flowers laugh before thee on their beds,*
> *And fragrance in thy footing treads:*
> *Thou dost preserve the stars from wrong;*
> *And the most ancient heavens through thee are fresh and strong.*

In a descriptive poem called " The Gypsies," there is a very striking instance of rapture immediately succeeding calmness : —

> The weary sun betook himself to rest ;
> Then issued Vesper from the fulgent west,
> *Outshining like a visible God*
> *The glorious path in which he trod.*

Again, observe how the imagination kindles and melts into rapturous idealization, and impetuously deifies the object of its sentiment, in the following short reference to the death of Coleridge : —

> Nor has the rolling year twice measured,
> From sign to sign, its steadfast course,
> Since every mortal power of Coleridge
> Was frozen at its marvellous source;
> *The 'rapt One of the godlike forehead,*
> *The heaven-eyed creature.*

In the sonnet which we now extract we have a specimen of that still ecstasy, so calm and so intense, in which Wordsworth stands almost alone among modern poets.

> A fairer face of evening cannot be;
> The holy time is quiet as a nun
> Breathless with adoration; the broad sun
> Is sinking down in its tranquillity;
> The gentleness of heaven broods o'er the sea :
> Listen ! the mighty being is awake,
> And doth with his eternal motion make

A sound like thunder — everlastingly.
　　Dear child ! dear girl ! that walkest with me here,
If thou appear'st untouched by solemn thought,
Thy nature is not therefore less divine :
　　Thou liest in Abraham's bosom all the year ;
And worship'st at the temple's inner shrine,
God being with thee when we know it not.

It is, however, in the sublime " Ode on the Intimations of Immortality from the Recollections of Childhood," that we best perceive the power of Wordsworth's imagination in all the various modes of its expression — descriptive, analytic, meditative, interpretative, abstract, and ecstatic ; and in this ode each of these modes helps the other ; the grand choral harmonies of the rapturous upward movement seeming to be born out of the intense contemplation, that hovers dizzily over the outmost bounds of human conception, to scrutinize, in the dim dawn of consciousness,

　　　　Those first affections,
　　　Those shadowy recollections,
　　　Which be they what they may,
　Are yet the fountain light of all our day,
　Are yet a master light of all our seeing.

It is from these that we have ecstasy almost as a logical conclusion ; for

　　　Hence in a season of calm weather,
　　　　Though inland far we be,

Our souls have sight of that immortal sea
Which brought us hither,
Can in a moment travel thither,
And see the children sport upon the shore,
And hear the mighty waters rolling evermore.

We have no space to particularize the felicity of
Wordsworth's muse in dealing with the affections, or
the depth and power of his pathos.   Before leaving the
subject of his genius, however, we cannot withhold a
reference to his " Ode on the Power of Sound," which
appears to be little known even to readers of the poet,
though in the thronging abundance of its ideas and
images, in the exquisite variety of its music, and in the
soul of imagination which animates it throughout, it
yields the palm to no ode in the language.

Wordsworth is most assuredly not a popular poet in
the sense in which Moore and Byron are popular ; and
he probably never will be so among those readers who
do not distinguish between being passionate and being
impassioned, and who prefer the strength of convulsion
to the strength of repose ; readers who will attend only
to what stirs and startles the sensibility, who read
poetry not for its nourishing but its inflaming qualities,
and who look upon poetic fire as properly consuming
the mind it animates.   Wordsworth is not for them,
except they go to him as a spiritual physician, in search

of "balm for hurt minds."   Placed in a period of time
when great passions in the heart generated monstrous
paradoxes in the brain, he clung to those simple but
essential elements of human nature on which true power
and true elevation must rest; and, while all around
him sounded the whine of sentimentality and the hiss
of Satanic pride, his mission, like that of his own beautiful blue streamlet, the Duddon, was "to heal and
cleanse, not madden and pollute."   His rich and radiant
imagination cast its consecrating and protecting light
on all those dear immunities of humanity, which others
were seeking to discard for the delusions of haughty
error, or the fancies of ripe sensations.   Accordingly,
though many other poets of the time have a fiercer or
fonder charm for young and unrestrained minds, he alone
grows upon and grows into the intellect, and " hangs
upon the beatings of the heart," as the soul advances in
age and reflection; for there is a rich substance of
spiritual thought in his poetry to meet the wants of
actual life — consolations for sorrow, help for infirmity,
sympathy for bereavement, a holy gleam of awful
splendor to irradiate the dark fear of death; a poetry,
indeed, which purifies as well as pleases, and penetrates
into the vitalities of our being as wisdom no less than
loveliness.

BRYANT.

———◆———

THE name of Bryant cannot be mentioned by any friend to American letters without respect as well as admiration. The instinctive feeling of the critic is to celebrate his positive qualities, rather than to indicate his limitations, or discuss his claims to be considered the greatest of American poets. A good portion of the men of the present generation read his most characteristic poems when they were boys, and object to any attempt to have their " pleasures of memory " disturbed. " The Ages," " Thanatopsis," " Green River," " Monument Mountain," are so blended with their most cherished sentiments and principles, and their power to purify and tranquillize the mind has been subjected to such tests of experience, that an interpretative criticism is slighted as needless, and a captious criticism is resented as impertinent.

The hold that Bryant thus has on the profoundest feelings of so large a portion of his countrymen is to be referred to the genuineness, delicacy, depth, and purity of his sentiment. A few other American poets may excel him in affluence of imagery and variety of tone and subject, but probably none is so essentially poetical in nature. He is so genuine that he testifies to nothing, in scenery or human life, of which he has not had a direct personal consciousness. He follows the primitive bias of his nature rather than the caprices of fancy. His sincerity is the sincerity of character, and not merely the sincerity of a swift imagination, that believes only while it is creating. He does not appear to have the capacity to assume various points of view, to project himself into forms of being different from his own, to follow any inspiration other than that which springs up in his own individual heart. As a poet, his nature is not broad, sensitive, and genial, but intense, serious, and deep; and we should suppose that his sensibility, pure and earnest as it is, within the bounds of his own individual emotions, would cool from sympathy into antipathy, when exercised on objects beyond its self-limited range. The charge of coldness, which is sometimes brought against him, must have reference to the limitation, not the force of his sympathies. The fire in his characteristic poems, though it may not roar and redden in a kind of conflagation of the passions, has a pure, intense, white heat, indicating the steady glow of feeling, which has fused together all the faculties of the man. His passion would appear to have more force if it were less purified from the recklessness of impulse and the taint and stain of appetite.

To this singular purity and depth of sentiment, he adds a corresponding simplicity, closeness, clearness, and beauty of expression. In language, indeed, he is so great an artist that no general terms can do justice to his felicity. The very atmosphere of his sentiment, the subtlest tone of his thought, the most refined modifications which feeling and reflection receive from individuality, are all tranfused into his style with unobtrusive ease. His style is literally himself. It has the form and follows the movement of his nature, and is shaped into the expression of the exact mood, sentiment, and thought out of which the poem springs. His compositions, therefore, with all their elegance and finish, — their " superb propriety " of diction, — always leave the impression of having been born, not manufactured or made. No melody of tone is ever introduced merely for the music, no flush of the hues of language is ever used merely to give the expression a bright coloring, but all is characteristic and artistic, indicating the subordination of the materials to the man, the poetry to the poet. It is for this reason that Bryant is so valuable a guide to young lyrists, who are so prone to be carried away by words, and who emerge from their tangled

20

wilderness of verbal sweets and beauties, without any essential sweetness and beauty of sentiment and imagination, and become, at best, authors of poetical lines and images rather than poems. A real poet, like Bryant, accepting the limitations of his nature, and never going beyond the point which separates inspiration from aspiration, creativeness from impressibility, the power of vital conception from the power of vividly appreciating the conceptions of others, may appear small in comparison with those adventurous spirits who would fuse Shakespeare, Spenser, and Shelley into their own little individuality, and by so doing lose their particular genius, instead of gaining the universality they seek. The genuineness of Bryant is, perhaps, too austerely conscientious, and, if any fault can be found with him in this respect, it is his repression of poetic instincts, which might, if cultivated, have given more variety to his muse. Surely, the little poem of "The Mosquito" indicates a vein of sentiment, delicate, playful, and genial, that might have been developed into many a piece of exquisite poetical wit and gracefully fanciful humor, which would have relieved the sad, sweet, earnest tone of his ordinary meditations.

Another characteristic of Bryant's poetical diction is its fulness of matter. Every line is loaded with meaning. This weight and wealth and compactness of

thought sometimes fail to impress the reader in his
blank verse, on account of its swift and slipping freedom
of movement ; but in his ringing rhyme they are forced
upon the attention. Take his lines in memory of William Leggett, and read them with a lingering emphasis
on the substantives and the substantial epithets, and
note how much life and meaning is condensed in the
four sounding stanzas : —

> " The earth may ring from shore to shore
>   With echoes of a glorious name,
>   But he whose loss our tears deplore
>   Has left behind him more than fame.
>
> " For when the death-frost came to lie
>   On Leggett's warm and mighty heart,
>   And quench his bold and friendly eye,
>   His spirit did not all depart.
>
> " The words of fire that from his pen
>   Were flung upon the fervid page,
>   Still move, still shake the hearts of men,
>   Amid a cold and coward age.
>
> " His love of truth, too warm, too strong,
>   For Hope or Fear to chain or chill,
>   His hate of tyranny and wrong,
>   Burn in the breasts he kindled still."

This solidity of thought is perhaps exhibited too
much in one direction, but still the one-sidedness

proceeds from a limitation of poetical sympathy, not from a limitation of intellectual power. It is, after all, the variety of sentiments bound up in a man's individual being which gives variety to his intellectual manifestation. Thus we find in Bryant all the faculties in vigorous manhood, — observation, judgment, understanding, fancy, imagination, — but, in poetry, obeying the direction of a few sentiments. Those who have followed his career as an editor, and have read his masterly prose articles on the principles, persons, and events of the time, know that the resources of his large, forcible, and teeming intellect are not confined to meditations like those which charm us in "Thanatopsis," but are equal to all the demands of statement, argument, and controversy ; and that political opponents come from the perusal of one of his scorching leaders in a less tranquil mood than that in which they come from the perusal of one of his tranquillizing poems. But doubtless the finer essence of the man's being is in his metrical compositions, though they may not fully indicate the diversity of his intellectual gifts.

In using the term "sentiment," in speaking of the direction of Bryant's genius, it may be as well to state what we mean. In our sense of the word it is the instinctive movement of the poet's mind to the objects which have a kind of magnetic affinity with its genius.

A poet, therefore, with a controlling sentiment, may almost reach perfection in the representation of some things, and be very mediocre the moment his mind is exercised on other things. Bryant has a true sentiment for external nature, and for the great ideas, abstracted from actual life and actual men, which the contemplation of nature evokes and nourishes ; but he has not, in addition to these, the sentiments which lead the intellect to explore the depths of human character, and find a joy in the concrete facts of human life. There are men who are said to have a feeling for nature simply because they yield naturally to the impressions which scenery excites in the most ordinary minds, — impressions which a city street or a masked ball will expel for others, which, in their turn, will not survive the hour. They require the actual *presence* of the forms, colors, hues, and sounds of objects, in order to receive their gladness or their gloom. This is not sentiment either for nature or for society. The poet of nature would be haunted by the images he saw and the sensations he experienced, in the *absence* of what excited them ; the poet of social life, or the dramatist, would be haunted in solitude by his perceptions gathered in the street and the ball-room. In both cases, the impressions would be lodged in the imagination, take a new and finer life there, be brooded over with delight, provoke more intense and deeper feelings as perceptions transformed than as perceptions immediately received, and at last would kindle the whole mind into activity — into a " noble rage " — to give them expression in language. This is the process by which nature is poetically described; this the process by which human life and character is poetically delineated. It is the same whether the object be a daisy or an Alp, — a Dogberry or a Hamlet.

Now we think it is plain that Bryant, as a poet, has not a sentiment for human life and character, though he has a deep one for external nature. There is no genial delineation of men and women, as individuals, in his writings. When he glows at the mention of a name, we find it is not a person he is celebrating, but some qualities of that person, abstracted from his personality, and idealized. His general tone toward society is harsh. Could he have seen the individual that hinted Falstaff, or Parolles, or Bottom, to Shakespeare, such a person would in him have excited simple aversion or contempt, as a hateful profligate, a lying braggart, or a stupid bore. In his poems he continually speaks of escaping from the crowd, of despising the frivolity of society, of hating the every-day work by which man, in this life, keeps up that interesting and slightly important connection between body and soul called

"getting a living." In this we are, of course, speaking
of Bryant as a poet, and of the feelings which animate
him as he contrasts the nature he poetically conceives
with the social life he prosaically apprehends. The
result is that, though perhaps the first of poets in
America, he is not especially an American poet, for
what nationalizes genius is not so much the scenery it
describes as the human life it idealizes. Why, Mr.
Jefferson Brick inquires, — why so much about American woods, fields, flowers, birds, beasts, ocean, and sky,
and so little that is characteristic about American men?
Indeed, the real concrete life of the nation, — that national life which even in meditative English poets, like
Wordsworth, forms the basis and inspiration of so many
lofty idealizations, — that peculiar something in almost
all English poets, which proves that their "limbs were
made in England," — seems to have no place in the
genius of Bryant. He appears rather to have for it a
subtle and supercilious antipathy, when, as a poet, he
gives himself up to the influences of nature. It is no
answer to this that some of his most glorious poems are
dedicated to what are called American ideas and sentiments, to Right, Truth, Independence, Freedom; for
these appear in his verse as abstracted, not only from
Americans, but almost from men, and smack of nothing
learned in town-meeting, or caucus, or congress, or

church, or assembly of reformers. A seraph singing in the air could hardly be more stainless and less characteristic.

We made these remarks in order to show all the more clearly the depth and intensity of the sentiment by which Bryant is led to nature and through which he becomes, not merely a worshipper at her shrine, but a priest of her mysteries, and an interpreter of her symbolical language to man. Though he resembles Wordsworth in this bias of his genius, he resembles him in little else, and imitates nobody. His thoughts, emotions, language, are all his own. He has earned the right to them by the contact of his mind with the objects to which they relate. The power of nature to heal, to gladden, to inspire, to sublime, to lift the mind above all anxious cares and petty ambitions, he has tested by consciousness. And it is not merely the external forms, but the internal spirit, with which he has communed. He sees and hears with his soul, as well as with his eye and ear. Nature to him is alive, and her life has coursed through the finest veins and passed into the inmost recesses of his moral being. It is this which compels us to mingle veneration and wonder with admiration and delight, in reading his works; it is this which gives his poems their character of depth.

Our readers may consider it an impertinence to give
them extracts from Bryant's poems; and, indeed, the
poems from which extracts would naturally be made
are so generally known that we almost fear to try the
experiment. But surely, the following lines on the
"Summer Wind" have in them a spirit of life and
beauty which keeps them ever young; and although we
have known them from a boy, they seem to us as fresh
as though they were now published for the first time.
Let the reader note how perfect the piece is as description, — how completely it calls up the images and sensations of the scene to his own mind, — and how the
various details melt into unity of effect, both in the
sense of impressing one picture on the imagination and
one mood on the heart, — and he will not regret reading
it for the twentieth time, if thereby he obtains a clear
idea of the difference between true description, and that
incongruous jumble of details which often takes its
name.

> "It is a sultry day; the sun has drunk
> The dew that lay upon the morning grass;
> There is no rustling in the lofty elm
> That canopies my dwelling, and its shade
> Scarces cools me. All is silent save the faint
> And interrupted murmur of the bee,
> Settling on the sick flowers, and then again
> Instantly on the wing. The plants around
> Feel the too potent fervors; the tall maize

Rolls up its long, green leaves; the clover droops
Its tender foliage, and declines its blooms;
But far, in the fierce sunshine tower the hills,
With all their growth of woods, silent and stern;
As if the scorching heat and dazzling light
Were but an element they loved.   Bright clouds,
Motionless pillars of the brazen heaven, —
Their bases on the mountains, their white tops
Shining in the far ether — fire the air,
With a reflected radiance, and make turn
The gazer's eyes awry.   For me, I lie
Languidly in the shade, where the thick turf,
Yet virgin with the kisses of the sun,
Retains some freshness, and I woo the wind
That still delays his coming.   Why so slow,
Gentle and voluble spirit of the air?
O, come and breathe upon the fainting earth
Coolness and life!   Is it that in his caves
He hears me?   See, on yonder woody ridge,
The pine is bending his proud top, and now
Among the nearer groves, chestnut and oak
Are tossing their green boughs about.   He comes!
Lo, where the grassy meadow runs in waves!
The deep distressful silence of the scene
Breaks up with mingling of unnumbered sounds
And universal motion.   He is come,
Shaking a shower of blossoms from the shrubs,
And bearing on their fragrance; and he brings
Music of birds, and rustling of young boughs,
And sound of swaying branches, and the voice
Of distant waterfalls.   All the green herbs
Are stirring in his breath; a thousand flowers,

By the roadside and the borders of the brook,
Nod gayly to each other; glossy leaves
Are twinkling in the sun, as if the dew
Were on them yet, and silver waters break
Into small waves and sparkle as he comes."

This is the true magic of poetry. How is it that the whole scene is thus made to " gush " into the reader's mind ? How is it that every small detail flows softly into its proper place to the sound of its own music, and, at the end, we are blessed with a summer picture, so alive with the inmost spirit of the reality that we hardly realize it is December as we read? It is this unanalyzable, inscrutable thing we call genius, that makes the critic, when he comes to the real mystery of the matter, throw by his pen in despair, and console his mortified analysis, as best he may, with Emerson's fine saying, " that it is the essence of poetry to spring, like the rainbow-daughter of Wonder, from the invisible, to abolish the past, and refuse all history."

The healing power there is in Bryant's philosophic meditation on life, the fine avenues through which his thought penetrates to what is deepest in the soul, and the beautiful serenity he not only feels but communicates, all are well illustrated in his poem on " The Return of Youth." With what winning sweetness of mingled reflection and imagination he smiles away all

the ugly associations connected with declining years, in
the following stanzas : —

> " Yet grieve thou not, nor think thy youth is gone,
>   Nor deem that glorious season e'er could die.
> Thy pleasant youth, a little while withdrawn,
>   Waits on the horizon of a brighter sky;
> Waits, like the morn, that folds her wing and hides
>   Till the slow stars bring back the dawning hour;
> Waits like the vanished spring, that slumbering bides
>   Her own sweet time to waken bud and flower.
>
> " There shall he welcome thee, when thou shalt stand
>   On his bright morning hills, with smiles more sweet
> Than when at first he took thee by the hand
>   Through the fair earth to lead thy tender feet.
> He shall bring back, but brighter, broader still,
>   Life's early glory to thine eyes again,
> Shall clothe thy spirit with new strength, and fill
>   Thy leaping heart with warmer love than then.
>
> " Hast thou not glimpses, in the twilight here,
>   Of mountains where immortal morn prevails ?
> Comes there not, through the silence, to thine ear
>   A gentle rustling of the morning gales;
> A murmur, wafted from that glorious shore,
>   Of streams, that water banks forever fair,
> And voices of the loved ones gone before,
>   More musical in that celestial air ? "

In regard to the versification of this poem, the
reader should note the movement and music of the

monosyllables. Contrast Pope's fleer at monosyllabic
words : —

> " And ten low words oft creep in one dull line,"

with this grand example of their felicitous use by Bryant : —

> " Waits, like the morn, that folds her wing and hides
> Till the slow stars bring back her dawning hour."

From the noble poem on the "Antiquity of Freedom," we extract a passage made of sterner stuff : —

> " O Freedom! thou art not, as poets dream,
> A fair young girl, with light and delicate limbs,
> And wavy tresses gushing from the cap
> With which the Roman master crowned his slave
> When he took off the gyves.   A bearded man,
> Armed to the teeth, art thou; one mailéd hand
> Grasps the broad shield, and one the sword; thy brow,
> Glorious in beauty though it be, is scarred
> With tokens of old wars; thy massive limbs
> Are strong with struggling.   Power at thee has launched
> His bolts, and with his lightnings smitten thee;
> They could not quench the life thou hast from heaven.
> Merciless power has dug thy dungeon deep,
> And his swart armorers, by a thousand fires,
> Have forged thy chain; yet, while he deems thee bound,
> The links are shivered, and the prison walls
> Fall outward; terribly thou springest forth,
> As springs the flame above a burning pile,
> And shoutest to the nations, who return
> Thy shoutings, while the pale oppressor flies."

In the last line we have a pertinent example of the amount of suggestion which can be conveyed by the movement of verse, independent of the exact meaning of the words. What a sneaking and snakelike suggestion there is in the way the verse slinks and halts, close on to its previous joyous tumult, —

> " *While the pale oppressor flies.*"

The concluding paragraphs of this poem we cannot resist the temptation to extract. The poet has just been speaking of the superior Antiquity of Freedom to Tyranny, and proceeds to detail the refinements that the latter learns in an advanced and civilized period of the world : —

> " Thou shalt wax stronger with the lapse of years,
> But he shall fade into a feebler age;
> Feebler, yet subtler. He shall weave his snares,
> And spring them on thy careless steps, and clap
> His withered hands, and from their ambush call
> His hordes to fall upon thee. He shall send
> Quaint maskers, wearing fair and gallant forms
> To catch thy gaze, and uttering graceful words
> To charm thy ear; while his sly imps, by stealth,
> Twine round thee threads of steel, light thread on thread
> That grow to fetters; or bind down thy arms
> With chains concealed in chaplets. Oh! not yet
> Mayst thou unbrace thy corselet, nor lay by
> Thy sword; nor yet, O Freedom! close thy lids

In slumber; for thine enemy never sleeps.
And thou must watch and combat till the day
Of the new earth and heaven. But wouldst thou rest
Awhile from tumult and the frauds of men,
These old and friendly solitudes invite
Thy visit. They, while yet the forest trees
Were young upon the unviolated earth,
And yet the moss stains on the rock were new,
Beheld thy glorious childhood and rejoiced."

But for sweetness, melody, rich description, rapt meditation, and high philosophy, all bathed in that softening and harmonizing light " which never was on sea or land," — for pure thought and emotion embodied in pure beauty of form, — we love the " Land of Dreams " almost beyond any other of Bryant's poems. Even those of our readers who have it by heart, and in their hearts, will pardon its reappearance to their eyes : —

" A mighty realm is the Land of Dreams,
    With steeps that hang in the twilight sky,
And weltering oceans and trailing streams,
    That gleam where the dusky valleys lie.

" But over its shadowy border flow
    Sweet rays from the world of endless morn,
And the nearer fountains catch the glow,
    And flowers in the nearer fields are born.

" The souls of the happy dead repair,
    From their bowers of light, to that bordering land,

And walk in the fainter glory there,
With the souls of the living hand in hand.

" One calm, sweet smile, in that shadowy sphere,
From eyes that open on earth no more, —
One warning word from a voice once dear, —
How they rise in the memory o'er and o'er!

" Far off from those hills that shine by day,
And fields that bloom in the heavenly gales,
The Land of Dreams goes stretching away
To dimmer mountains and darker vales.

" There lie the chambers of guilty delight,
There walk the spectres of guilty fear,
And soft low voices, that float through the night,
Are whispering sin in the helpless ear.

" Dear maid, in thy childhood's opening flower,
Scarce weaned from the love of childish play!
The tears on whose cheeks are but the shower
That freshens the early bloom of May!

" Thine eyes are closed, and over thy brow
Pass thoughtful shadows and joyous gleams,
And I know, by thy moving lips, that now
Thy spirit strays in the Land of Dreams.

" Light-hearted maiden, O, heed thy feet!
O, keep where that beam of Paradise falls,
And only wander where thou mayst meet
The blessed ones from its shining walls.

So shalt thou come from the Land of Dreams,
With love and peace to this world of strife;

And the light that over that border streams
　　Shall lie on the path of thy daily life."

In this notice of Bryant's poems. we have not done
justice to our conceptions of his poetic character and
genius, and, indeed, have attempted to do little more
than to assist, if possible, the circulation of his writings
among classes of readers to whom he may be still comparatively unknown.   There is a great deal of positive
intellectual and spiritual good which the American people can obtain from Bryant; for Bryant has, in large
measure, the very qualities in which the American people are deficient.   His works are wholesome food for
the mind and heart ; and although their circulation has
been extensive, in the sense in which we use that word
in speaking of the circulation of books of poems, it
has not been extensive in the sense of penetrating the
masses of that vast army of readers which, in our day,
we have seen engaged on one book.   We should be
delighted, as philanthropists as well as critics, to learn
that his poems were in every home in the land ; for,
unlike many books that by some means get into homes,
their mission is

" To heal and cleanse, not madden and pollute."

STUPID CONSERVATISM AND MALIG-
NANT REFORM.

———◆———

THE most comprehensive division of the human race
is into men who have common sense and men who
have not. This common sense has its general manifestation in individuals of mediocre but balanced minds,
who possess moderate powers orderly related; but its
noblest expression is in men of the highest order of
genius, who possess large powers harmoniously combined. Both in genius and mediocrity, however, the
distinguishing characteristic of the quality is moderation, the perception of things in their right relations,
and the refusal of the will to be whirled away by impulses from truths passionately misunderstood. The
general sum of intelligence and virtue in a community
is indicated by the degree of moderation evinced in the
conduct of its practical affairs. As this moderation includes in itself the whole science of limitations, and is
the condition of moral and mental health, wherever it
is absent principles subside into generalities, and virtues
fret themselves into vices.

Now it is one of the most significant characteristics of our day that this moderation is confounded on its moral side with pusillanimity, and on its mental side with commonplace. The natural consequence of this is, that all men who desire to obtain a reputation for virtue and intelligence — we say *reputation*, for virtue and intelligence themselves are not apt to have such a desire predominant — instinctively despise the common and rush off into some extreme. Intemperance in the advocacy of temperance, illiberality in the advocacy of liberalism, intolerance in sustaining toleration, are now the chief signs of that strange masquerade of the passions which passes with some, who are not by instinct philanthropists, under the name of philanthropy. To push one virtue to a fanatical excess and disturb the objective relations of things; to pour out a passionate flood of indignation at every seeming evil; to indulge more in invectives than facts, in interjections than arguments; to be, in short, a fifth-rate dialectician, and a first-rate word-piler, — these, the appropriate marks of the boy and the shrew, are now deemed the shining characteristics of a mind free from antiquated prejudices, and centuries in advance of the age. In a society which recognizes sensibility and the lungs as the grand peculiarities which distinguish human from brute nature, and which deifies the tongue to the

denial of thought, it is almost impossible for common
sense to obtain a hearing.   The opposition of the sensitive is crushed by a storm of abuse; the opposition of
the prudent is vented in an exclamation of disgust;
and, accordingly, the noisiest babbler that blows the
penny-trumpet of his rage is heard far above the still
small voice of a community's conscience and intelligence, and seems, to some wondering gapers, the great
man he affects.   The difference between a ball and a
bubble is, that one can stand the thrust of analysis, the
other collapses into suds the moment it is pricked.
Perhaps it would be well not to confine this test to
bubbles which have sprung from the marriage of soap
and water, but to extend it to those which have their
being in moral froth and mental wind.

The first obstacle to a trial of this process is the
sensitiveness of pretension, and the clatter which the
mere mention of examination rouses among its champions.   A person is sure to be honored with the invective of every professor of benevolence, if he attempt to
discuss the bad tendencies of any popular philanthropy,
from any position midway between fat and stupid conservatism and lean and malignant reform.   In every
age of the world, the fiercer class of tories and radicals,
that is, the class of men who do not reason, have
monopolized the vocabulary of passion, and plentifully

distributed the phrases of malice. Accordingly, those persons who have doubted the divine right of kings and the divine right of regicides, who have withstood the dictation of tyranny and the insolence of anarchy, who have, in short, striven hard to avoid being wrecked on the opposite shores of nonsense, have paid the penalty of their moderation in being placed between the two fires of fanaticism. It was a remark of Swift, that an honest man could be distinguished, from the fact that all the rogues were in confederacy against him. It is certain that a sensible one needs no other tribute to his intelligence than the vituperation of the insensible and the bigoted.

On the first blush it appears unjust to accuse any man, engaged in an assault on the evil of the world, and seemingly conscientious in his maddest outpourings of abuse, of envy, pride, and malice; but no student of history and human nature can have missed the fact, that the opinions of a saint and the actions of a savage are often found in the same person, and that when any portentous crime has been perpetrated, it has been commonly done on the plea of serving some great and just purpose. The world has had its full share of honest bigots and sincere tyrants; of men like Ximenes, who wished to rid the world of infidels; of men like Robespierre, who wished to rid the world of oppressors.

The principles of religion and liberty have ever been the cloaks of atheistical and despotic deeds. No man can act without some regard to his own conscience and the opinion of mankind; and few enormities have ever been committed without some fair pretext, which more or less deceived the author. Thus Cæsar conquered barbarous nations on the plea of civilizing them, and enslaved his country on the plea of reforming it; and the blood of a million men, shed to slake the measureless thirst of his ambition, was nominally a sacrifice to the genius of progress. Thus Cromwell easily connected the overthrow of the enemies of God with the triumph of the Parliamentarians, and his own conquest of the Parliament as the same military theology carried to its holiest logical consequences. Thus Napoleon never concluded to perform some act of self-aggrandizement, which involved a disregard or betrayal of the rights of others, without placing himself in the attitude of an injured man, and fiercely inveighing against the rascality or perfidy of his victims. These wolf-lambs and hawk-doves have cast ominous doubt on professions. The antithesis between tongue and heart, word and thing, is an old arrangement of depravity, — a pinchbeck gem from the antique which has lost none of its sparkle from age.

In treating this subject of Stupid Conservatism and

Malignant Reform, it is important to yoke them together, for they commonly exist as cause and effect. It is the peculiarity of both that they have no real vitality, no conception of the life and purpose of things, no perception of the organic in nature or society, no power of communicating intellectual and moral life. Apathy is the characteristic of the stupid phase of conservatism, anarchy is the characteristic of the malignant phase of reform. They both produce and detest each other; and, perhaps, if either could come to self-consciousness, it would detest itself. The moment any considerable number of men in a social system lose all perception of the spiritual bond which unites them, and become slaves to the forms of their concrete existence, they are ever sure to lapse into a contented, self-sufficing, stupid state, which inevitably stimulates the hatred and disgust of another class, who have loftier *opinions* of life, without ever having realized loftier *ideas* of it. Facts, institutions, social arrangements, are embodied ideas, — thoughts which originally were gifted with creative power, and forced themselves into things. Facts are either living or dead according as they are or are not animated and informed by ideas. Now the stupid conservative has no conception of the principles whence the institutions he defends draw their life, but simply has a hard prejudice for the forms in which he

finds them cast; resents all alteration of the forms even
when that alteration is merely the result of natural
growth; and, finding no safety for society except in
apathy, is the stagnant exponent and sluggish champion
of mental death, never so much delighted as when the
whole social body has the repose of a corpse. The
vices developed by such a state of mind are those naturally engendered by selfishness of purpose and littleness
of thought. They have produced, and are producing,
vast evils in the world; and among their many mischievous fruits we may emphasize the insurrection they
excite among sour, excitable, and self-willed spirits,
quick-witted enough to detect and despise the stupidities
of conservative selfishness, but without sufficient sweetness of disposition, depth of insight, and elevation of
character, to escape a virulent selfishness of another
kind. The theories and actions of stupid conservatism
are thus met and matched by the theories and actions
of malignant reform; enemies of each other, they are
jointly enemies of all the true wisdom, intelligence, and
moderation of the community in when their feuds rage
and foam; and together they do all in their power to
discredit and bring into contempt both the cause of
conservatism and the cause of reform.

Influence, good or bad, comes not from the opinions
a man professes, but from the character he has formed,

and the life he leads ; and malice uttering the commonplaces of meekness, or selfishness prating glibly in the
phraseology of benevolence, can only communicate to
others the life of malice and selfishness ; and thus it is
that so much of the Satanic in disposition finds a vent in
the propositions of charity and love, and that opinions
on which angels might gossip often come from lips
touched with a fire not from heaven. Now the source
of popular misjudgments in this matter is in confounding moral commonplaces with moral character, and in
calling a man of philanthropical or reforming opinions
by the name of philanthropist or reformer, without regard to his possession of the ideas, sentiment, spirit, and
character which distinguish philanthropy from misanthropy, and reform from lawlessness. The inward,
essential life of the man, which is the real thing to be
computed, as it is the real thing communicated, is overlooked in doing homage to the abstract truth of his
propositions ; and thus, in the popular estimation, a
person gifted only with the form without the spirit of
philanthropy is considered a philanthropist, just as a
person doggedly blind to everything but the form of
conservatism, is dignified by the title of conservative.

But perhaps the great strength of the malignants who
infest the profession of benevolence proceeds from the
ingenious combination of truth and falsehood in their

opinions. A system of thought compounded of truisms and paradoxes, one part intended to flatter the sagacity of superficial understandings, and the other part to foment the passions of discontented hearts, and both parts true to nothing in the concrete life of the community it is shaped to disturb, exactly realizes that union of shallow thought and vehement sensibility which is the condition of mental and moral anarchy. Facts and things being the creation, not of mechanical understandings but of living men, and as organisms rejecting the tests of exterior rules and principles, cannot stand a criticism which does not recognize their root in human nature, their appropriateness to the ends they were created to serve, or the internal processes by which they are to be renovated and reformed. Here is the work of the human race, — there are the opinions of Mr. Somebody, himself no better than the majority of the race, and without any power in himself to create anything; and we are informed that because facts do not square with his notions, have not been manufactured after his pattern, and do not agree with his arithmetic, that they are only worthy of being the objects of his indignant rhetoric, — which is degrading them, indeed. In addition to this, we are told that the imperfections he detects in existing institutions are not visible to other men, but that the discovery was the precious re-

ward of his superior insight; whereas, in fact, his whole
system of thought proceeds on the principle of rejecting
insight, vision into the interior constitution of things,
for a string of generalities which any child can as readily perceive, and as triumphantly apply as himself. He
criticizes society, indeed, as Rhymer or Dennis criti-
cized Shakespeare, and the generalities of his sterile ethics are about on a par with the generalities of their
barren taste.

Now if a man of moderate mental and moral powers,
neither better nor worse than the majority of the community in which he lives, starts with the capital mistake
of ignoring facts and deifying opinions, the process by
which he gradually sours into a malignant reformer is
exceedingly simple. His character is not up to what
he is pleased to call his principles, and the moment he
announces the latter he is subjected to annoyances calculated to fret his temper and stimulate his pugnacity.
Convinced in his own mind of the truth of his darling
propositions, he finds to his amazement that they are
doubted by some, denounced by others, treated with
a certain smiling indifference by still more; and he
knows no readier way of solving the problem of this
opposition than by charitably imputing it to selfishness,
knavery, or folly. His conceit of his own virtue, benevolence, and wisdom enlarges with each consignment

of other people into the category of knaves and fools;
and, accordingly, in an extremely limited period we
find him chuckling over the discovery that he is some
centuries in advance of his age, and glorying in the
greatness of being a prophet of the future.   While he
is revelling in this soft delirium of vanity, up starts fat-
witted conservatism, and in an agony of fear for the
salvation of stupidity, pitches at him all the moss-
covered phrases of its antique vocabulary ; and while the
words " fool," " incendiary," " rebel," and " fanatic " are
whizzing over his head, they flash into it the delicious
thought that he is a martyr.   This last revelation fin-
ishes his education.   From that moment he takes out
a patent for execration, and devotes his time to hating
men and loving man, misanthropy eating into his heart
as fast as philanthropy dances from his tongue.

In truth, it is not sufficiently considered that to be a
philanthropist is to reach that highest grace of character in which strength is united to sweetness, power to
love ; that the severest trial of philanthropy is to war
with selfishness without catching the disease ; that it
begins in love to individuals, and widens gradually into
love for mankind ; that by a certain divine felicity of
nature it returns magnanimity for meanness, love for
hatred, meekness for arrogance ; that it is hopeful,
genial, disinterested, patient, forbearing, persistent, in-

fluential, radiating light and warmth from its own fulness of life, and above the littleness of wreaking the
grudges of vanity and self-will in the invectives of
malice. In short, the thing itself is still rare, although
the word has been amazingly cheapened; and the word
has power to stir associations so beautiful, elevated, and
serene, that it would be a worthy ambition for some
knight-errant of language to rescue it from the contempt into which it has fallen, since it has been made
the convenient cover of so much acid and acrimonious
misanthropy.

But it may be objected to all this celebration of the
virtues peculiar to philanthropy, that it is a cheap way of
avoiding the responsibility of doing anything for mankind, and that the serpent of selfish indifference peeps out
from among its rose-leaves of rhetoric. A sour reformer
might retort that the practical question is, how are we
to upset the stupidities and rascalities of society and
government, strong as they are in all the strength of
stupidity, keen as they are in all the keenness of rascality? Will bright words, and beautiful sentiments,
and sweet rebukes do it? No; the rack and the hot
iron must be called in; and the whole set subjected
to a torture which, if it result not in victory, "will
be at least revenge." The real fact of the case, our
opponent would argue, is this, — that the whole affair

is a dog-and-cat fight between rascality and honesty,
and that in such a contest we must scratch and bite
and snarl with a beautiful adaptation of our powers to
the exigency of the occasion.   Stupidity has a force of
its own, against which the gods themselves are power-
less; it cannot be reached by weapons forged in celestial armories; and, accordingly, we prefer to dart scorn
and hatred at it, — to fret, tease, caricature, and torment
it, — and, as it is insensible to the honey of benevolence,
to make it wince under the sting.   If the fight be thus
a fight between stupidity and malice, — the two nega-
tives in the social sentence, — we do not know but that
the majority of sensible people should be as blandly
indifferent to the issue as was the amiable old lady who
witnessed her husband's struggle with the bear.   At
any rate, it is curious that a man should claim to be a
philanthropist on the ground that he has renounced the
first principle of philanthropy, and considers moral
power as too valuable a thing to be wasted on the
rogues he would still convert.   The assumption reminds us of a theory which regulates the epistolary
compositions of a gentleman of our acquaintance, who
considers grammar and orthography as too expensive
luxuries to be squandered in his private correspondence.

As these remarks are strictly confined to the malignants of benevolence, to those small, sharp, aggressive minds, who glory in the conceit of being prophets and martyrs, in virtue of dipping soulless ethical truisms in the gall of unloving hearts, we shall not attempt an analysis of that phase of philanthropy in which a real enthusiasm for right and duty, springing from comprehensiveness of feeling, is combined with intense and elevated, but somewhat narrow thought in conceiving plans. Philanthropists of this kind do not always bear the shock of collision with what is base and stupid, without having their austerity sour into moroseness, and without infusing a little vitriol into their virtue; but they still draw their inspiration from the benevolent instead of the malignant instincts, have few opinions which are not vitalized into principles and organized into character, and are of course to be discriminated from that other class who are engaged in a scheme of cheapening all the moral virtues by a process which dilutes love and condenses malice.

It is evident that in our enlightened age, so given up to the brag of benevolence, a malevolent spirit could not animate so many reforming schemes without breaking into literature, and insisting on having its representatives in romance. The form it has commonly assumed, in order to push its doctrines, is that best calculated to reach the largest number of readers, namely, the novel; and certainly it has displayed in this a good deal of shrewdness, for if it had relied on its plain ethics and metaphysics, it would simply have increased the number of deaths by gaping. It has, however, succeeded to a great extent in corrupting romance with a new nonsense and a new immorality; and though many of its productions are as stupid as they are brazen, and are about the dearest things which a prodigal can obtain for his shilling, some of them bear the signs of misdirected talent and morbid genius. So extensive has the evil become, that one can hardly take up a new novel without some expectation of being conducted through a series of imagined characters and events in which virtue is exhibited as mere conventional convenience, and crime as the road by which great souls reach the knowledge of their natural rights. As the didactive malignants would overturn existing facts and institutions, in order to satisfy the anarchical demands of their truisms, so the romantic malignants would subvert the organized morality and religion of society, by paradoxes which are merely inverted truisms.

Now this literature has been for a considerable period creating the taste which it addresses. From its bookstall intrenchments it has invaded kitchens, fought its way into parlors, and now constitutes a large portion of the people's reading. Altogether, it has come to be a greater public evil than smooth scholars and dainty critics are inclined to believe, as it is day by day forming in the public mind thoughts which eventually promise to be things. England is kind enough to furnish ruffians, and France to furnish philosophies, to help on the Satanic cause both with representatives and systems of diabolism; and Jonathan Wild can here fraternize with George Sand. Every element of blackguardism and false sentiment which our country can furnish is blended with the importation, and the result is a compound mass of passionate nonsense, immorality, and irreligion, passing under the nickname of popular literature.

Now it is evident that the extension of such a taste as these monstrosities of romance pander to will soon be more or less felt throughout the profession of letters. The purity of literature depends on the decency of readers ; authors, relying on the public for their subsistence, must furnish the article most in demand ; and if blasphemy, ribaldry, and licentiousness be the demand, blasphemy, ribaldry, and licentiousness will be the supply. Such appears to be the most universal law which can be generalized from literary history ; but stupid conservatism has an instinctive contempt for the power as well as the profession of letters, — is utterly

22

blind to the influence of literary talent, both in its good
and its perverted exercise, — and has ever done its
best to drive needy authors to that perilous point,
where they are compelled to choose between starvation and the prostitution of their powers. But it has
done even more than to stigmatize authors and refuse
its patronage to their works. It not only delights to
force talent into discreditable shifts for existence, but
it furnishes within itself the social abuses on which
perverted talent bases its opposition to social institutions. Thus the irruption of celebrated murderers and
highwaymen into romance might be traced to the
abuses of English criminal law. Stupid conservatism
treated the suspected or convicted felon with unwise
severity; as a matter of course, malignant reform lifted
him into the object of its peculiar interest and affection
and then nothing was left for the novelist to do but to
exalt him into a hero.

Among the many writers belonging to this Satanic
and sensual school of romance, there are doubtless
some whose talents are brilliant, and whose inten-
tions are not consciously bad. With opinionated understandings directed by imbittered sentiments, they are
continually mistaking their passionate hatred of wrong
for an impassioned love of right, and their pampered
egotism for a conscience emancipated from prejudice.

Deceived by their own sophistries, they take a moody delight in detaching the minds of their readers from all those institutions in which morality and religion are organized, and in enticing them into a freer region of thought and action, where each may follow out his instincts without any impertinent intrusion of fear or remorse, — two emotions which are apt to disturb the equanimity of free souls in actual life. Moral principles underlie, animate, and shape social institutions; the power and life of those principles are indicated by their having sufficient force to pass out of abstractions into things ; and, as far as regards the welfare of the generality of men, an assault on the institutions in which morality is embodied is an assault on moral principles. However imperfect may be the body of institutions in which morality is organized, they at least recognize the truth that man is not to be governed by will and impulse, but by law. Now the leading characteristic of the malignants and sentimentalists of romance is the denial of law and deification of impulse. Everything is brought to the test of individual will or individual whim. Their system excludes the ideas of truth, obedience, self-denial, and the like, for it always exalts the subject thinking or feeling over all the *objects* of thought and emotion. Thus these gentlemen love truth; but their truth is ever a darling paradox of their own minds, declining the authority of any common standard, and therefore nothing but a subtle egotism and love of self. The same principle runs through all their notions of virtue and excellence. Disinterestedness with them is never sacrifice of individual comfort for the benefit of others, but sacrifice of individual comfort for the delights of individual opinion. The result of such a morbid selfishness, tricked out in the most flaring sentimentalities of emotion and the gaudiest sophistries of thought, is to make obedience to self the highest virtue; and thus sensuality and wilfulness, the lust of the heart and the lust of the brain, are practically inculcated as the proper springs of conduct. Such a code inevitably brings them into opposition to all the concrete morality of civilized society, for the peculiar excellence of that morality consists in its being a system of checks equally upon the caprices of thought and passion. In order to make their opposition palatable, they strive to pervert the natural action of conscience; and here the egotistic character of their system becomes curiously manifest, for conscience with them only gives a certain sacredness to selfishness, and baptizes their passionate impulses as inalienable rights. Duty is lost sight of except as an underling to selfishness, — a man's duty consisting in battling for his rights. In this the romancers have altogether distanced the metaphysicians; for the austerest of transcendental thinkers has said that conscience both commands and allows; what it commands is duty, what it allows is right. But with the romancers, conscience is the mere pimp of passion, allowing everything, and commanding us to obtain everything it allows. Their theories, however, are principally obnoxious for the practical result to which they lead, namely, the disconnection of individual conscience from institutions in which the general conscience is embodied. The conscience of a community naturally reposes on things, is educated and sustained by institutions, and would die out if it had no other sustenance than moral opinions, however elevated. This is proved by the readiness with which the majority of men give way to sensual excesses, when the restraints of civilized society are withdrawn, and "you ought" is altogether substituted for "you shall." Those persons are therefore to be suspected who, on the ground that institutions are imperfect, would substitute moral theories for facts and things which embody morality. Unless their characters and lives are obviously higher than what they attack, it is a shrewd conjecture that their quarrel with institutions is on account of the imperfection of their evil, rather than the imperfection of their good. A man whose notions of human rights leads him to call property theft must be considered as opposed to the laws which protect property, because they shackle his desire to thieve rather than his power to bless; and a romancer who prates against the institution of marriage because it does not always unite souls commonly ends in exalting adultery into a virtue. Indeed, the universal process of the malignants of letters is dexterously to exaggerate the abuses of social institutions, to confound abuses with uses, and then to apply a rose-colored theory of duty, which dispenses with self-denial, and identifies right with pleasure. Injustice to individuals is the great social wrong, disorganization of society is their great social remedy; but to disorganize is to deprave, however seemingly fine may be the sentiments and abstractly true the propositions, on which the disorganization proceeds. Society is really improved and reformed only by communicating to it a higher life, — a life which penetrates into its organic substance, mixes with and modifies its inmost spiritual character, and there, at the heart of things, creatively shapes new forms, or puts new vitality into old ones. Such a life, it is true, can never proceed from a stupid, apathetic, purblind conservatism, without faith, without energy, without anything deserving the name of life; but neither can it be communicated by morbid and acrid spirits, who announce elevated opinions from a low level of character, and whose opposition to social institutions results from that good element in them which checks the caprices of their self-will and bridles their aggressive passions.

These hurried remarks on a prevailing imposture of the day have occasionally, we fear, betrayed in their style of expression a combination of the dulness of the conservative with the bitterness of the reformer, which vividly exemplifies the faults they have attacked. We have not pretended, however, to quarrel with any system, conservative or philanthropic, which justifies its adoption of the name by illustrating the qualities of the thing, but simply to express the dislike of a somewhat enraged common sense against two forms of selfishness, the apathetic and the malignant, which now strut and bluster as the chosen champions of order and liberty. If order consists in social stupidity and mental death, if liberty be nothing more than the triumph of malevolent mediocrity, then the sooner they destroy each other, and their names are dismissed from the dictionaries, the better it will be for all that is real in order and inspiring in liberty. But it would seem that their hostility is not so much calculated to be mutually destructive, as it is to inflame the worst qualities of each. The men who stand between the two, in a medium position, are distinguished for the moderation of their opinions rather than for possessing the life of

moderation, and they therefore have little influence as
positive forces. Vital moderation is what is wanted;
a moderation which discerns the essential relations of
things, and acts in accordance with its insight, — a
moderation which is not synonymous with commonplace but with comprehensiveness. Such a moderation
would be too austerely just and too broadly intelligent, to defend existing institutions or advance beneficent reforms on any other principles than those of justice and intelligence; and in its vigorous grasp of
things, and comprehensive discernment of relations, it
could afford to dispense with that rabble of resounding
words which the poisonous vitality of opinionated malevolence has now almost organized into a vocabulary
of execration.

THE END.